CONVEYANCING 2009

CONVEYANCING 2009

Kenneth G C Reid WS

Professor of Scots Law in the University of Edinburgh

and

George L Gretton WS

Lord President Reid Professor of Law in the University of Edinburgh

with a contribution by Alan Barr of the University of Edinburgh

Avizandum Publishing Ltd
Edinburgh
2010

Published by
Avizandum Publishing Ltd
58 Candlemaker Row
Edinburgh EH1 2QE

First published 2010

ISBN 978-1-904968-40-5

British Library Cataloguing in Publication Data
A catalogue record for this book is available from the British Library.

Typeset by Waverley Typesetters, Warham, Norfolk
Printed and bound by Bell & Bain Ltd, Glasgow

CONTENTS

PART III: OTHER MATERIAL

PART IV: COMMENTARY

PART V: TABLES

PREFACE

This is the eleventh annual update of new developments in the law of conveyancing. As in previous years, it is divided into five parts. There is, first, a brief description of all cases which have been reported or appeared on the Scottish Courts website (www.scotcourts.gov.uk) or have otherwise come to our attention since *Conveyancing 2008*. The next two parts summarise, respectively, statutory developments during 2009 and other material of interest to conveyancers. The fourth part is a detailed commentary on selected issues arising from the first three parts. Finally, in part V, there are three tables. A cumulative table of decisions, usually by the Lands Tribunal, on the variation or discharge of title conditions covers all decisions since the revised jurisdiction in part 9 of the Title Conditions (Scotland) Act 2003 came into effect. Then there is a cumulative table of appeals, designed to facilitate moving from one annual volume to the next. Finally, there is a table of cases digested in earlier volumes but reported, either for the first time or in an additional series, in 2009. This is for the convenience of future reference.

We do not seek to cover agricultural holdings, crofting, public sector tenancies (except the right-to-buy legislation), compulsory purchase or planning law. Otherwise our coverage is intended to be complete.

We gratefully acknowledge help received from Alan Barr, John Glover, Bill Gordon, Graeme Henderson, Mary McIlroy Hipwell, John MacLeod, Norman Macleod, Ross MacKay, Roddy Paisley, Graeme Reid, Ann Stewart, Neil Tainsh, Andrew Weatherley and Scott Wortley.

Kenneth G C Reid
George L Gretton
15 March 2010

TABLE OF STATUTES

TABLE OF ORDERS, RULES AND REGULATIONS

TABLE OF CASES

PART I

CASES

CASES

The full text of all decisions of the Court of Session and of many decisions of the sheriff court is available on the Scottish Courts website: http://www.scotcourts.gov.uk.

Since 1 January 2005 all Court of Session opinions are numbered consecutively according to whether they are decisions of the Outer House or Inner House. Thus '[2009] CSOH 4' refers to the fourth Outer House decision of 2009, and '[2009] CSIH 15' refers to the fifteenth Inner House decision of 2009. This neutral method of citation is used throughout this volume.

MISSIVES OF SALE

(1) Mitchell v Caversham Management Ltd
[2009] CSOH 26, 2009 GWD 29-465

This case was about whether sellers (to a property development company) were entitled to withdraw from missives. See **Commentary** p 95.

(2) Smith v Stuart
2009 GWD 8-140, Sh Ct

This is a continuation of *Smith v Stuart* 2004 SLT (Sh Ct) 2 (digested as *Conveyancing 2003* Case (9)). The original decision was appealed to the Court of Session, which allowed the pursuer to amend her pleadings, and remitted the case back to the sheriff court. The facts of this case were unusual. In 1995 the defender undertook in writing:

> I . . . hereby confirm that I will enter into a formal Minute of Agreement with my sister [designed] to the following effect: (1) In the event of the sale of [certain identified land] for agricultural or development purposes half of the sale proceeds will fall to be paid to my sister . . .

The remaining clauses provided further detail. More than five years passed, and the minute of agreement was not entered into. The sister sued to compel performance. The brother pled that his obligation had prescribed. The pursuer argued it was an obligation relating to land and so subject to the 20-year prescription: see Prescription and Limitation (Scotland) Act 1973 sch 1 para 2(e). One puzzle about the case was why it was thought necessary to have two agreements, namely the undertaking followed by the minute of agreement. We have no explanation to offer.

An obligation begins to prescribe when it becomes enforceable. At the rehearing, the learned sheriff (D J Cusine) took the view that the obligation to enter the minute of agreement did not become enforceable unless and until the land was sold. Since the land had not been sold the pursuer's action was premature and hence was dismissed. (The sheriff expressed the view that as and when the land was sold, the relevant prescriptive period would be five years, not 20.) Thus it seems that the decision is a technical victory for the defender but a substantive victory for the pursuer.

(3) Forbo-Nairn Ltd v Murrayfield Properties Ltd
[2009] CSOH 47, 2009 GWD 16-251 affd [2009] CSIH 94

Forbo-Nairn Ltd concluded missives to sell some land to the defender for £1 milllion. The missives called for a real burden to be inserted into the buyer's title, but the parties could not agree on its terms. See **Commentary** p 99.

(4) F M Finnieston Ltd v Ross
[2009] CSOH 48, 2009 GWD 16-250

The pursuer built new flats and the defender concluded missives to buy 24 of them. When the defender did not pay, the pursuer rescinded the contract and remarketed the properties. They were resold, but the prices obtained fell short of the original price, and accordingly the pursuer then raised this action of damages, claiming £880,000. (For an earlier stage of the case, concerned with procedural matters, see 2009 SC 106.)

There were 24 separate sets of missives, all in identical terms, and all of the familiar 'builders' missives' type. Clause 3.1 in each case said that payment on the date of entry was 'of the essence', and that if payment were not made within seven days of the date of entry that would constitute material breach giving the seller the right to rescind. (The two parts of this provision are contradictory, because 'of the essence' means that if payment is not made on that day, that is material breach: see *Conveyancing 2006* pp 89–90. But this was not an issue in the case.) When was date of entry? This was the key issue. Clause 3 said:

> The date of entry will be fourteen days from the later of (a) the date on which the plot has been inspected and passed by Local Authority as habitable and fit for occupation (whether or not a formal certificate to that effect by the Local Authority is available at that time) and (b) the date on which a cover note has been issued by NHBC/Zurich Municipal/Premier Guarantee confirming that a final inspection has been carried out by them and that a new home warranty for the plot will be provided; or such earlier date within the fourteen day period as is mutually agreed. The Purchaser accepts that any remedial work outstanding at the date of entry will be carried out in terms of Condition 12 and will not delay the date of entry or payment of the full price. Entry and vacant possession and the keys released to the Purchaser will be given

only on payment of the full purchase price (including the price of any extra items not previously paid for) and any interest due on the purchase price. Consignation of the price will not be accepted.

The local authority inspected the properties on 17 August and approved them, but the seller did not actually apply for completion certificates until 1 October. They were issued on 3 October. On the basis that the date of entry was 17 August + 14 days = 31 August, the pursuer required payment on that date. Eventually, on 1 November, the pursuer rescinded.

The defender argued that the pursuer had not pled a relevant case, since the missives could not mean that the date of entry could arrive without a completion certificate having been applied for. At para 12 the Lord Ordinary (Glennie) comments:

> The inspection envisaged by clause 3 is the inspection which is part of the statutory application for a Completion Certificate.... I cannot accept that the date of entry and the obligation to pay can be triggered by an inspection and approval given by the Local Authority which was not linked to an application for a Completion Certificate.

The Lord Ordinary also comments (para 13):

> It is, to my mind, axiomatic that a purchaser will, upon paying the price, be entitled to enter into the property immediately. He would be amazed if, having done so, he was told that he would have to wait for entry, indeed that it would be unlawful for him to move in, because there was as yet no Completion Certificate nor any written permission for temporary use and occupation of the property. That would, in my opinion, also be the reaction of a reasonably informed third party. It would be of no comfort to such a purchaser to be told that he should apply to the local authority for temporary permission to use or occupy the premises. Why should he have to bear the risk of any delay by the Local Authority in granting such permission? Why should he have to bear the risk that they will not in fact grant it?

This remark is, we think, *obiter,* for it seems to go beyond the central point that clause 3 presupposed that an application for completion certificate had been made. It would mean, as we read it, that even if the seller had on 17 August applied for a completion certificate, the date of entry would not happen 14 days later unless by that time a completion certificate had actually been issued.

If, as we think, the Unfair Terms in Consumer Contracts Regulations 1999, SI 1999/2083, apply to builders' missives (see *Conveyancing 2008* p 84) then it seems likely that unreasonable provisions about entry do not bind buyers. That said, since Mr Ross was buying 24 flats, it seems likely that he was not acting as a consumer.

(5) Cala Management Ltd v Messrs A & E Sorrie
[2009] CSOH 79, 2009 GWD 40-687

In 2002 the pursuer entered into two contracts with the defenders relating to land at Inverurie. One was an option to acquire certain land at 87.5% of its development value. The other was a contract to buy certain other land for £1.25 million, conditional on planning permission. The grant of planning permission was conditional on a s 75 agreement. Such an agreement has to be signed by the owner, and the defenders refused to sign. The question was whether they were justified in this refusal. See **Commentary** p 99.

(6) Aberdeen City Council v Stewart Milne Group Ltd
[2009] CSOH 80, 2009 GWD 26-417

Aberdeen City Council sold some land to the defender. The missives contained a complex provision that an additional sum was to be payable in the event that the buyer resold the land at a profit. The buyer resold the land to another company in the same group at a price which was, averred the Council, far below the market value. The low price would mean that the additional sum payable to the Council would be zero. Had the land been resold at its market value, averred the Council, the additional sum payable would have been about £1.7 million. The Council raised an action for declarator that the additional sum should be calculated on market value and not on the price actually paid.

The wording of the contract was less than clear on this point, but it was **held** that the Council's interpretation was to be preferred. The Lord Ordinary (Glennie) commented (para 11):

> It seems to me to be plain that the parties, in approaching the calculation of the profit share in the event of a sale, must have contemplated a sale at arm's length and at open market value. Otherwise it would be within the power of the purchasers in every case to defeat the sellers' entitlement to receive any amount by way of profit share. This is something which, so it seems to me, the parties cannot have intended.

(7) McPhee v Black
20 June 2008, Glasgow Sheriff Court

This is the sequel to the case digested as *Conveyancing 2006* Case (5). Buyers rescinded missives on the ground that what was disclosed by the title deeds was unacceptable to them. The sellers resold the property at a lower price and sued the original buyers for damages. The question was whether the original buyers had been entitled to pull out. See **Commentary** p 90.

(8) R & D Construction Group Ltd v Hallam Land Management Ltd
[2009] CSOH 128

Hallam had an option on some land and then concluded missives to sell the land to R & D, with a condition that the sale would proceed only if the option price proved satisfactory to Hallam. When Hallam refused to proceed with their contract with R & D, the latter sued Hallam to enforce it. See **Commentary** p 92.

(9) Scottish Coal Company Ltd v Danish Forestry Co Ltd
[2009] CSOH 171, 2010 GWD 5-79

The pursuer had an option to acquire the defender's land. If it did so it had to grant to the defender (ie the seller) a standard security to secure future payments. The option contract said that the seller would have to enter into a ranking agreement with the buyer's bank. Was this unenforceable as being an 'agreement to agree'? See **Commentary** p 94.

(10) Park Ptrs (No 2)
[2009] CSOH 122, 2009 SLT 871

Can missives be concluded by fax? See **Commentary** p 85.

COMMON PROPERTY

(11) Gavin v Junor
2009 SLT (Sh Ct) 158 affd 2009 SLT (Sh Ct) 162

The pursuer sought to interdict the defender, a fellow co-owner of a private road which served various parts of a former estate, from using the road to reach property which had not been part of the original estate. **Held**: that such use could not be said to be 'extraordinary', and so there were no grounds for the interdict. See **Commentary** p 105.

(12) Mason v Jones
2009 GWD 9-152, Sh Ct

A private road provided access to four houses, and was owned in common by the proprietors of these houses. In 1983 the owner of 'Headways', the final house on the road, constructed an alternative and exclusive means of access from the other side. Thereafter he and his successors in effect incorporated the final section of road into their garden, building a wall (with a gate which had long ceased to open), planting shrubs, erecting a greenhouse and so on. In the same spirit, the owners of the next house along (3 Lagg Cottage) planted shrubs on 'their' side of the boundary.

When the pursuer bought Headways with her late husband in 2005 they decided that they wanted the original access opened up, apparently so that they could meet or visit their neighbours and also in case of emergency. They raised the present action seeking (i) interdict against the owners of 3 Lagg Cottage from obstructing access, eg by the planting of shrubs or parking of cars, and (ii) ordaining the defenders to remove the existing shrubs so to restore the *status quo ante*. Crave (ii) was dropped, and the sheriff principal later refused an amendment to reinstate it.

The sheriff principal (B A Lockhart) found for the pursuer on the law. Common property could be used for 'ordinary' purposes unless there was an agreement to the contrary among all the owners. No such agreement had been reached. It was true that, by usage, a use (such as growing shrubs) which was initially 'extraordinary' could become 'ordinary' and acceptable but, even so, such a use could only supplement (and not replace) what was otherwise an ordinary use. So the road remained available for access. See **Commentary** p 106.

Nonetheless the sheriff principal found for the defenders. Interdict was not an appropriate remedy because there was no suggestion that there might be *future* obstructions (and crave (ii), dealing with past obstructions, and hence essential to the actual use of the road, had been dropped). The sheriff principal added (para 17):

> I am bound to notice the fact that, by seeking interdict, the appellant is in effect seeking to vindicate her one-quarter *pro indiviso* right of property in the access road. She does so at a time when she enjoys exclusive use of that part of the common access road to the east of what is now the line consisting of wall, mature hedging and gate. The curtilage of Headways is that much the greater by her usurpation of that portion of the common access road.... The greenhouse pertaining to Headways is partially built on the common access road. It appears to be the case, while seeking to vindicate her right of access in the common access road, at the same time she deprives the other common owners, and in particular the respondents of their right to use that part of the common property which is now, as a result of the boundaries constructed by the appellant's predecessors, within the exclusive use of the appellant. Although it is not necessary for the determination of whether or not interdict should be granted, I think this does add weight to the proposition that it is not, in all the circumstances, appropriate.

(13) Sutherland v Sutherland
2008 Fam LR 151, Sh Ct

In a divorce action, one of the questions at issue was the valuation of houses which were co-owned by the parties to the marriage. In refusing to value each party's half share separately, the sheriff (D A Kinloch) explained (at para 24) that:

> While title to the heritable properties and endowment policies is in joint names, that joint ownership is in the form of a one-half *pro indiviso* share, rather than a separate and distinct one-half share as is the case with property held in common. So, there is here only one estate vested in them *pro indiviso*, and the property subject to a transfer order is their *pro indiviso* share in that single estate, which ought accordingly to have a single valuation.

As far as it goes, this is an accurate account of the difference between joint and common property. The trouble is that property co-owned by husband and wife is an example of the latter and not of the former. That has been settled since at least Lord Cooper held in *Magistrates of Banff v Ruthin Castle* 1944 SC 36 at 68 that common property is the normal type of co-ownership and that joint property is confined to trusts and unincorporated associations. For a discussion of the development of the distinction, see K G C Reid, *The Law of Property in Scotland* (1996) paras 19 and 20.

(14) Sutherland v Sutherland
22 February 2009, Stonehaven Sheriff Court

After spouses separated, the husband, who remained in the matrimonial home, carried out £30,000 worth of improvements. Subsequently, the wife raised an action of division and sale. **Held**: the £30,000 fell to be top-sliced in favour of the husband out of the sale proceeds.

The basis of this decision is unclear. The sheriff relied on the statement in para 23.37 of Macphail's *Sheriff Court Practice* (3rd edn) that 'considerations of equity can properly be taken into account in determining the method of division and the distribution of proceeds of sale'. But any claim for unequal division of sale proceeds must have some legal basis, such as contract or unjustified enrichment, and it is hard to see how either applied on the facts of the present case.

TENEMENTS

(15) Stewart v Malik
[2009] CSIH 5, 2009 SC 265, 2009 SLT 205

The defender owned a shop in Maybole. The pursuers owned the flat above the shop. The defender obtained a building warrant for works which involved the removal of a load-bearing wall and its replacement by a central supporting column. The work was carried out by an independent contractor. In the event, something went wrong and there was a loss of support causing damage to the pursuers' flat. The pursuers averred that this was because the contractors failed to build the central supporting column.

Two propositions are well established in this area of law. First, while a lower proprietor owes an obligation of support to the upper, liability for damage caused is not strict but requires negligence (*Thomson v St Cuthbert's Cooperative Association Ltd* 1958 SC 380). Secondly, in general an owner carrying out repairs has no liability for an independent contractor (as opposed to an employee).

It was held by the sheriff principal that, following English law, there can be liability for an independent contractor if the operation in question is inherently hazardous: see 2008 GWD 14-232 (*Conveyancing 2008* Case (9)). On further appeal to the First Division, the court reserved its position on whether such a general exception existed, but decided, by analogy with the English House of Lords case of *Dalton v Angus* (1881) 6 App Cas 740, that where (as here) there is a duty of support under the general law, such a duty cannot be avoided by use of an independent contractor. In the words of Lord President Hamilton (para 26):

> In Scotland the law of the tenement, similarly in my view, casts on the 'servient' proprietor a positive duty in carrying out works which may affect support to avoid endangering the 'dominant' property. That duty, which is personal to him, cannot, in my view, be elided by the instruction of an independent contractor to execute the works.

A proof was accordingly allowed.

(16) Morris Amusements Ltd v Glasgow City Council
[2009] CSOH 84, 2009 SLT 697

The pursuer owned most of a six-storey Victorian building in central Glasgow. There was a fire in an adjacent building. A notice was served by Glasgow City Council under s 13 of the Building (Scotland) Act 1959 requiring demolition of the fire-damaged building. The Council itself took over the site and, in due course, instructed the second defenders as independent contractors. During the course of the work, the gable of the pursuer's building was seriously damaged. In this claim for damages, based on both negligence and nuisance, the pursuer sued the Council and also the contractor. **Held**: proof before answer allowed (subject to further procedure on the too sketchy averments of loss).

In relation to the claim against the Council, Lord Emslie took a more robust view than the First Division in *Stewart v Malik* (above) as to the liability for independent contractors in circumstances where the works were inherently hazardous. 'For well over a century', Lord Emslie said (para 43), 'the "inherently hazardous" nature of operations has been thought sufficient to deprive the responsible landowner or employer of the protection of the ordinary rule relieving him of liability in law for the acts or omissions of an apparently competent independent contractor.'

(17) Mehrabadi v Haugh
June 2009, Aberdeen Sheriff Court

The pursuer owned one of the attic flats at 20 Summerfield Terrace, Aberdeen. Spurred on by a letter from Aberdeen City Council encouraging proprietors to maintain their properties, he obtained estimates for roof repairs and circulated them to the other owners in the tenement. Some replied and others did not, and it is unclear whether (or to what extent) consent was given for the repairs. Be that as it may, the pursuer went ahead with the works, using a different contractor. The total cost was £7,000. In this action the pursuer sought to recover a proportionate share from one of the owners. The action was defended on the basis that (i) the pursuer had gone ahead without majority agreement, and in any event (ii) that part of the bill relating to the dormer windows was the sole responsibility of the pursuer and the owner of the other attic flat.

The sheriff **held** that argument (i) was ill founded, because it was based on the Tenements (Scotland) Act 2004 which 'does not apply in circumstances where the titles contain express provisions regulating responsibility for repairs'. But argument (ii) was correct: although real burdens provided for the maintenance of the roof, the dormers had been added much later and were not covered by the burdens.

While the decision on (i) is correct (although not, we think, for the reason given by the sheriff), the decision on (ii) seems incorrect. We would stress, however, that we have not seen the titles and that some of the other factual details are unclear.

On (i), the 2004 Act does in fact apply to all tenements, but is subject to the title deeds of the tenement in question. In particular, the Tenement Management Scheme (set out in sch 1 of the Act) applies only to the extent that its subject matter is not otherwise covered by the titles: see s 4. So the fact that (as in the present case) real burdens apportion liability for the roof means that the default provisions for such liability (in TMS rule 4) do not apply (subject to the position of dormers, discussed below). On the other hand, unless the titles make provision for decision-making (which they appear not to), TMS rules 2 and 3 will apply. These provide that, in relation to repairs, decisions must be made by a majority. And to drive the point home, s 16 of the Act disapplies the rule of the common law that, where something is owned in common (as, here, in the case of the roof) any owner, acting alone, can carry out necessary repairs and recover the cost. So the position is clear: an owner who jumps the gun and carries out repairs without majority agreement must usually bear the cost himself. To this rule, however, there is at least one important exception. By s 8 of the Act the owner or owners of the roof must keep it in repair and, by s 10, can recover the costs from the other owners in the same way as if majority agreement had been reached. That exception would appear to apply to the pursuer in the present case.

The position on (ii) is more complex than might at first appear. The sheriff is probably correct to say that the real burdens in respect of roof maintenance are restricted to the roof in its original state and do not extend to the roof surrounding the dormer windows. But to the extent that title provisions do not apply, the TMS does. Whatever the position may be under the titles, a dormer window (other than the window frame itself) is part of the roof and therefore 'scheme property'. See TMS rule 1.2(c) (and see also the discussion of the issue at para 5.8 of the Scottish Law Commission's Report on the *Law of the Tenement* (Scot Law Com No 162 (1998), available at www.scotlawcom.gov.uk). Hence, even although it is not covered by the real burdens, the dormer falls to be maintained by all the owners under rule 4.2(b).

It is understood that the sheriff's decision has been appealed.

(18) McKenzie v Scott
19 May 2009, Lands Tr

4 Fettes Row, Edinburgh came to be divided into four flats. The flat on the first floor was the first to be split off. The disposition, granted in 1944, conveyed the flat itself:

> together with the whole fittings and fixtures in the said dwellinghouse so far as belonging to me, also a right in common with me as proprietor of the remaining dwellinghouses in said building (One) to the solum on which the same are built (two) to the flight of stairs and entrance platt in front of said building, the common entrance hall and stair, hatchway leading to the roof, as also the roof itself, rhones and rain water pipes, chimney stacks, drains and all others common to the houses in said building with free ish and entry by the said hatchway for the purpose of cleaning vents and

all other necessary purposes; and (three) to use the garden ground behind the said building for the purpose of drying and bleaching clothes with right of access thereto by the existing back stair leading to the said garden ground; and the whole other parts, privileges and pertinents of the house hereby disponed and my whole right title and interest present and future therein.

The remaining split-off writs, dating from 1957, were in similar terms. A dispute arose as to the nature of the right to the garden. Was it a mere servitude (of drying and bleaching)? Or was it a right of common property?

The Lands Tribunal **held** that the right was one of servitude only. This, the Tribunal thought, was the obvious conclusion from the language of the pertinents clause which, while conferring rights 'to' the solum and stairs, conferred in respect of the garden only a right 'to use'. Although, on this view, ownership of the garden was not expressly dealt with, that was governed by the general law, which would confer ownership solely on the proprietor of the basement flat.

While the decision is plainly correct, it proceeds on the basis of the common law of the tenement despite the fact that, even in respect of pre-2004 tenements, that law has been replaced by the Tenements (Scotland) Act 2004. Fortunately, the rule as to ownership of garden ground is the same: see 2004 Act s 3(3).

[Another aspect of this case is digested at (42) below.]

SERVITUDES

(19) Holms v Ashford Estates Ltd
[2009] CSIH 28, 2009 SLT 389, 2009 SCLR 428

A parking space was burdened by a right of access in favour of another parking space. This prevented the first space from being used for its primary purpose, ie parking a car, although it could still be used for other purposes, eg parking a bike or sitting in the sun. **Held** that there was no reason to suppose that the servitude was invalid as repugnant with ownership. See **Commentary** p 180.

[Another aspect of this case is digested at (52) below.]

(20) Greig v Middleton
2009 GWD 22-365, Sh Ct

Adjacent houses in the High Street at Earlsferry – 'Ardsheiling' and 'Ashdene' – were for many years the property of the same person. When that person died, in 1955, his legatees agreed that Ardsheiling should be exposed for sale 'without right of access to Links Road'. This referred to the fact that only Ashdene had direct access to the street at the rear (Links Road), and was presumably designed to prevent access to Links Road being taken through the rear garden at Ashdene. In the event, Ardsheiling was acquired by one of the legatees and Ashdene by another. The two – sister and brother – lived in their respective houses for many years. For reasons not explained, the disposition of Ardsheiling in favour of the sister was not recorded until 1977. Faithful to the 1955 agreement, this specified 'free ish and entry thereto from High Street only'.

Later Ashdene passed out of the family, and a dispute arose as to whether there was a right of pedestrian access from Ardsheiling through Ashdene to Links Road. A declarator was sought by the owners of Ardsheiling. **Held**: absolvitor. Although the short-cut had been used quite often over the years, the usage had varied in frequency and intensity. Nor was it clear that the possession was of the right type. On the contrary, the two deeds – one recorded as recently as 1977 – argued against the existence of a servitude. And the fact that the owners of the two properties were close relatives suggested that the true explanation for the usage was tolerance rather than an attempt to establish a right by prescription. After all, would the daily use of a connecting door between a granny flat and a main house – allowing mother and daughter to pass through – create a servitude after 20 years? The sheriff (G J Evans) doubted that that would be so. The present facts were analogous.

(21) Garson v McLeish
2010 GWD 5-88, Sh Ct

The defenders' house was reached by a track or road which, at the point where it joined the main road, was the property of the pursuers. The track was unmetalled except at the bell mouth on to the main road. A servitude of access had long since been established by prescription.

The defenders applied for and were granted planning permission for the erection of a second house, but on condition that they improved the access at the point where the track joined the main road. After consultations with the planning authority, it was agreed that this could be done by widening the tarmacked width from 2.5 metres to 3.25 metres. This involved converting grass verge into road for a length of 5 metres. The pursuers sought to interdict the defenders from carrying out this work. After a proof, interdict was granted.

In the view of the sheriff (Daniel Kelly QC), there were several reasons why the work could not be carried out. (i) The evidence was that the verge was almost never used, except occasionally by large vehicles. As possession determines extent, that meant that the verge was not subject to the servitude (paras 65–67). (ii) Works that are absolutely necessary might be permitted, but these works did not fall into that category (para 68). (iii) Works that were reasonably necessary might also be allowed, but in this case the main gain would not be to the enjoyment of the servitude (eg by improving safety) but to the physical condition of the servient tenement (by replacing a grass verge which is easily damaged by vehicles with tarmacadam) (paras 69–71). (iv) There was a special rule for roads which prevented improvements which either changed their character or which promoted a use which would increase the burden. The building of an additional house would increase the burden (paras 73–74).

In reaching his decision, the sheriff paid close attention to paras 12.124–12.127 of D J Cusine and R R M Paisley, *Servitudes and Rights of Way* (1998). The reasoning, however, is not always clear. For example, if ground (i) is established, it is hard

to see why it was necessary to consider any other: for if the verge is exempt from
the servitude, then that is the end of the matter. Grounds (ii) and (iii) are, in
effect, founded on the idea that a servitude holder has certain ancillary rights. In
Moncrieff v Jamieson 2008 SC (HL) 1 such rights were held to be based on an implied
term of the original grant of servitude and so to depend on what was within the
contemplation of the parties at that time. How (or even whether) this rule can
operate for servitudes created by prescription is unclear, and was not considered
by the sheriff. Finally, the sheriff's finding that the proposed use, for a second
house, would increase the burden on the servient tenement might have been a
separate reason for preventing the defenders' ultimate plans, independently of
whether the track needed to be upgraded.

(22) Compugraphics International Ltd v Nikolic
[2009] CSOH 54, 2009 GWD 19-311

Where ductwork on the wall of a building encroached into the airspace of
neighbouring property, it was **held** that the encroachment (which had been in
position for more than 20 years) could be justified as a servitude of overhang (*jus
projiciendi*). See **Commentary** p 104.

   [Another aspect of this case is digested at (90) below.]

(23) SP Distribution Ltd v Rafique
2009 SCLR 891, 2010 SLT (Sh Ct) 8

An express servitude of access to cellars under a street which were approached
from an external basement area was **held** not to include, by implication, a right to
construct a flight of steps on the basement area to improve access to the cellars.
See **Commentary** p 101.

(24) Patersons of Greenoakhill Ltd v SP Transmission Ltd
[2009] CSOH 155, 2009 GWD 39-666

When the pursuer terminated a voluntary electricity wayleave, the defender
applied to the Scottish Ministers for a statutory wayleave under sch 4 para 6 of
the Electricity Act 1989. Nonetheless the parties continued to negotiate the terms
of a possible voluntary wayleave. This continued for three years during which
time the application to the Scottish Ministers was sisted with the agreement of
both parties. Eventually the defender decided to do without the wayleave and
removed the electricity lines. The pursuer claimed £1 million compensation
for the defender's use during the three years of negotiations. The pursuer had
various arguments. One was that, although the Act did not provide expressly
for compensation during a transitional period such as this, such compensation
was implicit in the legislation. Another was that the three-year period must be
viewed as an extension of the previous wayleave. A third was that compensation
was due 'under common law'. All three failed. One argument which was not tried
was unjustified enrichment.

REAL BURDENS

(25) Braes v Keeper of the Registers of Scotland
[2009] CSOH 176

A right of pre-emption in a disposition of 1982 was **held** not to be a real burden because (i) the express nomination of a benefited property was unacceptably vague, and (ii) no benefited property could be implied because the rule in *J A Mactaggart & Co v Harrower* (1906) 8 F 1101 did not apply to pre-emptions and in any event could not apply to a deed with an express (albeit flawed) nomination. See **Commentary** p 114.

Temporary Judge M G Thomson QC also had something to say about the test of praedial benefit (now s 3(3) of the Title Conditions (Scotland) Act 2003) as applied to pre-emptions. As there is so little authority on this point, the passage (para 66) is worth quoting in full:

> A clause of pre-emption creates an opportunity for the servient tenement to be joined together with the dominant tenement in the common ownership of the dominant proprietor. There must, in my opinion, be some benefit to the dominant tenement to satisfy the requirement of praedial interest. Such a conjoining of properties might improve the amenity of the dominant tenement. It might enable a commercial operation carried out on the dominant tenement, such as farming, to be carried out more efficiently or more profitably. There could be many reasons for the value of the dominant tenement to be enhanced by being in the same ownership as the servient tenement.

[Another aspect of this case is digested at (58) below.]

(26) Clarke v Grantham
2009 GWD 38-645, Lands Tr

Two properties – the House and the Maltings – were separated by a courtyard. Ownership was shared, part of the courtyard belonging to the House and a smaller part to the Maltings. The split-off disposition of the Maltings prohibited parking on the courtyard and undertook to impose a similar restriction in the split-off writ for the House. This restriction was not, however, imposed. It was **held** (i) that no restriction having been imposed on the part of the courtyard belonging to the House, the restriction could not be enforced by the owner of the House in respect of the part belonging to the Maltings, and (ii) that in any event there would be no interest to enforce. The Tribunal, however, rejected an argument that the restriction was void from uncertainty. See **Commentary** p 116.

[Another aspect of this case is digested at (34) below.]

(27) Perth and Kinross Council v Chapman
13 August 2009, Lands Tr

A disposition granted in 1945 provided as follows:

And whereas the said small field or park before gifted to our said disponees is at present leased for use as Tennis Courts it is hereby provided and said disponees by acceptance hereby agree that the said field shall be used only for outdoor recreational purposes which agreement and restriction is hereby declared to be a servitude over the subjects hereby disponed ... in favour of us the said British Linen Bank and our successors in the Property in Kinross retained by and now belonging to us.

The validity of this restriction was attacked on two grounds. (i) The word 'servitude' was used whereas in fact what was being attempted was a real burden. (ii) The description of the benefited property was insufficiently clear. Both grounds were rejected.

In relation to (i), the Tribunal emphasised the traditional rule which says that no *voces signatae* are necessary for real burdens. In relation to (ii), the Tribunal said that, under the law in force in 1945, there was a difference between what was required for the burdened and for the benefited property. The former had to be properly identified. The latter did not have to be, and indeed a benefited property could even be implied. The reason for the difference, the Tribunal speculated, was interest to enforce (para 26): the outer limits of the benefited property did not matter because only an inner part of that property would carry the necessary interest. This argument does not, however, explain why it is not necessary to define the inner limits. Compare the result reached on this point with the decision in *Braes v Keeper of the Registers of Scotland* (Case (25) above).

The result would be different if the burden were created today. The modern law requires the use of the term 'real burden' (or equivalent) and also that the benefited property be identified: see Title Conditions (Scotland) Act 2003 s 4(2).

[Another aspect of this case is digested at (35) below.]

VARIATION ETC OF TITLE CONDITIONS BY LANDS TRIBUNAL

The full opinions in most Lands Tribunal cases are available at http://www.lands-tribunal-scotland.org.uk/records.html. Section 98 of the Title Conditions (Scotland) Act 2003 provides that the Tribunal is to grant an application for variation or discharge of a title condition if it is reasonable to do so having regard to the 10 factors (factors (a)–(j)) set out in s 100. A table listing all the applications so far made under the 2003 Act, and their result, will be found in Part V.

(28) Melville v Crabbe
19 January 2009, Lands Tr

Numbers 84 and 86 Forsyth Street, Greenock were, respectively, the upper and lower flats in a Victorian villa. The applicant owned 84 and the respondent 86. Each owned part of the basement. The applicant obtained planning permission for conversion of her part of the basement into a separate flat. But to do so would contravene a condition in a feu disposition of 1880. The application was to vary this condition to the extent of allowing the conversion.

The application was refused. As often happens in such cases, the Tribunal began by considering the purpose of the condition (factor (f)). Plainly, this was 'the type of planning control commonly exerted by superiors in the era before public planning control' (para 45). 'To that extent', the Tribunal said, 'the conditions belong to a bygone age' (para 55). But in addition (para 45):

> [T]here was also a purpose of providing not just for the building of the two villas but maintaining their amenity at least to some extent for the benefit of the owners. The deed envisages up to two owners at each villa, does not reserve to the superior any right to waive, and takes proprietors bound to bind their successors. There is no express *ius quaesitum tertio*, but, although it is not necessary to decide this specific issue, there would appear to have been a strong argument for its implication.

That purpose, the Tribunal thought, was a continuing one (para 55), and had not been defeated by any change in circumstances (factor (b)).

As usual in such cases, much depended on the balance of advantage as between the parties (factors (b) and (c)). Obviously, 'inability to develop one's property as one wishes, even purely for financial gain, significantly impedes one's enjoyment of the property'. But the disadvantage to the respondent seemed worse. To the existing flat above there would be added a new flat below. The respondents would be vulnerable to noise, to smells from cooking, and so on. It was accepted by both parties that the value of the respondent's flat would be reduced by 8.75%. One approach would be to grant the application and to order compensation. But the disadvantage to the respondent seemed particularly serious, and was made worse by the absence, as yet, of a building warrant and hence of fully detailed plans.

The burden's age (factor (e)) favoured the application, particularly in view of the subdivision in recent years of many properties in the area (factor (a)). Nonetheless, on balance, the Tribunal concluded that the application should not be granted.

On 16 April 2009 the Tribunal awarded expenses to the respondent but reduced by one fifth to reflect (i) the lengthy and 'unreasonably argumentative' correspondence emanating from the respondent's law firm, and (ii) the respondent's unsubstantiated insistence, in pleadings, correspondence and in her own evidence, that the applicant's proposals were contrary to the respondent's property rights (para 8).

It is noteworthy that, while both sides gave copious citation of case law, not a single case was mentioned in the Tribunal's own reasoning. Instead the Tribunal made do with the laconic remark that 'the general approach to deciding applications of this kind is familiar and … uncontroversial' (para 36). And indeed the Tribunal tends to avoid analysing or even relying on its own previous decisions: often, one feels, its decisions are almost intuitive, relying heavily on the impression made by a site inspection. As was said in another case from 2009, *Graham v Lee* (Case (38) below), at para 26: 'Each case depends on its own facts and circumstances, with our own inspection at the location being important and reference to previous decided cases of limited assistance.'

(29) McClumpha v Bradie
2009 GWD 31-519, Lands Tr

A small housing estate in Fishcross, near Alloa, was developed in three phases. In the first phase, of eight detached houses, the provision of garden ground was very generous. Both the applicant and the respondent owned phase 1 houses, and the applicant's plot was not much short of an acre. In the subsequent phases, however, the gardens were of 'normal' size.

The applicant obtained planning permission for the erection of four additional houses, but this was contrary to a no-building restriction in the split-off disposition for her plot. This was assumed to be a community burden, enforceable by everyone in the estate. The application was for the complete discharge of the burden. The Tribunal granted the application, but only to the extent of permitting four detached houses each with a plot size of not less than 600 square metres.

The Tribunal had little difficulty in reaching its decision. On the one hand, there was little benefit to the respondent from the burden (factor (b)). The new development would barely be seen from the respondent's house, which in any event faced in the opposite direction. Owners much closer had not objected. And the proposed development was similar in scale to phases 2 and 3 of the original development. On the other hand (factor (c)), it was obvious from a visual inspection that the land available to the applicant was 'considerably in excess of what might be considered normal or appropriate for a house of the applicant's size or type' (para 26). This 'must create difficulties, if not potential expense, in maintenance' (para 33). Further, the burden prevented the applicant from realising the proceeds of development 'which the applicant would, but for the burden, be entitled to expect from her ownership' (para 33).

(30) Matnic Ltd v Armstrong
2009 GWD 31-520, Lands Tr

The applicant owned three retail units on the ground floor of a modern block of flats. This was part of a 300-unit, largely residential development in Bridge of Don. Units 1 and 2 were quite small (1,000 square feet) while unit 3 was almost 4,000 square feet. The applicant had managed to let unit 2 but was seeking tenants for unit 1 and most of unit 3. There were good prospects of letting unit 1 as a small convenience store, but only if the store could sell alcohol. That was contrary to the deed of conditions which governed the development. The applicant accordingly applied for variation of the deed of conditions, in so far as affecting the three units, so as to allow the sale of alcohol. Only one owner (in the same building as the units) opposed the application.

The Tribunal accepted (factor (c)) 'that the condition, although by no means fatal, does represent quite a significant burden on the applicants' investment' in respect that it was making the units difficult to let. On the other hand (factor (b)), it protected the respondent against, not only a convenience store (which would make little difference to his amenity) but also a supermarket (which would increase noise and traffic). The burdens were only five years old (factor (e)), 'which we consider an important factor particularly where we have not found any significant changes of circumstances supporting the reasonableness of the application' (para 26). The almost complete lack of opposition was, however, a point in the applicant's favour (factor (j)).

The Tribunal granted the application, but in a restricted form. It could only apply to the smaller units (thus eliminating the risk of a supermarket), and alcohol must not be sold later than 8 pm.

(31) McGregor v Collins-Taylor
14 May 2009, Lands Tr

In 1988 land was split off from the policies of Lannhall House, near Tynron in Dumfriesshire. In terms of the disposition there was a prohibition on the erection of any building without the consent of the owner of the House. The applicant, and owner of the land in question, had obtained outline planning permission for the erection of four houses. This had been opposed by the owner of the House – the respondent in the present application – and there seemed little prospect that he would give his consent. Hence this application for discharge of the condition.

Since the proposed new houses could not be seen from Lannhall House, the Tribunal thought that the condition was of little benefit to the respondent (factor (b)). In any event, there had been a significant amount of house building, including by the respondent himself, since 1988 (factor (a)). It was true that the proposed houses would be visible from the driveway but, due to the recent building activity, and the consequent access rights, the driveway could no longer be seen as part of the policies of the House.

The respondent emphasised that he did not oppose the houses in principle but merely wanted the opportunity to control the detail. But even if this was correct, the Tribunal did not think the point a strong one:

> We do not accept that there is any sound basis for a finding that variations of the particular detail of the buildings would be a factor of any great significance to the amenity of the house. We are not concerned with the particular taste of Mr Collins-Taylor. The matter must be viewed objectively. Other proprietors of Lannhall House might have quite different preferences.

If, however, the condition was not of much benefit to the respondent, it was a material burden to the applicant (factor (c)). 'A requirement of a tolerable personal relationship between the current parties before the subjects can be developed' – apparently lacking in this case – 'is a significant additional aspect of the burden'.

The Tribunal discharged the condition, but only to the extent that was needed to match the planning permission obtained by the applicant. As to the form of the order, the Tribunal explained that:

> [I]t is no longer the practice of the Tribunal to make an Order expressed by reference to the terms of the planning consent. We seek to identify the essential conditions so that they can appear explicitly in the title. In some cases this requires applicants to provide additional detail allowing, where appropriate, explicit restriction on height

or location, and style. In the present case, for example, we are not satisfied that it is necessary to specify the precise positioning of the houses or the extent of garden ground to be allocated to each. But we think certain points from the terms of the outline planning permissions should be included.

In short, we are satisfied that it is reasonable to vary the condition so as to allow construction of four separate dwelling-houses on the subjects; each to be single storey with a roof of traditional pitch and clad in slates; and with sash and case windows of predominantly vertical form. We have not identified any specific issue of detail likely to have a particular impact on the benefited subjects. In particular, we consider that little purpose would be served by attempting to specify screening measures.

On 10 September 2009 expenses were awarded to the applicant subject to a deduction of 15% to reflect (i) the fact that the application was for a complete discharge, and (ii) the failure of the applicant to seek the respondent's consent to the development as approved by the planning authorities. The Tribunal rejected the suggestion that expenses should be awarded to the respondent 'based on the proposition that the outcome of the case was what he had always been aiming at'. If this was true, the position should have been communicated to the applicant.

(32) Scott v Teasdale
22 December 2009, Lands Tr

In 1962 the owners of a row of six substantial Victorian houses in Kilmalcolm bought the vegetable garden of an adjoining mansion house, extending to about an acre. This was then divided among the six houses, giving each a substantial extension to the rear garden. Detailed burdens were imposed, both in the feu disposition by the owner of the mansion house and also in the subsequent feu disposition splitting up the ground, and were mutually enforceable. Essentially, no building was to be permitted, but there could be garages or greenhouses if approved of by a two-thirds majority.

The applicants were the owners of the two villas at the end of the row. They proposed to combine their part of the former vegetable garden and had obtained outline planning permission for the erection of a two-storey house. The application was to vary the burdens so as to allow this. All the other owners in the row of villas were opposed to the application, and the owners of the two closest houses were respondents.

The Tribunal refused the application. Considerable weight was placed on the purpose of the conditions (factor (f)). This was to protect the private amenity of the villas. The 'clear and detailed provisions can be contrasted, for example, with the type of general building restriction which could often be seen as being in the nature of a general planning restriction conceived substantially in the interests of the superior or developer' (para 43). 'It is perhaps unusual', the Tribunal added (para 44), 'to come across arrangements so clearly applicable to, and in the interest of, all the owners.' There were no changes of circumstances which would prevent that purpose from continuing to be fulfilled (factor (a)). It was true, of course, that not being able to develop the land would impede the applicants' enjoyment of their property, and their chance to benefit financially (factor (c)). But, given the upwards slope of the plot, the proposed house would impact very considerably on the respondents' properties. It would 'remove the environment on one side, substituting a dominating, close building for a significant part of the immediate surroundings' (para 36). Further it would lead to a significant reduction in the value of their properties.

The Tribunal asked whether, despite the prejudice to the respondents, the application should nevertheless be granted but on the basis of the payment of compensation – which would be calculated as the diminution in the value of the respondents' properties (respectively £30,000 and £15,000). 'The legislation', the Tribunal commented, 'clearly envisages such an approach in an appropriate case.' The Tribunal added (para 56):

> It is sometimes appropriate in relation to a proposal to build a house, or perhaps a substantial extension, in the face of a title restriction, even where, as in this case, the benefited proprietors make clear their primary position that they wish the application refused. In this case, however, we consider that the impact of the proposed house on at least the owners of Ardgryffe and St Ronans would have such an effect on their enjoyment of their properties that it would not be reasonable simply to compensate them with a monetary award.

Finally, the Tribunal made the following comment about the potential difficulty for applicants who have only outline planning permission (para 26):

> We did at first wonder whether it might be difficult for the applicants to satisfy us that it would be reasonable to grant the application, when they were only seeking variation on the basis of an outline planning consent. The result of granting the application would be to allow them to build any two-storey house for which they could get full planning consent. It is understandable that burdened proprietors may consider it appropriate to try to achieve variation of the burden before undertaking the full planning application, but this can sometimes be to their disadvantage in contested applications to the Tribunal, particularly where they are seeking, in the face of a building restriction in the titles, to develop on what may be seen as a sensitive site.

In the present case, however, the applicants' plans were sufficiently advanced for the Tribunal to have a clear idea of what was being proposed.

(33) Hollinshead v Gilchrist
2010 GWD 5-87, Lands Tr

The applicants sought variation of two sets of real burdens to the extent that they should be allowed (i) to park private cars in front of the building line of their house, and (ii) to carry out internal alterations. It was not clear that, following feudal abolition, the burdens remained valid, or that the respondent owned a benefited property, or indeed that the burdens (if valid) prohibited (ii). But because the application was so modest in scope, the Tribunal was able to grant it without having to engage with these questions. An application for compensation was refused. It should perhaps be added that it seems unlikely that a neighbour would have had interest to enforce in respect of these matters.

(34) Clarke v Grantham
2009 GWD 38-645, Lands Tr

In 2004 Pitlessie House in Fife was sold in two lots. One lot, purchased by the respondent, comprised the House itself. The other lot, purchased by the applicants, comprised outbuildings which had been converted into a house known as the 'Maltings'. Between the two was an open courtyard, one-quarter of which was conveyed with the Maltings and the remaining three-quarters with the House. In terms of the disposition of the Maltings, there was to be no parking in the courtyard, and the disponer undertook to impose a similar restriction in the disposition of the House. In the event this was not done.

The application was for discharge of the parking restriction or alternatively for a declaration that the restriction was invalid and unenforceable. The Tribunal found that, at present at least, the burden was unenforceable: see Case (26) above. In relation to the application for discharge, the Tribunal had greater difficulty. The restriction could not be said to confer much benefit on the respondent, having regard in particular to the fact that she parked freely in her own part of the courtyard (factor (b)). Viewing the matter objectively, however, it must be borne in mind that a future owner of the House might not park there and might therefore value the prohibition on parking in respect of the Maltings. So far as the applicants were concerned, it could not be said that the restriction was much of an impediment to enjoyment of the Maltings, particularly as two other areas were available for parking. On balance, however, the Tribunal decided to grant the application and discharge the restriction. As the restriction was likely to remain unenforceable, it was confusing to leave it on the Register. But even if the restriction had been enforceable, the decision would have been the same 'as we would then have been of the view in the circumstances that in the absence of any similar condition in the title of the House, it would be unreasonable to leave the House owner in a position to enforce the burden' (para 49). On 27 October 2009 expenses were awarded to the applicants: see 2010 GWD 1-10.

Arguably, the last substantive point extends reasonableness too far. The Tribunal's concern should have been solely with the burden on the applicants and not with the absence of a corresponding burden on the respondents. It is common for a burdened owner to be subject to a condition which does not affect the benefited owner. Why this inequality should matter is hard to see. Nor should it make any difference that the inequality came about by accident.

(35) Perth and Kinross Council v Chapman
13 August 2009, Lands Tr

In 1945 the British Linen Bank donated a plot of land to Kinross Town Council. The disposition contained the following provision:

> And whereas the said small field or park before gifted to our said disponees is at present leased for use as Tennis Courts it is hereby provided and said disponees by acceptance hereby agree that the said field shall be used only for outdoor recreational purposes which agreement and restriction is hereby declared to be a servitude over

the subjects hereby disponed … in favour of us the said British Linen Bank and our successors in the Property in Kinross retained by and now belonging to us.

The plot was next to Kinross High School, and in 1978 the tennis courts were relocated to another site in Kinross and the original courts were built over and incorporated into the school, apparently without objection. Now the school itself was to be relocated and the site sold for development. To clear the title, Perth and Kinross Council applied for the discharge of the restriction. The application was opposed by the owners of two houses on the benefited property.

The application was granted. The benefit conferred by the restriction was said to be relatively modest (factor (b)). Unless it was removed the plot might not find a buyer, in which case the buildings would remain; and even if the plot were to revert to outdoor use, there is no guarantee that that use would be congenial to the respondents, or promote tranquillity. On the other hand, the restriction was self-evidently a severe impediment to the applicant (factor (c)). The fact that a building had stood on the plot for 30 years 'with either the agreement of the benefited proprietors or at least no attempt to enforce it' (para 43) was an important change in circumstances since the burden was first created (factor (a)). Also significant was the fact that the purpose of the restriction – to provide outdoor recreational facilities – was now being met by the new tennis courts (factors (f) and (j)).

Although the point was not taken (para 27), presumably the restriction had been substantially extinguished by negative prescription, for it had been many years since the original breach. But it is natural that the applicant should want the comfort of a formal Tribunal discharge.

[Another aspect of this case is digested at (27) above.]

(36) Fleeman v Lyon
2009 GWD 32-539, Lands Tr

This was an application for preservation of a real burden, following execution and service of a discharge of a community burden under s 33 of the Title Conditions (Scotland) Act 2003 in so far as it affected one particular property. The application was by the immediate neighbour.

Although the Tribunal indicated that it would have been willing to vary the burden to the extent of allowing the respondent's plans (which were to build a second house), it was not prepared to allow a complete discharge. The application for preservation was therefore granted. See **Commentary** p 120.

(37) Fenwick v National Trust for Scotland
2009 GWD 32-538, Lands Tr

A mill conversion in Perth undertaken by the National Trust for Scotland resulted in a building comprising office premises (owned by the Trust) and seven flats, each in separate ownership. The Trust's deed of conditions, dating from 1989, regulated the property. As well as the usual kinds of condition, this reserved to the Trust extensive powers of management (including the power to act as manager or appoint someone else), and also made provision in relation to sheltered or retirement housing, such as a requirement that residents be at least 60, and the operation of a community alarm call system.

This was an application under s 91 of the Title Conditions (Scotland) Act 2003 – the first (we think) to have been considered by the Lands Tribunal. Section 91 allows applications by the owners of one-quarter of the units in a development for the variation of community burdens, including the provision of new or replacement burdens. It thus supplements the provision for majority variation contained in s 33 of the Act (and considered in the previous case). The present application was made by the owners of three flats. It was opposed by the Trust and by the owners of two other flats.

The proposal was for the complete discharge of the deed of conditions. It had, the applicants argued, become badly out of date. The Trust did not in practice exercise any management functions. There was no longer a community alarm call system. The development could not properly be classified as sheltered housing, and the age restriction should be lowered to 55. In the long term there should be a new deed of conditions, but to vary the existing one would be cumbersome and it would be better to start again with a clean sheet. Until a new deed of conditions could be prepared and agreed, it would be acceptable for the building to be governed by the default rules set out in the Tenement Management Scheme (ie sch 1 of the Tenements (Scotland) Act 2004).

The application was refused. It was true, the Tribunal said, that there had been changes in circumstances, as the applicants indicated (factor (a)). But the deed of conditions continued to confer a great deal of benefit (factor (b)), for which the Tenement Management Scheme would not be an adequate substitute. Apart from anything else, the age restriction, which everyone agreed was desirable (with some disagreement as to the figure), would be lost. Conversely, there was very little benefit from discharging the conditions (factor (c)). If the applicants wished to dispense with the existing conditions, they should have proposed replacement ones. In fact they seemed unduly optimistic that such conditions could be readily agreed. The opposition to the present application by three of the owners was significant in this regard, and a factor against the application being granted (factor (j)).

Subsequently, the Tribunal awarded expenses against the applicants: see 2010 GWD 5-84.

It seems worth adding that the reservation of management rights to the Trust was a manager burden which had now expired under s 63 of the Title Conditions Act, leaving the building without a management structure. At least in this respect the building would have been better off with the relatively sophisticated provisions offered by the Tenement Management Scheme.

(38) Graham v Lee
18 June 2009, Lands Tr

Recently, land at Upper Bowertower, Bower, Wick was divided into three lots – two quite substantial (lots 1 and 2), and the third very small. The present application was by the owners of lot 2 and was opposed by the owners of lot 1.

Lot 1 was sold first, in 2001. The disposition created a reciprocal servitude of access over a proposed road which ran through all three lots. In the event, this road came to be only partially made up, and then only on lot 1. The disposition also reserved a servitude over lot 2 'to install a septic tank or septic tanks and soakaways'. The applicants sought the discharge of the access servitude and a restriction of the drainage servitude to the septic tanks and soakaways already installed.

In relation to the servitude of access, the Tribunal thought that it was of little real benefit to the respondents (factor (b)), given that it had never been properly completed, that they had constructed another road on their own land which did some of the work of the servitude, and that they could readily construct another which would do the rest of the work. Equally, however, its continued existence had little impact on the applicants (factor (c)), other than the minor inconvenience of having to share an access. The Tribunal granted the application on condition that the applicants were willing to discharge their own reciprocal rights of access over lot 1 (which they were), and the respondents were given an opportunity to claim compensation for the increased costs of making a section of new road (modest compensation was agreed between the parties).

The Tribunal refused the application in respect of the septic tanks. The purpose of the servitude was to promote reasonable development on plot 1 (factor (f)). That was an important benefit (factor (b)). The corresponding burden on the applicants was slight (factor (c)).

Both parties claimed expenses but on 24 November 2009 the Tribunal decided that, in view of the divided success, none should be awarded. If expenses had in fact been awarded, the Tribunal indicated that it would have decided (narrowly) to sanction the employment of junior counsel, adding (para 9):

> Applications under this jurisdiction often do not justify the employment of counsel, but in this case we would have been persuaded that the issues were just complex enough to justify sanction, considering also the particular sensitivies of a case in which there had been considerable animosity and a complicated tale of an unsuccessful settlement agreement.

(39) Colecliffe v Thompson
2009 GWD 23-375, Lands Tr

When part of a rear garden was sold off as a building plot in 1997, the plot could only be reached by a driveway running through the parent property. Accordingly, the 1997 disposition included a servitude of pedestrian and vehicular access. Subsequently, the owners of the plot obtained a servitude of access from West Lothian Council which allowed them to take access from the front, to a different street. This became the main access, and the original access – less convenient in a number of respects – ceased to be much used. Both properties changed hands. The present application was by the owners of the parent property to have the original servitude discharged. The application was opposed.

The application was granted. The new servitude was a change in circumstances (factor (a)). Now that it was available, the original servitude conferred little in the way of benefit (factor (b)). Although the applicants did not have any other use in mind for the driveway (eg to build on it), it would obviously be of benefit not to have to share it with the respondent (factor (c)); and 'the ability to park, or the potential to make some other use of the driveway or part of it (perhaps for a garage or other building) would be of some benefit' (para 23).

The Tribunal, however, refused to award the applicants' expenses. The parties were on bad terms (para 29):

> It seems to us that this application became necessary as a result of the unfortunate loss of goodwill between the parties. It may well be that there is blame on both sides, and it is not for us to judge that, but we certainly did not have the impression that the applicants were blameless. They appeared to us to have adopted an intransigent and almost intimidatory approach when a more reasonable approach might perhaps have avoided the need for these proceedings.

(40) G v A
26 November 2009, Lands Tr

The facts were close to those of the previous case – a connection made by both the applicant and the Tribunal. The only material difference was that the servitude over the applicant's driveway was the only means of entering the respondent's garage. This was because of the location of the door, which could not be reached by vehicle from the respondent's own property. Thus to grant the application would be to deprive the respondent of access to his garage. In practice, however, the respondent did not use the garage for his car, and the garage was relatively dilapidated.

The Tribunal granted the application, but on the basis that the respondent should have the opportunity to apply for compensation. As the Tribunal explained (paras 32–33):

> The legislation provides for awards of compensation for substantial loss or disadvantage suffered in consequence of such a discharge. In other words, the answer can sometimes be that the discharge will cause substantial loss but it would nevertheless be reasonable to discharge the condition on the basis that the loss can be compensated. The statutory provisions ensure that the respondent can have a claim for compensation decided, and indeed compensation paid, before the discharge is ordered.
>
> We have reached the view that that is the position in this case. We think that the loss and inconvenience to the respondent could reasonably be met by monetary compensation. If the discharge is granted, the respondent will have options including to re-align the garage, to build a new garage or perhaps simply to do nothing and use the garage building as a store.

(41) Gibb v Kerr
2009 GWD 38-646, Lands Tr

The applicant owned an end-terraced house in Eaglesham, number 56 Hill Road. The respondent owned the next-door house, number 58. Access to the rear of number 58 was by a path along the far side of number 56, and this was formally constituted as a servitude in the split-off writ for number 56 granted in 1981. This nominated a fixed route identified by reference to a plan. In 2003 the applicant built a conservatory at the side of her house and made some other changes as a result of which it became necessary to move the path. This work was carried out shortly before the respondent bought number 58.

The application was to allow the re-routing of the servitude which had already taken place on the ground. Helpfully, if unusually, the Tribunal was willing to offer a general rule on the issue (para 17):

> Each case has to be decided on its own facts and circumstances, although it is fair to say that applications for specific variations of access routes will often be held reasonable if the alternative route proposed fulfils the purpose of the condition and is reasonably comparable in quality and convenience with the original route. This is because the purpose of the condition will continue to be fulfilled and there will be no real benefit to the benefited proprietor to set against the detriment to the burdened proprietor if the original route is maintained with the result of preventing reasonable development.

That general rule was applied in the present case. Thus the application was allowed subject to a requirement that the new route should be of minimum width of 0.9 metres. At one point – where the path turned the corner – it was narrower than this and, in the view of the Tribunal, too narrow. The change could, however, be made without altering the conservatory. Expenses were awarded to the applicant but reduced by 50% to take account of the applicant having already carried out the works and the fact that she did not achieve complete success.

Although the Tribunal tended to dismiss the point (para 19), it seems likely that the new route was already established by acquiescence and that the application was therefore unnecessary. See E C Reid and J W G Blackie, *Personal Bar* (2006) paras 6–46 to 6–55, and in particular the decision in *Millar v Christie* 1961 SC 1.

(42) McKenzie v Scott
19 May 2009, Lands Tr

4 Fettes Row, Edinburgh is divided into four flats. The applicants, who owned the basement flat and the back garden, sought the discharge of a servitude right to dry clothes in that garden which was held by the owners of the other flats. The right had not been used for many years and so had almost certainly been extinguished by negative prescription. But the Lands Tribunal has no jurisdiction to consider validity in relation to servitudes (as opposed to real burdens), and so the application proceeded on the basis that the servitude was still live. The application was opposed by the owners of the other flats.

The Tribunal granted the application. Given how little the servitude had been used, the benefit to the respondents was small (factor (b)). And technological change (factor (a)) – the invention of the tumble dryer – meant that it was quite normal today for flats not to have access to a drying green – 'apart from environmental considerations, which some take seriously' (para 55). On the other hand, the use of the back garden by the other proprietors was plainly intrusive from the applicants' point of view (factor (c)).

[Another aspect of this case is digested at (18) above.]

(43) Cassidy v McAdam
2009 GWD 17-274, Lands Tr

An application was initially opposed by a number of neighbours, but the opposition fell away, although the last objector to withdraw did so only four days before the hearing was due to take place. In the absence of opposition, the Tribunal granted the application, as it is required to do by s 97 of the Title Conditions (Scotland) Act 2003. The applicants then sought an award of expenses. The Tribunal declined to make the award. Expenses could only be due in respect of matters caused by the objectors – in this case the cost of answering objections and of preparation for the hearing. But these were modest. Further, the applicants were to some extent to blame for the initial opposition in respect that they did not, apparently, consult the neighbours first, and that the initial application was skeletal.

(44) Ballantyne Property Services Trs v Lawrence
3 February 2009, Lands Tr

The application having been refused (*Conveyancing 2008* Case (28)), it was uncontroversial that expenses should be awarded against the applicants. But the applicants opposed certification of junior counsel and of an experienced residential solicitor as an expert witness. The Tribunal allowed the former, but only in respect of the hearing itself, and refused the latter. In relation to the former it emphasised the complexity of the case and the fact that the issue in question had not been previously considered.

EXECUTION OF DEEDS

(45) Gibson v Royal Bank of Scotland plc
[2009] CSOH 14, 2009 SLT 444, 2009 SCLR 364

An offer in respect of an option to buy heritable property contained the following clause:

8. FORMAL DOCUMENTATION REQUIRED

Neither the Grantor nor the Grantee shall be bound by any acceptance hereof or any other letter purporting to form part of the Option Agreement or any amendment or variation of the Option Agreement unless the same satisfies the requirements of Section 3 of the Requirements of Writing (Scotland) Act 1995.

In the event, the acceptance was signed but not witnessed – in other words was executed in accordance with s 2 of the 1995 Act but not in accordance with s 3. While Lord Emslie felt that there was 'some force' in the argument that no contract had been concluded, he was not prepared to exclude the averments on the subject from probation (paras 10–11):

> On a proper construction of the 1995 Act, it does not seem to me that s 3 contains any 'requirements' worthy of the name. The primary requirements of the Act are to be found ss 1 and 2, and by comparison s 3 does no more than identify particular circumstances in which a presumption regarding the granter's subscription will arise. Had cl 8 referred simply to 'the requirements of the Act of 1995', I do not think that the informed reader would have contemplated looking for these in s 3. To my mind, therefore, it is a matter of speculation whether the wording of cl 8 was deliberately intended, and if so what that wording was supposed to convey.
>
> In my opinion, a party desiring to stipulate for particular formalities in a contract must do so clearly and in a fair manner. Clause 8 here was not highlighted in any way as being of special or unusual importance; on the contrary it appeared among other clauses on a different page from cl 10 [which provided for immediate written acceptance]; where there was no obvious point in having a solicitor's signature witnessed, its terms might strike even a careful reader as containing a misprint for s 2 of the Act; and in the circumstances I regard it as preferable to defer any decision on the relevancy of the challenged averments until after any proof at which the matters in issue might be raised with relevant witnesses. It is not clear, for example, whether clauses of this type are in common use among conveyancers. The bank make no averments of custom and practice in that regard. And at this stage I do not feel able to rule out the possibility that, after proof, cl 8 will be held to have been an unclear source of doubt and confusion – a trap for the unwary – and thus a purported stipulation to which effect could not fairly be given.

The court's reasoning is unconvincing. Although it is true that compliance with s 3 is not required for formal validity, it is going too far to say that s 3 does not lay down any 'requirements'. Three are listed in s 3(1). In any event, what the parties wanted is not in doubt. If parties wish that a document should take a particular form, then it is not clear on what basis a court can, or should, refuse to give effect to that choice. There seems no basis for supposing that 's 3' was a 'misprint' for 's 2'. To require a document to be in probative form is not unusual. We do not see why it is significant that the provision was 'not highlighted' or that it was on a 'different page' from clause 10. Nowadays courts are more willing than formerly to interpret contracts according to their real intent rather than their literal meaning, but here the court seems to be interpreting the contract not only against the literal meaning but also against the real intent.

[Another aspect of this case is digested at (59) below.]

PUBLIC RIGHTS OF WAY AND ACCESS RIGHTS

(46) Aviemore Highland Resort Ltd v Cairngorms National Park Authority
15 January 2009, Inverness Sheriff Court rev 2009 SLT (Sh Ct) 97

It was **held** that the local authority cannot use s 14 of the Land Reform (Scotland) Act 2003 to require removal of hedges etc that already existed when the 2003 Act came into force. See **Commentary** p 169.

(47) Forbes v Fife Council
2009 SLT (Sh Ct) 71

A path that was not a public right of way was closed by the owners because of anti-social behaviour. When the Council ordered that it be reopened, by serving a notice under s 14 of the Land Reform (Scotland) Act 2003, the owners appealed and were partially successful. See **Commentary** p 168.

(48) Tuley v Highland Council
[2009] CSIH 31A, 2009 SC 456, 2009 SLT 616

The owners of land welcomed the public on to their land, but did not allow riding on certain paths because they were unsuitable for riding. The Council ordered the owners to open up all paths to riders and the sheriff found for the Council (2007 SLT (Sh Ct) 97, digested as *Conveyancing 2007* Case (24).) The Inner House has now reversed that decision. See **Commentary** p 165.

(49) Creelman v Argyll and Bute Council
2009 SLT (Sh Ct) 165

A land owner who charged visitors for tours wished to include a neighbouring property in his tours, without paying the owners. They refused. The Council then ordered them to comply and they appealed. See **Commentary** p 164.

(50) Hamilton v Dumfries and Galloway Council
[2009] CSIH 13, 2009 SC 277, 2009 SLT 337, 2009 SCLR 392

This is the latest, and presumably final, stage of a long litigation. For earlier stages see [2006] CSOH 110 (*Conveyancing 2006* Case (37)); [2007] CSOH 96, 2007 GWD 20-347; [2007] CSIH 75, 2007 GWD 34-582 (*Conveyancing 2007* Case (22)).

The only access to a small housing estate was by means of a road belonging to the petitioner. When the Council adopted the road, against the petitioner's wishes, he sought a declarator that the road was not a 'road' within the Roads (Scotland) Act 1984 in respect that it was not subject to a 'public right of passage'. At first instance Lady Smith decided that such a right could be, and had been, established by usage falling short of the 20 years needed for a public right of way under s 3(3) of the Prescription and Limitation (Scotland) Act 1973: see [2008] CSOH 65, 2008 SLT 531 (*Conveyancing 2008* Case (37)). The petitioner appealed. **Held**, allowing the appeal, that, in requiring a 'public right of passage' the 1984 Act was working with traditional and well-established concepts. Consequently, 20 years' usage was required. As this had not occurred in the present case, the petitioner was entitled to his declarator. See **Commentary** p 157.

(51) Hamilton v Nairn
[2009] CSOH 163, 2010 GWD 1-11

The pursuers were in the process of buying land near Aberdeen. The land abutted a public road but was separated from it by a verge of up to 7 or 8 metres. Part of this verge was grassed and maintained by the council, but closer to the pursuers' land the verge was rough grassland and scrub and overgrown in places. A track, capable of taking vehicles, led from the pursuers' land across the verge to the public road. The junction was marked by a bell mouth. The defender, apparently opposed to the use to which the pursuers now proposed to put the land (a cattery and livery stables), bought the verge and challenged the pursuers' right to take access over it. The access had not been in place for long enough for a servitude to have been established by prescription.

The extent of the road, as listed, included the whole of the verge right up to the boundary of the pursuers' land, and it was conceded for the defender that the whole verge was a 'verge' for the purposes of the Roads (Scotland) Act 1984 and hence, by s 151(1), part of the road. After a proof it was **held** that a public right of passage had been constituted over the verge by use for the prescriptive period (eg for horse-riding or by vehicles having to move to the side of the (narrow) road to let an oncoming vehicle past). Hence the pursuers (as members of the public) were entitled to take access in that way. But Lord Glennie further indicated that, if a road is subject to a public right of passage and adopted, that right must be taken to extend to the whole road as adopted, including the verge. See **Commentary** p 157.

WARRANDICE

(52) Holms v Ashford Estates Ltd
[2009] CSIH 28, 2009 SLT 389, 2009 SCLR 428

The defender converted an office into flats and sold one of the flats to the pursuers. A car-parking space was included, and was reached by means of an adjacent parking space in the car-parking area. A servitude of access over that space (and other parts of the parking area) was also granted. In the event, the adjacent space was sold to a third party who used it to park her car, thus preventing the pursuers from reaching their own space. The pursuers sought damages from the defender for breach of warrandice in respect of the defective servitude. Damages of £15,000 were awarded by the sheriff and this was confirmed by the sheriff principal on appeal: see 2006 SLT (Sh Ct) 70 and 2006 SLT (Sh Ct) 161 (digested as *Conveyancing 2006* Case (40)). The defender appealed to the Court of Session. **Held**: As the pursuers' servitude was not obviously defective, there could not be said to be the 'unquestionable' defect which is needed for extra-judicial eviction. Hence there was no basis for a claim in warrandice. See **Commentary** p 180.

[Another aspect of this case is digested at (19) above.]

REVERSIONS

(53) Burgess-Lumsden v Aberdeenshire Council
2009 SLT (Sh Ct) 117

By a feu charter granted in 1855, the Earl of Kintore feued subjects at Leylodge, Kintore, Aberdeenshire, to the Kirk Session of the Parish of Kintore. The pursuers claimed to be the successors of the Earl of Kintore (though whether personal successors or successors as owners of his land – a controversial issue in this area of law – is not disclosed by the report). The defender was the statutory successor of the Kirk Session. The subjects were feued under the School Sites Act 1841 to provide a site for a school. In terms of the feu charter, they were to be held 'under and for the use of the said Minister and Kirk Session of Kintore and myself and our respective successors foresaid as trustees for the purposes of the said Acts'.

Sometime during the 1970s the property ceased to be used for a school, and in 1979 it was sold and a disposition granted which was recorded in the Register of Sasines. By s 2 of the 1841 Act, a school site reverts to the 'estate' of the original granter if it has ceased to be used for its statutory purposes. That provision has been interpreted, in Scotland at least, as a right to a reconveyance, and s 86 of the Title Conditions (Scotland) Act 2003 has now converted that right – from the day the provision came into force (4 April 2003) – to a claim for the value of the property. Accordingly, this was an action for payment of the property's value.

The pursuers had a claim under s 86 only if, immediately before 4 April 2003, their statutory right of reversion had been still in existence. Implicit in the sheriff's judgment is the idea that the pursuers (or their predecessors) would have had two distinct claims in 1979. One was against the Council. The other was against the persons buying from the Council. Following the recording of the disposition any claim against the Council would presumably have resolved into a claim for damages for failure to reconvey. But, since the disponees would have bought with constructive notice of the statutory reversion, their title would have been reducible at the instance of the pursuers on the basis of the rule against offside goals (for which see K G C Reid, *The Law of Property in Scotland* (1996) paras 695ff).

The Council's argument was that any right held by the pursuers had prescribed. Some of the difficulties of founding on prescription in this context were discussed by the Scottish Law Commission at para 10.52 of its Report on *Real Burdens* (Scot Law Com No 181 (2000)) but this passage does not seem to have been referred to the court. It was **held** that prescription had indeed operated. On the one hand, any claim against the Council had been lost by the long negative prescription; on the other, the title of the purchasers had become exempt from challenge by the pursuers ten years after the date of recording of the disposition. The pursuers' rights having prescribed prior to the coming into force of s 86 of the Title Conditions Act, it followed that no claim could be made under that provision.

The sheriff added that any right of the pursuers to receive the proceeds of sale would also, and separately, have prescribed after five years. This, however, seems to go further than was necessary: under the 1841 Act the pursuers' claim was to the property (which failing to damages) and not to the sale proceeds. The decision is, however, a helpful analysis of how prescription might operate in this difficult area of law.

One other matter deserves mention. On the wording of the original feu charter, the sheriff was firmly of the view that a trust had been created, but he rejected the suggestion that 'another trust arose by implication' when the site ceased to be used for a school (para 31). The significance of this finding is that the rights of trust beneficiaries are imprescriptible (Prescription and Limitation (Scotland) Act 1973 sch 3 para (e)), opening up the possibility of a claim by the pursuers for breach of trust. No doubt the sheriff was correct to say that there was no new trust, but if the feu charter set up a trust for the purposes of the 1841 Act, it is hard to see how these purposes did not extend to the obligation to reconvey in the event of the reversion being incurred.

LAND REGISTRATION

(54) PMP Plus Ltd v Keeper of the Registers of Scotland (No 2)
19 March 2009, Lands Tr

This is the sequel to *PMP Plus Ltd v Keeper of the Registers of Scotland* 2009 SLT (Lands Tr) 2 (*Conveyancing 2008* Case (42)). In the first phase of the case the Lands Tribunal held that the developer had title to the area of ground in question, and accordingly that, when it disponed that ground to PMP Plus Ltd, the Keeper had no reason to exclude indemnity on the basis of any nullity in the disponer's title. That left the question whether the disposition by the developer might be voidable because of the 'offside goals' rule, the idea being that the developer had already contracted to convey the ground to the various other buyers in the development. That issue was considered in this second phase of the case. However, neither the Keeper nor any of the individual buyers made any representation to the Tribunal that the disposition would be voidable. In the absence of objections, the Tribunal ordered the Keeper to register the title of PMP Plus Ltd without exclusion of indemnity.

(55) Turnberry Homes Ltd v Keeper of the Registers of Scotland
22 July 2009, Lands Tr

The facts of this case were similar to the facts of the previous case, *PMP Plus* (which was decided later), but the appellant had not run the argument that had proved successful in that case and had accordingly been unsuccessful: see *Conveyancing 2008* Case (41). It subsequently appealed to the Court of Session, which remitted the case back to the Tribunal. Given the decision in *PMP Plus*, the Keeper no longer opposed the appellant's position. Accordingly the Tribunal **held**, contrary to its decision at the earlier hearing, that the appellant was entitled to be registered without exclusion of indemnity.

(56) McCoach v Keeper of the Registers of Scotland
22 October 2009, Lands Tr

After the Land Register was rectified against Mr and Mrs McCoach, their appeal against the rectification failed: see *Conveyancing 2008* Case (43). The present phase of the case was about expenses. The Tribunal has now made an award of expenses (with certain modifications) against the appellants, in favour of the Keeper and also in favour of the City of Edinburgh Council, the owner of the property in question, in whose favour rectification had been made.

(57) Kinnaird v Keeper of the Registers of Scotland
30 April 2009, Lands Tr

This was an appeal against the Keeper's decision not to rectify the Register. In the end it was conceded that the Register was inaccurate and should be rectified. The decision deals with questions of expenses in cases of this sort.

(58) Braes v Keeper of the Registers of Scotland
[2009] CSOH 176

In this case the Keeper was sued for compensation outwith the framework of the Land Registration (Scotland) Act 1979. See **Commentary** p 128.
 [Another aspect of this case is digested at (25) above.]

COMPETITION OF TITLE

(59) Gibson v Royal Bank of Scotland plc
[2009] CSOH 14, 2009 SLT 444, 2009 SCLR 364

By an exchange of letters on 8 February 2005 Mr Macalister granted a two-year purchase option to Mr and Mrs Gibson in respect of his house in St Andrews. As well as provisions of the usual kind, clause 4 of the option agreement bound Mr Macalister not to 'give, grant, lease, dispose or in any other way deal with the Grantor's heritable interest in the Option Subjects during the Option Period'. The Gibsons exercised the option almost at once, with a date of entry of 8 February 2006. Shortly before this date, Mr Macalister granted a standard security to the RBS which was recorded on 6 February. The Gibsons raised an action against the RBS for reduction of the security.
 In granting the security, Mr Macalister was plainly in breach both of (i) the option agreement (and in particular clause 4) and also (ii) the warrandice implied into the contract of sale which had been created by exercise of the option. Assuming, therefore, that the RBS was in bad faith in the sense of knowing

of these obligations on Mr Macalister (which was disputed), the security was potentially reducible on the basis of the 'offside goals' rule. But the prospects of success might depend on whether the RBS could be shown to know of the existence of (ii) as well as of (i). If the RBS knew of (ii), then the Gibsons would succeed, on the authority of *Trade Development Bank v Crittall Windows Ltd* 1983 SLT 510 (a view confirmed by Lord Emslie at para 39 of the present case). But if the RBS knew only of (i) – and so did not know that the option had been exercised – the Gibsons would encounter two difficulties.

First, it had been held in *Wallace v Simmers* 1960 SC 255 that the offside goals rule did not apply to breaches of all personal rights but only of personal rights capable of being made real (such as missives of sale). An option agreement, on one view, is not capable of being made real because it is no more than a power to enter into another personal right (ie the contract of sale which results from the exercise of the option). Although a real right will or should be the end result, that real right is at one stage removed from the option agreement. On the other hand, the rule in *Wallace* was perhaps not inviolable. It is possible to read *Trade Development Bank v Warriner & Mason (Scotland) Ltd* 1980 SC 74 as a challenge – for the right in that case (to prevent the granting of leases) was not capable of being real – although it is possible that the decision, which was vaguely expressed, was not about offside goals at all. Be that as it may, clause 4 of the option agreement was similar in nature to the clause considered in *Warriner & Mason* and it was arguable that the result should be the same (ie the reduction of the offending deed).

Secondly, there is recent Outer House authority to the effect that the offside goals rule cannot be pled in respect of an unexercised option: *Advice Centre for Mortgages v McNicoll* [2006] CSOH 58, 2006 SLT 591 (for which see *Conveyancing 2006* p 104). This disapproved an earlier decision to the opposite effect: *Davidson v Zani* 1992 SCLR 1001. The basis of the decision in *Advice Centre for Mortgages* was that the granting of a deed which defeated the option was not in itself a breach of the option agreement: see para 46.

Lord Emslie allowed a proof before answer. But in the course of a thoughtful opinion he expressed some interesting, and sometimes controversial, views on this area of law.

On the assumption that the RBS knew of (ii) (the exercise of the option) as well as (i) (the option agreement), the position, Lord Emslie said, was on all fours with *Crittall Windows*, so that the Gibsons would succeed. For the RBS it had been argued that the granting of a security *before* the Gibsons' date of entry was not in itself a breach of the option because it might turn out to be temporary and the title be clear by the date of entry. But that, said Lord Emslie, was a matter of 'fact and degree' (para 39), and in the present case the Gibsons were offering to prove that the security was registered just before the date of entry.

Even if the RBS was shown, at proof, to know only of (i), however, Lord Emslie would be inclined to find for the Gibsons. There were two reasons. '[O]n a broad view of the *Wallace* limitation, it seems to me that such rights – even if unexercised – ought *prima facie* to qualify as "... capable of being made real" or "... capable of becoming a real right", and that breach of an explicit prohibition against alienation should be sufficient to satisfy any further legal requirement in that connection' (para 50). But in any event, the *Wallace* limitation should not be seen as a rigid one. The statement by the First Division that the right must be capable of being made real 'was arguably intended, not as a rigid universal requirement to be met in all cases, whatever their circumstances, but rather as a means of expressing the court's refusal, on the particular facts under discussion, to allow the established precedence of recorded real rights to be subverted' (para 45). No doubt the offside goals rule did not apply to breaches of *all* personal rights. Nonetheless, 'the bad faith exception may be applied in a wide range of different circumstances. It would be unusual (and undesirable) for an equitable exception to be more rigidly confined' (para 49).

Three comments may be made about this decision. First, it proceeds on a perhaps questionable view of the purpose of the offside goals rule. A conventional view would be to say that the rule is about competition of real rights, actual or potential, and is designed to penalise a person whose own right, knowingly, was granted in breach of a right held by a competitor. But for Lord Emslie good faith seems to be virtually a requirement of the acquisition of real rights at all, at least in so far as they relate to land ('recognising that the settled general rule is designed to protect an acquirer of heritable rights who, in good faith, relies on the face of the public records' (para 44)).

Secondly, the decision makes a striking contrast with its immediate predecessor, *Advice Centre for Mortgages*, in respect of its attitude to the offside goals rule. In *Advice Centre for Mortgages* Lord Drummond Young noted (at para 42) the potential of the rule to 'subvert' the distinction between real and personal rights. Lord Emslie, by contrast, seems to be a more enthusiastic supporter of the rule, referring in the context of the *Trade Development Bank* cases to 'the court's willingness, in modern conditions, to penalise contractual bad faith in circumstances where a subsequent transaction puts the granter in breach of some prior personal obligation relating to heritable subjects' (para 47).

Thirdly, the decision leaves the law less certain than it found it. For a number of years now, academic lawyers have tried to tame the offside goals rule by setting out a (small) group of mandatory requirements. The latest attempt can be found at the end of the article by Ross Gilbert Anderson and John MacLeod (2009 SLT (News) 93) commenting on the decision. Lord Emslie's approach is different (para 43):

> On a fair reading of the various authorities cited to me, I am not convinced that any of them can be regarded as comprehensively prescribing the circumstances in which recorded real rights may be susceptible to challenge on bad faith grounds. On the contrary it may be said that a universal rule would be difficult to devise, and that in consequence individual decisions have tended to turn on their own particular facts.

In particular, Lord Emslie opens up the *Wallace* limitation – the requirement, accepted by most commentators, that the right of the challenger must be capable of becoming real.

The decision has been widely commented on. In addition to the article by Anderson and MacLeod already referred to, there have been contributions by Robert Rennie (2009 SLT (News) 187), and Peter Webster (2009) 13 *Edinburgh Law Review* 524. All, to a greater or lesser degree, are hostile.

[Another aspect of this case is digested at (45) above.]

(60) McGraddie v McGraddie
[2009] CSOH 142, 2009 GWD 38-633

2009 was the year of the Homecoming. But 'not every homecoming', Lord Brodie observes (para 1), 'is free from complications'. In the present case the pursuer and his wife had lived for many years in Albuquerque, New Mexico. When his wife became seriously ill, the pursuer determined to return to Glasgow and commissioned his son, the first defender, to buy a flat. Money was sent for that purpose. The flat was duly bought and the pursuer came home to live in it. The son had, however, taken title in his own name. A year or so later, the pursuer gave his son a second sum of money and again a house was bought, and this time taken in the name of the son and his wife (the second defender). The litigation was a result of disagreement as to the basis on which the money was handed over. The pursuer's case was that his son was simply being appointed as agent, to buy the houses on the pursuer's behalf. Accordingly, the pursuer sought an order that the houses be conveyed to him. The defenders' position was more complicated but in its essentials amounted to saying that the first house was to be used for the benefit of the defenders' family, and that the second cheque was an outright gift.

Following a proof, Lord Brodie preferred the evidence of the pursuer to that of the defenders. The result, he said, was that the houses were held in trust for behoof of the pursuer (para 29):

> When an agent obtains money for the specific purpose of purchasing a property for a principal and takes title in his own name then his title will be taken to be that of trustee only, the beneficial owner being his principal: *Bank of Scotland v Liquidators of Hutchison Main & Co* 1914 SC (HL) 1, Lord Shaw of Dunfermline at 15.

Accordingly, the pursuer was entitled to the houses.

RIGHT-TO-BUY LEGISLATION

(61) McCreight v West Lothian Council
[2009] CSIH 4, 2009 SC 258, 2009 SLT 109, 2009 SCLR 359, 2009 Hous LR 21

There was a secure tenancy of a house in Broxburn. Following the tenant's death, her cohabitant applied for the tenancy to be transferred to him, and that was done. Thereafter he was convicted of having murdered her. He was sentenced to life, with a minimum period in prison of 18 years. After being convicted, he applied to buy the property. The local authority argued that the fact of the murder meant that he had no title to the tenancy, because of the common law rule that an unlawful killer cannot profit from the crime. The Tribunal ruled that it had the jurisdictional competence to consider this defence. At this stage, before the Tribunal had made a final decision on the application, the applicant appealed, arguing that the Tribunal was bound to grant his application.

The Inner House **held** that the Tribunal lacked the jurisdictional competence to decide whether the local authority's defence was sound, and that the proper course would be for the Tribunal to sist the case until such time as the matter could be determined by the ordinary courts. The decision is based on the speciality of the fact of the unlawful killing, but there seems also to be a broader *ratio* that the Tribunal lacks the jurisdictional competence to determine whether a secure tenancy exists. The result of the Inner House's decision is thus, in substantive terms, an open one: there is as yet no decision as to whether the applicant does or does not have the right to buy.

The court's rejection of one particular argument by the applicant deserves note. Lord Justice Clerk Gill said (para 14):

> Counsel for the appellant has taken the *ratio* of that case [*East of Scotland Water Authority v Livingstone* 1999 SC 65] a stage further by submitting that the respondent's failure to serve an offer to sell or a notice of refusal precludes it from even denying the appellant's right to be tenant. On that argument, it would seem to follow that a squatter in a public sector dwelling house who made a speculative application to purchase it would become entitled to enforce the purchase if by an administrative error the authority failed to serve a notice of refusal. In my view, section 71 [of the Housing (Scotland) Act 1987] cannot have the effect of conferring a right to a conveyance upon an applicant whose right to the tenancy is in dispute.

(62) Taylor v Renfrewshire Council
2010 GWD 4-68, Lands Tr

The Housing (Scotland) Act 2001 sch 1 para 9 says:

> A tenancy is not a Scottish secure tenancy if the house forms part of, or is within the curtilage of, a building which (a) is held by the landlord mainly for purposes other than the provision of housing accommodation, and (b) mainly consists of accommodation other than housing accommodation.

Such a tenancy would therefore fall outwith the right to buy. In the present case the question was whether a janitor's house was 'within the curtilage' of a school. As the Tribunal noted at para 15, '"curtilage" is a necessarily imprecise word, so that each case must be decided on its own facts and circumstances'. Nevertheless a certain amount of case law has developed, of which the Tribunal made use. After careful consideration of the facts of the case it was **held** that the house was within the 'curtilage' of the school with the result that the application to buy it failed.

(63) Fotheringham v Hillcrest Housing Association Ltd
2009 Hous LR 99

Fotheringham had been a tenant of Hillcrest Housing Association since 1990. She applied to buy her house. The application was refused on the ground that tenancies with housing associations do not attract the right to buy, except for those dating before 2 January 1989: see Housing (Scotland) Act 1988 s 43. The applicant said that she had once been a tenant of Dundee City Council. This point was held not to be relevant. The applicant also said that when she took up the tenancy in 1990 she had been told by the housing association that she would have the right to buy. It was held that, even if this could be proved, it was irrelevant because it would still not give her the right to buy. The application was dismissed with expenses awarded against the applicant. We note that on the internet there seem to be differing views as to the right to buy from housing associations and that s 43 is sometimes overlooked.

(64) Warren v South Ayrshire Council
17 April 2009, Lands Tr

The Housing (Scotland) Act 2001 introduced the concept of 'pressured areas'. If an area is so designated, the right to buy is suspended for that area in relation to tenancies commenced after the date of the designation. In this case the applicant had inherited her tenancy from her late husband after the date when the area had been designated, but the tenancy itself had commenced before the designation. Section 61B(3)(b)(ii) of the Housing (Scotland) Act 1987 (as inserted by the 2001 Act) made it clear that the relevant date was the date when the applicant succeeded to the tenancy. Accordingly the application was dismissed.

The Tribunal also considered whether the 'obscurely worded' Housing (Scotland) Act 2001 (Scottish Secure Tenancy etc) Order 2002, SSI 2002/318, helped the applicant but concluded that it did not.

LEASES

(65) Douglas Shelf Seven Ltd v Co-operative Wholesale Society Ltd
[2009] CSOH 3, 2009 GWD 3-56

The pursuer was the landlord (head lessee) of a shopping centre in the Whitfield area of Dundee. The defender was a sub-tenant, holding on a lease running from 15 May 1970 until 15 May 2033. The property was a supermarket. Notwithstanding a 'keep open' clause in the sub-lease, the defender closed the supermarket in 1995 and it has remained closed. In an earlier litigation the landlord succeeded in an action for damages for breach of contract: see [2007] CSOH 53, 2007 GWD 9-167 (*Conveyancing 2007* Case (37)). In this new action, the landlord sought (a) to compel the tenant to carry out repairs conform to a schedule of dilapidations, and (b) to require the tenant to pay for security services. It was **held** by the Lord Ordinary (Menzies) that the latter was outwith the terms of the lease.

(66) Robert Purvis Plant Hire Ltd v Brewster
[2009] CSOH 28, 2009 Hous LR 34

The pursuer took from the defenders a five-year lease of ex-industrial premises at Ratho at £45,000 per annum. Clause 5.14 said that the tenant was 'to use the premises only for the storage of bulk road materials or for such other purposes as may from time to time be approved in writing by the Landlords'. When the pursuer began to use the site for storage and also for recycling, the operation immediately gave rise to complaints from neighbours about dust and noise. Within two weeks the local authority served an enforcement notice on the ground that there was no planning consent for the use being made of the site. The tenant raised the present action against the landlord, arguing that the lease had been terminated by frustration, because the proposed use of the site had become unlawful. **Held**: that the lease had not been frustrated, because the lack of planning permission for the intended use predated the lease.

The pursuer had a separate argument that the lease was void *ab initio* because the intended use would be unlawful. This argument too was rejected. As the Lord Ordinary (Hodge) said at para 20, 'the flaw in that case is clause 5.14, which creates a mechanism by which the pursuers can use the site legally by applying to the landlords for approval for a use which is authorised under planning legislation'.

(67) Scottish Coal Company Ltd v Trs of Fim Timber Growth Fund III
[2009] CSOH 30, 2009 SCLR 630

The pursuer entered into a contract with the owners of afforested land whereby they acquired an option to be granted a mining lease. Later the owners sold to the defender in this action. At the time of the sale the option contract was novated, so that it became a contract between Scottish Coal Co Ltd and the buyers. The buyers thereafter denied that they were bound by it because the contract presupposed that the original owners would remain the owners. This argument was rejected by the court.

(68) Wing v Henry Tse & Co Ltd
2009 GWD 11-175, Sh Ct

Section 2 of the Law Reform (Miscellaneous Provisions) (Scotland) Act 1985 says that, before irritating a lease for non-payment of rent, the landlord must first serve a pre-irritancy notice, and that the notice must state a deadline for payment to be made for the tenant to avoid the irritancy. That deadline must be 14 days or such longer period as the lease may provide. In the present case there were rent arrears of £27,000 and the landlord served a pre-irritancy notice. But the notice did not state a payment deadline. It said only that 'you require to make full payment of the said sum with interest thereon at the rate of …' **Held**: that the notice was not valid as a pre-irritancy notice.

(69) Primary Health Care Centres (Broadford) Ltd v Ravangave
[2009] CSOH 46, 2009 SLT 673

Over the years we have more than once mentioned that leases to partnerships are a fertile source of difficulty. *Primary Health Care Centres (Broadford) Ltd v Ravangave* [2008] CSOH 14, 2008 Hous LR 24 (*Conveyancing 2008* Case (52)) was an example. The present case was not an appeal but a new action and was, not surprisingly, met by a plea of *res judicata*. The plea was sustained.

(70) Multi-link Leisure Developments Ltd v North Lanarkshire Council
[2009] CSOH 114, 2009 SLT 1170 rev [2009] CSIH 96, 2010 SLT 57

The pursuer took a lease from the defender. The property was a golf course. The lease had a purchase option. The tenant exercised the option. The parties disagreed as to the price. The tenant argued it should be the property's market value as undeveloped land. The landlord argued that the price should reflect potential development value. The lease said:

> The price to be paid in terms of this Clause ('the Option Price') shall, if the Option to purchase is exercised within the first year of the period of let, be the sum of ONE HUNDRED AND THIRTY THOUSAND POUNDS (£130,000) STERLING. The Option Price, if the Option to Purchase is exercised subsequent to the first year of let, shall be equal to the full market value of the subjects hereby let as at the date of entry for the proposed purchase (as determined by the Landlords) of agricultural land or open space suitable for development as a golf course but, for the avoidance of doubt, shall be not less than the sum of 130,000 …

The landlord stressed the words 'the full market value' while the tenant stressed the words 'of agricultural land or open space suitable for development as a golf course'. The Lord Ordinary (Glennie) preferred the tenant's view. The defender reclaimed, and the Inner House preferred the landlord's view. The decision does not fix the price, but only the basis for its calculation. But we know that the tenant was willing to pay £500,000, while the landlord was asking for £5.3 million. For the background to the dispute, we quote para 4 of the Inner House opinion:

> The underlying reason why this issue is important to the parties is that, in 2006, the Glasgow and Clyde Valley Structure Plan identified the South Cumbernauld Community Growth Area, which includes the subjects of the lease, as one of three priority growth areas. In 2008 the North Lanarkshire Finalised Draft Local Plan identified the area as a potential area for housing-led area expansion.

Because the tenant pressed the 'exercise option' button, the consequence is presumably that it is now committed to going ahead, even though the price will turn out to be higher than hoped for.

(71) Kodak Processing Companies Ltd v Shoredale Ltd
[2009] CSIH 71, 2009 SLT 1151

In commercial contracts, including leases, one side often argues that a notice is for some reason not valid. Sometimes the objection is to the contents of the notice (as in *A W D Chase de Vere Wealth Management Ltd*, below), and sometimes to its service (eg that it has not been served at the address stipulated in the contract). In the present case the notice was served by sheriff officer, and the question was whether that was valid service.

The tenant was in arrears of rent. The landlord served a pre-irritancy notice as required by s 4 of the Law Reform (Miscellaneous Provisions) (Scotland) Act 1985. But it served it by sheriff officer, whereas s 4(4) says that 'any notice served under subsection (2) above shall be sent by recorded delivery'. The sheriff held that this would have been fatal if the 1985 Act had used the technical term 'recorded delivery *service*' but it had not done so. The shorter phrase, 'recorded delivery', was not, the sheriff held, limited to recorded delivery service but meant any method whereby there was formal recording of delivery, which could therefore include delivery by officer of the court.

The defender appealed to the Inner House, which reversed, holding that the 1985 Act in using the expression 'recorded delivery' meant recorded delivery service.

As a postscript we might mention that the Recorded Delivery Service Act 1962 does not seem actually to say what 'recorded delivery service' means. This issue was not, however, raised in the case.

(72) A W D Chase de Vere Wealth Management Ltd
v Melville Street Properties Ltd
[2009] CSOH 150, 2009 GWD 38-652

In 2004 Melville Street Properties Ltd leased a property to AWD Wealth Management Ltd for ten years, with a break option in 1999. By error the tenant was named as 'Thomsons Wealth Management Ltd', a name that it had once had but which it had changed before the time when the lease was entered into. Although the case was about an error in the tenant's name, in fact it was not about *that* error: no one queried whether the lease itself was valid. When the tenant decided to exercise the break option, its solicitors sent a notice to that effect to the landlord, but did so on behalf of 'AWD Group Services Ltd', an entirely different company. The landlord took the view that the notice was invalid. In the present action AWD Wealth Management Ltd sought declarator that the break option had been validly exercised. (The summons seems to have got the name right.) **Held**: that the notice was valid and that accordingly the lease had come to an end.

This result is unsurprising given the Inner House decision in *Ben Cleuch Estates Ltd v Scottish Enterprise* 2008 SC 252 (*Conveyancing 2007* Case (47)). As the Lord Ordinary (Glennie) put it, 'the question was how a reasonable recipient, circumstanced as the actual recipient was, would have understood the notice' (para 7). Notwithstanding the error, the landlord could have been in no real doubt. Although the errors proved in the end to be non-fatal, there is clearly a lesson to be learnt here about getting company names right.

(73) Macdonald Estates plc v National Car Parks Ltd
[2009] CSOH 130 affd [2009] CSIH 79A, 2010 SLT 36

Macdonald Estates plc contracted with National Car Parks Ltd to grant a 35-year lease, conditional on planning permission. Planning permission was granted, and whilst Macdonald Estates plc was happy with its terms, National Car Parks Ltd was not. The contract provided that in the event of a dispute of this nature the matter would be referred to an expert. The expert took the view that the terms of the planning permission were satisfactory. National Car Parks Ltd asked the expert to state a case to the Court of Session. That would be competent only if the expert had the status of arbiter. The expert consulted senior counsel who advised that the expert was acting as arbiter and accordingly the expert requested submissions preliminary to a stated case. Macdonald Estates plc responded by raising this action for declarator that the expert was not in the position of an arbiter and accordingly could not state a case. The effect of the action, if successful, would thus be that the original decision in favour of Macdonald Estates plc would stand. The Lord Ordinary (Hodge) **held** in favour of Macdonald Estates plc and the Inner House subsequently affirmed that decision.

For another recent case in which it was held that a surveyor was acting as expert, not arbiter, see *Holland House Property Investments Ltd v Crabbe* [2008] CSIH 40, 2008 SLT 777, 2008 SCLR 633 (*Conveyancing 2008* Case (55)).

(74) Wright v Shoreline Management Ltd
2009 SLT (Sh Ct) 83

Section 20 of the Land Registration (Scotland) Act 1979 allows tenants-at-will to buy the land from their landlord at a mouth-watering 96% discount. In this case it was held at first instance that the applicant did not in fact hold a tenancy-at-will and that in any event the sheriff court lacked jurisdiction in such matters: see *Conveyancing 2008* Case (60). The applicant appealed. The sheriff principal has now **held** that the sheriff court does have jurisdiction, but on the substantive issue adhered to the sheriff's decision that the applicant did not in fact hold a tenancy-at-will. The leading case on the 'what is a tenancy-at-will?' question remains *Allen v McTaggart* 2007 SC 482 (*Conveyancing 2007* Case (40)).

STANDARD SECURITIES

(75) Royal Bank of Scotland plc v Wilson
[2009] CSIH 36, 2009 SLT 729

This case, which is about the way that standard securities can be enforced, reverses the decision of the sheriff reported at 2008 GWD 2-35 (*Conveyancing 2008* Case (61)). See **Commentary** p 177.

(76) Webb Resolutions Ltd v Glen
2009 GWD 38-634, Sh Ct

The pursuer raised an action to enforce a standard security and obtained decree in absence. The defenders then sought to be reponed so as to enable them to make an application under the Mortgage Rights (Scotland) Act 2001. It was **held** that in principle this could be a ground for seeking to be reponed, but that the defenders had not explained why they had not entered appearance and had failed to persuade the court that an application under the 2001 Act would have prospects of success. The reponing note was refused.

(77) Salvesen Ptr
[2009] CSOH 161, 2010 GWD 4-57

Natural House Co Ltd was a Scottish company. It bought some land in England. Mr Salvesen was the main shareholder and also a director. He and his wife made loans to the company, secured by mortgages over the land. These mortgages were duly registered in HM Land Registry. Natural House Co Ltd had previously granted a floating charge to Royal Bank of Scotland plc, and a ranking agreement was entered into whereby RBS agreed that the mortgages would have priority over the floating charge. Later the company became insolvent and went into administration. At this stage it was noticed that the mortgages had not been registered in the Companies Register as required by s 410 of the Companies Act 1985 (now replaced by pt 25 of the Companies Act 2006). Section 410 requires most types of charge granted by companies to be registered in the Companies Register within 21 days on pain of nullity. Section 420 of the 1985 Act allows the court to authorise a charge to be registered late. The Salvesens applied for authorisation. The application was refused. The Lord Ordinary (Hodge) commented at para 12:

> The onset of formal insolvency, as a general rule, fixes the position of creditors, who are ranked on the insolvent estate in accordance with their strict legal rights. From then on, the insolvency practitioner holds the company's assets for the benefit of the creditors in accordance with the rights which the general law gives them as to ranking. For the court thereafter to interfere with that ranking would be a serious step.

(78) Ferro Finance UK Ltd v Akintola
2009 GWD 33-550, Sh Ct

The lender obtained decree in absence for the enforcement of a standard security, and proceeded to evict the debtors. Before sale had taken place, the debtors sought to be reponed against the decree. **Held**: that the fact of eviction meant that it was too late to be reponed.

SOLICITORS, ESTATE AGENTS, SURVEYORS

(79) Halifax Life Ltd v DLA Piper Scotland LLP
[2009] CSOH 74, 2009 GWD 19-306

On 29 May 2008 missives were concluded for the sale of property in West George Street, Glasgow for £8.8 million. The seller was Halifax Life Ltd. The buyers (for whom DLA Piper Scotland LLP bore to act) were identified simply as 'the Members of the 227 Syndicate'. There was no such 'syndicate'. The seller resold at a loss and sued DLA Piper Scotland LLP for damages. The action was dismissed. See **Commentary** p 107.

(80) Frank Houlgate Investment Co Ltd v Biggart Baillie LLP
[2009] CSOH 165, 2010 GWD 4-71

Frank Houlgate Investment Co Ltd advanced money against a standard security over land in Fife owned by John Cameron. The standard security was signed by a different John Cameron, a fraudster. The lender sued the firm of solicitors who acted for the fraudster. The action failed. See **Commentary** pp 108 and 127.

(81) Bothwell v D M Hall
[2009] CSOH 24, 2009 GWD 10-165

The pursuer ran several nurseries, one of which was at 226 Braid Road, Edinburgh. She sold it to a developer for £1,825,000, conditional on planning permission. In the end it became clear that planning permission would not be granted for the type of development intended, and the developer withdrew. The nursery business went into decline. The pursuer considered that this was because local parents and also staff had learned of the intended sale. She sued her agents for damages, her case being that they had failed to inform her of a letter from the planning department saying that permission for a substantial development was unlikely, and also that they had failed to disclose this letter to the prospective purchasers. Had the letter been disclosed the whole idea of a sale would have been dropped at an early stage and as a result there would have been no damage to her business. After proof it was **held** by the Lord Ordinary (Hodge) that there had been no negligence or breach of contract, and accordingly decree of absolvitor was pronounced.

(82) Christie Owen & Davies plc v Campbell
[2009] CSIH 26, 2009 SC 436, 2009 SLT 518

A property was sold for £46,000. The commission charged by the estate agents was £9,360.05. They posted this letter to the solicitors:

> We understand that missives have now been concluded in respect of the assignation of the Waldorf Bar. On speaking with Mrs Anne Campbell she advises that the purchase price has been placed in joint deposit until a letter is issued confirming the assignation of the lease.
>
>   In this instance, we remit to you our fee note in respect of the assignation in advance of the consideration being released. We understand that receipt of the assignation letter from the landlord is imminent and therefore look forward to receiving payment in early course.

Enclosed with the letter (but not referred to in it) was a copy of the agency agreement. One of the clauses read:

> We hereby authorise the vendor's solicitors … Valance Kliner, Cambridge House, Cambridge Street, Glasgow G2 3B1 … to pay out of money received by such solicitors the fees requested by you.

The solicitors did not pay the estate agents and the latter sued them. The sheriff held in favour of the defenders. The pursuer appealed to the sheriff principal who also held in favour of the defenders: see 2007 GWD 24-397 (*Conveyancing 2007* Case (53).) The sheriff commented that 'I am not prepared to hold that a solicitor is under an obligation to read every document sent to him or that a solicitor is deemed to have read all such documents'.

The pursuer appealed again and the Inner House has now held in favour of the pursuer. We would agree with the comments on the case by R G Anderson at (2009) 13 EdinLR 484. We would also suggest that if the Inner House's interpretation of the law is sound, then there must be a doubt as to whether the law is in a wholly satisfactory state.

(83) Dickson v A & W M Urquhart WS
[2009] CSOH 38, 2009 GWD 13-210

In 1987 the pursuers bought a property in Leith from the liquidator of a company. At the same time another person, Strachan, bought the neighbouring property, also from the liquidator. Both dispositions contained real burdens restricting the use of each property. Each burden was enforceable by the owner of the other property. Many years later the Dicksons wished to change the use of their property but the neighbour objected. The Dicksons now sued the solicitors who had acted for them in the purchase, saying that the real burden had been inserted without their knowledge or consent. Although no file evidence could be produced showing that the Dicksons had agreed to the real burden, it was **held** after proof that the balance of evidence was that the Dicksons must have been informed and must have consented.

(84) Upton Park Homes Ltd v Macdonalds
[2009] CSOH 159, 2010 GWD 3-38

Upton Park Homes Ltd concluded missives to sell some land to Wishaw and District Housing Association. Clause 4 provided:

> There are no overriding interest or interests within the meaning of section 28(1) of the Land Registration (Scotland) Act 1979 affecting the subjects save, if appropriate, in so far as disclosed in the Land Certificates exhibited in respect of the subjects.

After settlement of the transaction it emerged that there was an underground sewerage facility, over which building was not possible. This meant that the housing association could not develop the land as planned. The pursuer did not deny that it was in breach of contract. One of the directors of Upton Park Homes Ltd happened to own some land adjacent to the site, and the housing association agreed to accept from her a gratuitous conveyance of this extra land, which would enable them to complete the development to their satisfaction. With the conveyance of the extra land, the dispute between the housing association and Upton Park Homes Ltd ended. A new dispute now began. Upton Park Homes Ltd claimed that the law firm that had acted for it in the sale should not have concluded missives with clause 4 in them. The company averred that that negligence had caused the company loss, and it sued the law firm for £311,159.25. The basis of the calculation was the amount of damages the company would have had to pay the housing association had the extra land not been conveyed, and in turn that amount was calculated on the basis of the capitalised value of the loss of rental income that the housing association would have suffered.

The action was dismissed on the ground of relevancy. (1) The claim that the housing association would have had against the company would not have been based on the lost rental income. 'In my opinion', said the Lord Ordinary (Uist) at para 36, 'their claim for breach of contract falls to be calculated as the difference between the value of the land without the overriding interest and its value with the overriding interest'. Hence that aspect of the pursuer's case was not relevantly pled. (2) 'There was no legal obligation on the part of the pursuers to pay Mrs Collins [the director] the value of the land she conveyed.' Accordingly the pursuer had suffered no loss.

We offer one thought. Even if the law firm had been negligent in agreeing to clause 4, did that in fact cause the problem? Was the problem not the simple fact that the existence of the sewerage facility meant that the land was not worth as much as the company had hoped? If that is the right approach, then it is difficult to see how the law firm could have been liable for the loss of value. Cf *Hay v Gourley McBain* 2008 SLT (Sh Ct) 101 (*Conveyancing 2008* Case (70)).

(85) Legal Services Centre Ltd v Miller Samuel LLP
[2009] CSOH 141, 2009 GWD 36-616

This litigation concerned the building that houses the Glasgow procurator fiscal office. The story begins in the 1980s. Glasgow City Council owned the site. The

Council was to lease it to Scottish Development Agency which was to sub-lease it to Legal Services Centre Ltd which was to construct the building and then sub-sub-lease it (for a duration of 60 years) to the Secretary of State. The sub-sub-lease had a rent-review clause, and in this action the pursuer sought damages from the defender for having allegedly failed to draft it correctly. The case centred on a proof as to what exactly had happened more than 20 years previously. It was **held** that there had been no negligence and accordingly decree of absolvitor was granted. At para 142 the Lord Ordinary (Glennie) comments:

> I am satisfied that the pursuers' case on liability fails. The defenders were never given clear instructions as to what was to be achieved by the clause. Mr Rodie's drafting seems to me to have been largely responsive to decisions taken at meetings at which he was often not a party and to suggestions made both by Mrs Bevan and by Messrs Clapham and Tulloch (and possibly Mr Hart). In other words, his role was to put into legal form that which he understood to have been agreed between the parties. He was not 'driving' the transaction, nor was he given any clear indication that his role was to produce a clause which would achieve a certain result. But even if I am wrong about this, it is clear that the suppositions and disregards in the clause as finally agreed on were the subject of discussion and assent between principals.

COMMUNITY RIGHT TO BUY

(86) Hazle v Lord Advocate
16 March 2009, Kirkcaldy Sheriff Court

This concerned the community right to buy under part 2 of the Land Reform (Scotland) Act 2003, and was a successful challenge to three entries in the Register of Community Interests in Land on various grounds including (i) that the maps accompanying the applications omitted the OS grid references required by the Community Right to Buy (Specification of Plans) (Scotland) Regulations 2004, SSI 2004/231 (for which see *Conveyancing 2004* p 34), (ii) that the decision letters by Ministers did not indicate which of the alternatives in s 38(1)(b) applied, and (iii) in respect of one of the entries, that there was *Wednesbury* unreasonableness because Ministers adopted a particular position (that red and grey squirrels can co-exist) without addressing the landowner's argument to the contrary. For a discussion, see Malcolm M Combe, 'Access to land and to landownership' (2010) 14 *Edinburgh Law Review* 106 at 110–13.

BOUNDARIES, ENCROACHMENT AND PRESCRIPTION

(87) North Atlantic Salmon Conservation Organisation v Au Bar Pub Ltd
2009 GWD 14-222, Sh Ct

In this summary cause action for recovery of possession, the underlying dispute was about the ownership of a small area of ground. The pursuer held on a Sasine title. Title to the defender's flat was registered in the Land Register and, in the usual way for tenements, was said to lie 'within' land edged red. The disputed area lay within the land edged red. **Held**: that where a property was said to lie 'within' land edged red, it did not follow that the property was co-extensive with that area. Accordingly, the dispute between the parties could be resolved only by considering the respective Sasine titles. On that basis, the claim of the pursuer was the stronger. See **Commentary** p 174.

(88) Clydesdale Homes Ltd v Quay
[2009] CSOH 126, 2009 GWD 31-518

This was a fact-specific dispute between neighbours about whether a particular boundary of the defenders extended to 40 metres or only 37.5 metres. The pursuer had erected a fence on the basis of the latter measurement. The defenders contended that this fence encroached on their property to the extent of the disputed 2.5 metres. As both titles were on the Land Register, the dispute should, in principle, have been capable of being resolved by reference to the title plans. But these plans do not give boundary lengths and are on too small a scale to resolve this kind of dispute with confidence.

The task for the court was described by Lord Malcolm in this way (para 30):

> [T]heir [ie the defenders'] property is defined by the title plan referable to their registered title. That plan does not provide the same detail as the feu plan. The issue boils down to the exact length of a line on the title plan. Neither surveyor can be certain as to his evidence given the margin of error involved. The difference between them is more or less within that margin for error.

That the deed plan is more detailed and on a larger scale than the title plan is a common complaint about registration of title.

The court found for the pursuer. The pursuer's expert witness was marginally to be preferred. While the plan in the defenders' split-off writ did indeed show the relevant boundary as 40 metres, it could not be assumed that this plan was accurate. The court accepted the evidence led for the pursuer (but disputed by the defenders) to the effect that the current fence was constructed on the same line as a previous fence, thus indicating that the boundary had always been at 37.5 metres. See **Commentary** p 176.

(89) Stuart v Stuart
27 July 2009, Stonehaven Sheriff Court

A boundary dispute involving two adjacent houses both of which were held on Land Register titles. When the defenders removed a *leylandii* cypress hedge, the pursuer sought declarator of ownership and also damages in respect of the hedge. After considering expert evidence on both sides the sheriff found for the pursuer. See **Commentary** p 176.

(90) Compugraphics International Ltd v Nikolic
[2009] CSOH 54, 2009 GWD 19-311

A duct for air conditioning, attached to the wall of the pursuer's building, passed over the neighbouring ground of the defender, supported by metal posts secured into that ground. The pursuer sought declarator that it was heritable proprietor of the duct and associated support structures. **Held**: (i) that the pursuer's (Sasine) writ was *habile* to acquire the ductwork by prescription, and (ii) that it was competent for ductwork above the ground to be held as a (conventional) separate tenement. See **Commentary** p 171.

[Another aspect of this case is digested at (22) above.]

MISCELLANEOUS

(91) Luminar Lava Ignite Ltd v Mama Group plc
[2009] CSOH 68, 2009 GWD 19-305

Luminar Liquid Ltd owned premises in Edinburgh's Lothian Road and sold them to Mama Group plc. The missives bound the buyer not to compete with Luminar Lava Ignite Ltd (a company in the same group as the seller) in its business at nearby premises. The latter then claimed that the defender was in breach of the undertaking and sought interdict. **Held** after proof that the defender was not in breach of the undertaking.

(92) Glasgow City Council v Scottish Information Commissioner
[2009] CSIH 73, 2010 SLT 9

This is a decision of considerable importance for the law of freedom of information. For conveyancers its interest is smaller but it is nevertheless a case worth noting. For background, see *Conveyancing 2007* p 62 and *Conveyancing 2008* p 72.

On 17 February 2005 MacRoberts LLP made numerous FoI requests on behalf of an undisclosed client. It requested: (1) the register of private water supplies; (2) the register of public roads maintained under the Roads (Scotland) Act 1984; (3) all outstanding statutory notices. The information was to be provided free of charge. Glasgow City Council did not comply and MacRoberts appealed to the Scottish Information Commissioner, who decided in favour of MacRoberts. The Council appealed to the Inner House which has reversed the Commissioner's decision. A parallel case involving Dundee City Council was heard at the same time, with the same outcome.

The court helpfully gives, at para 88, a summary of its reasons for allowing the appeal:

1. The requests were invalid in that they were not requests for 'information' within the meaning of the Act.
2. The requests were in addition invalid in that they did not disclose the name of the applicant, namely the second respondents [Millar & Bryce Ltd].

3. The Commissioner erred in reaching his decisions on the basis that copies of statutory notices constituted 'information' within the meaning of the Act.

4. The Commissioner erred in reaching his decision in the Glasgow case on the basis that a preference expressed by the applicant in terms of s 11 was relevant to the application of s 25.

5. We question whether, in any event, a request for copies of specified documents falls within the scope of s 11, but we do not require to express a concluded opinion on the point.

6. The Commissioner further erred, in relation to s 25, in failing to proceed on the basis that information which is made available in accordance with an authority's publication scheme, any payment required being specified in, or determined in accordance with, the scheme, is deemed to be reasonably obtainable.

7. The Commissioner further erred, in relation to s 25(1), in failing to take into consideration the nature and characteristics of the applicant.

8. The Commissioner failed to comply with his duty to act fairly in reaching his decisions, in relation to s 33(1)(b), in both the Glasgow case and the Dundee case.

9. The Commissioner's decision in the Glasgow case was, in addition, irrational in that it dealt with the contentions in respect of s 12 and s 25 on inconsistent bases.

(93) Kerr of Ardgowan v Lord Lyon King of Arms
[2009] CSIH 61, 2009 SLT 759

The question was whether the Lord Lyon was entitled to refuse to recognise a territorial designation ('Kerr of Ardgowan', 'Goldstraw of Whitecairns' and 'Ayre of Kilmarnock') on the ground that the petitioners had no substantial landholding, but only a (now abolished) superiority. Lyon refused recognition. That decision was reversed in the Outer House: see [2008] CSOH 34–36 (*Conveyancing 2008* Cases (80)–(82)), but the Inner House has now reversed in turn, thus reinstating the original decision of the Lord Lyon.

(94) Manson v Manson
2009 SLT (Sh Ct) 175

Robert Nisbet was the owner of 'Everglades', a house in Shetland. When his sister, Catherina, married a Mr Manson, Robert allowed her and her husband to live there, rent-free. Later Catherina and her husband were divorced. Catherina continued living there with her daughter, Avril. Eventually Robert decided he wished to gift the property to Catherina, or to Avril, or to both. He discussed the transfer with his solicitor. The possibility of transferring title to both Catherina and Avril was considered, and also an arrangement whereby Avril would take sole title and Catherina would take a liferent. Eventually what happened was that he disponed the property to Avril alone. A good deal of the case involved evidence as to what Robert had instructed and as to whether the solicitor had in fact carried out those instructions. At the end of the day the sheriff took the view that the point did not matter for the purposes of the present action, but he commented on the obscurity of the evidence. He also noted a certain lack of clarity as to whether the solicitor was acting for Avril as well as for her uncle.

The property was very run-down and Avril, now the owner, was able to borrow money against a standard security so as to renovate it, and that was done. Later she and her mother fell out, the main reason being that her mother was unhappy about her daughter's new boyfriend. Catherina began excluding Avril from the house. Avril raised the present summary cause action to recover possession. The defence was that Avril was personally barred from removing her mother, because the latter had made financial contributions to the household in the belief she would be allowed to stay. After a proof, the sheriff (W H Summers) found that the scale of the household contributions had been minimal and granted decree against the defender.

(95) Longmuir v Moffat
[2009] CSIH 19, 2009 SC 329

The question sometimes arises as to whether an asset is partnership property, the present case being an example. Mr Longmuir (junior) and his parents were in partnership. They farmed two adjacent farms in Lanarkshire, Netherfield Farm and Merchanthall Farm. Mr Longmuir (senior) died, and later, in 1994, Mrs Longmuir died, and the partnership thus came to an end. A dispute then arose between Mr Longmuir (junior), on the one hand, and his three sisters, Mrs Moffat, Mrs McLean and Mrs McLaren, on the other hand, as to whether Merchanthall Farm had been partnership property or whether, on the contrary, it was the property of Mr Longmuir (junior). The dispute went to arbitration. The arbiter found that, although the recorded title to Merchanthall Farm had been taken in the name of Mr Longmuir (junior) without mention of the partnership, and although there were certain other circumstances also suggesting that it was not partnership property, the balance of the evidence was in favour of the view that it was partnership property. In particular, it had been purchased with partnership funds and it had been included as a partnership asset in the partnership's annual accounts.

At this stage the arbiter stated a case to the Court of Session. The third of the three questions posed was about expenses. The first two were:

1. Whether a properly registered heritable title which is not otherwise impugned or subject *ex facie* to any qualification as to the real right of ownership, may nevertheless be successfully contradicted by a body of extrinsic or circumstantial evidence (including the inclusion thereof in the balance sheet of a farming partnership's accounts), some of which evidence has been construed or found to have somewhat contrary effect?
2. Whether in the whole circumstances of the arbitration, the deeming provision contained in the Partnership Act 1890 section 21 falls to be rebutted?

The first question was not difficult to answer. It has always been accepted that the way that title has been taken is not conclusive as to whether property is partnership property or not, and indeed it is doubtful whether Mr Longmuir seriously asserted the contrary. As for whether accounts are competent evidence, the court quoted (para 17) with approval the statement in the joint *Report on Partnership Law* (Scot Law Com No 192 (2003) para 2.21, n) by the Law Commission and Scottish Law Commission:

> The partnership accounts are often a good guide as to whether an asset is partnership property. If every partner has agreed to the inclusion of an asset in the balance sheet, this will normally be sufficient agreement.

The court held that the second question also fell to be answered in the affirmative, there being sufficient evidence before the arbiter to support the conclusion that the farm in question was a partnership asset. The decision is to be welcomed as a clear statement of the law (though a purist would point out that strictly speaking it is not correct to describe the partnership as having the 'beneficial ownership' of the farm).

(96) Moderator of the General Assembly of the Free Church of Scotland v Interim Moderator of the Congregation of Strath Free Church of Scotland (Continuing) (No 2)
[2009] CSOH 113, 2009 SLT 973

In 2000 the Free Church of Scotland (Continuing) split off from the Free Church of Scotland. There followed litigation as to the assets. In that litigation the Free Church of Scotland was successful: *General Assembly of the Association or Body of Christians known as the Free Church of Scotland and for administrative purposes only as the Free Church of Scotland (Continuing) and others v General Assembly of the Free Church of Scotland and others* 2005 SC 1. The present action was not about the assets in general, but about the church and manse at Broadford in the parish of Strath on Skye. The Free Church (Continuing) was in possession and the Free Church sought to recover possession. Given the earlier decision the case was a strong one and the claim succeeded. For discussion see F Lyall, 'Non-established church property in Scotland: a further case' (2010) 14 *Edinburgh Law Review* 113.

(97) Tayplan Ltd v Smith
[2009] CSOH 93

Tayplan Ltd, a property company, went into administration, and the administrator sued the directors, Alan Smith and Lee Smith, to recover funds which, it alleged, they had misappropriated. The case is about company law, but we mention it because of one of the background events and what was said about it by the defenders. Tayplan's bank wished it to reduce its indebtedness. One of the directors bought one of the company's properties, funding the purchase by a secured loan from the Mortgage Business. The latter was not willing to lend more than 75% of valuation. The price stated in the disposition by the company to the director was £1,100,000. The bank advanced £825,000, ie 75% of £1,100,000. We quote from para 43 of the opinion of the Lord Ordinary (Hodge):

Mr Alan Smith explained that in the commercial world, valuation was a matter of professional opinion and a commercial man could instruct several valuers, informing them of the valuation which he sought, to see if one would provide a valuation which suited his purposes. The price stated in the disposition was what had to be stated in order to obtain the loan of £825,000 and did not reflect the commercial reality. The documents were, he said, a means to an end to allow the agreement to be carried out. Mr Lee Smith similarly described the valuation at £1.1 million as a means to an end.

PART II

STATUTORY DEVELOPMENTS

STATUTORY DEVELOPMENTS

Flood Risk Management (Scotland) Act 2009 (asp 6)

This Act was passed primarily in order to transpose the Floods Directive (2007/60/ EC). It is a substantial piece of legislation, running to 97 sections and 4 schedules. Conveyancers may wish to note in particular s 21, which requires SEPA (Scottish Environment Protection Agency) to draw up, by 22 December 2013, 'flood hazard maps' and 'flood risk maps' which are (s 25) to be public, and also s 62, which requires local authorities to create, for their areas, 'Registers of flood protection schemes'. To what extent the Act will affect conveyancing practice remains to be seen.

Climate Change (Scotland) Act 2009 (asp 12)

Scotland accounts for only 0.2% of global greenhouse gases. But the new Act shows a determination to bring about a further reduction. Section 1(1) provides that 'The Scottish Ministers must ensure that the net Scottish emissions account for the year 2050 is at least 80% lower than the baseline'. An interim reduction of 42% is required by 2020 (s 2(1)). Scottish Ministers must lay a 'land use strategy' before the Scottish Parliament by 31 March 2011, and must provide by regulations for owners of buildings to increase energy efficiency and to reduce the emission of greenhouse gases (ss 63 and 64). Apparently the Government will try voluntary measures first. For this and other aspects of the legislation, see an article by Gordon McCreath in the October issue of the *Journal of the Law Society* (p 18).

Two provisions of the Act are of particular interest to conveyancers. First, s 68 introduces a new kind of personal real burden known as a 'climate change burden'. A personal real burden is a real burden in favour of a person (as opposed to a property) and is regulated by part 3 of the Title Conditions (Scotland) Act 2003: see *Conveyancing 2003* pp 124–28. A climate change burden must consist of an obligation, in the event of the burdened property being developed, for the property to meet specified mitigation and adaptation standards. It can only be created in favour of the Scottish Ministers or a conservation body or a trust. For a discussion, see Euan Sinclair, 'A new burden is born' (2009) 54 *Journal of the Law Society of Scotland* Dec/58. As Mr Sinclair points out, 'mitigation and adaptation' standards are to be found in legislation, meaning that the legislation would have to be copied out if the burden is to comply with the rule that the full terms of a real burden must be contained within the four corners of the deed. Mr Sinclair goes on to note that the narrow class of those permitted to hold such burdens means that 'the St Vincent Crescent Preservation Trust can impose a climate change burden on its property sold for development, but not Scottish Water, SEPA, Scottish Enterprise, HIE etc'.

The other provision is much more modest in scope. Section 69 expands the definition of 'maintenance' in the Tenement Management Scheme so as to include the installation of insulation. This allows a majority of owners in a tenement to make a 'scheme decision' under rule 3.1(a) of the TMS to put in insulation, and, under rule 4.2, to divide the cost amongst all the owners.

Stamp duty land tax

Further changes to SDLT are made by the **Finance Act 2009 (c 10)**. See **Commentary** p 183.

Sale and rent-back schemes and FSA regulation

The **Financial Services and Markets Act 2000 (Regulated Activities) (Amendment) Order 2009, SI 2009/1342,** brings sale and rent-back arrangements within the scope of 'regulated activities' for the purposes of the Financial Services and Markets Act 2000. For background see http://www.hm-treasury.gov.uk/consult_sale_rent.htm.

Development Management Scheme

The Development Management Scheme was enacted by the **Title Conditions (Scotland) Act 2003 (Development Management Scheme) Order 2009, SI 2009/729,** and came into force on 1 June 2009. The matching provisions in part 6 of the Title Conditions (Scotland) Act 2003 were brought into force on the same day by the **Title Conditions (Scotland) Act 2003 (Commencement No 2) Order 2009, SSI 2009/190.** The Act is now fully commenced. Consequential changes are made to the Lands Tribunal for Scotland Rules 2003, SSI 2003/452, by the **Lands Tribunal for Scotland Amendment Rules 2009, SSI 2009/259,** while fees are set by the **Lands Tribunal for Scotland Amendment (Fees) Rules 2009, SSI 2009/260** (amending the Lands Tribunal for Scotland Rules 1971, SI 1971/218, as amended).

For the Development Management Scheme, see **Commentary** p 130.

The two Northern Rocks

Northern Rock is being split into two. The **Northern Rock plc Transfer Order 2009, SI 2009/3226,** transfers a large portion of the assets (including, we believe, tens of thousands of standard securities) from Northern Rock plc to a new company. Though the order does not itself say so, we understand that Northern Rock plc is to be renamed Northern Rock (Asset Management) plc and that the new company is to be renamed Northern Rock plc. (This may be called the 'second' Northern Rock plc, which, as explained, will be a separate company from the original Northern Rock plc.) Hence in future it would be a mistake to think that the company called Northern Rock plc is the same company as has hitherto been the company called Northern Rock plc. Nor can it be assumed that an existing standard security in favour of Northern Rock plc will in future be held by the second Northern Rock plc because we understand that some standard securities will not be transferred and will thus continue to be held by the first Northern Rock plc (ie Northern Rock (Asset Management) plc). Moreover, it may well be that the second Northern Rock plc will not seek to complete title to the standard securities transferred to it. In that case such securities will be vested in Northern Rock (Asset Management) plc, but under the name of Northern Rock plc (the first), while Northern Rock plc (the second) will hold an uncompleted title thereto.

Registration of private landlords: exemption for insolvency practitioners

The **Private Landlord Registration (Modification) (Scotland) Order 2009, SSI 2009/33**, extends the existing exemptions from registration by inserting into the Antisocial Behaviour etc (Scotland) Act 2004 a new s 83(6)(m). This applies to a house owned by a person acting as an insolvency practitioner within the meaning of s 388 of the Insolvency Act 1986 for a period not exceeding six months. A similar exemption already applies in respect of executors and heritable creditors.

New information fees at Registers of Scotland

The **Fees in the Registers of Scotland Amendment Order 2009, SSI 2009/171**, which came into force on 31 May 2009, introduces new fees – some higher a few lower – for the provision of information from Registers of Scotland. In the Land Register, fees have generally been increased by around 6%, but the cost of searches in Registers Direct has been reduced from £3.30 to £1.80. A complete list is:

Register of Sasines

For a search in the Presentment Book (per item searched for)	£1.80
For a search in the Minute Book (per item searched for)	£1.80
For each search sheet viewed	£1.80

(Note: There is no fee for searching the indices of persons or places. Nor will a fee be charged for a search that produces a nil return.)

Land Register New Fee

Land Register

For a search of the Application record (per item searched for)	£1.80
For a search of the Title Sheet record (per title sheet searched for)	£1.80
Per view of a title sheet for an interest in land	£1.80
Per index Map search	£1.80
Per Property Price search/Scotland's House Prices	Nil

(Note: If you search for a title number by name, address or title number and then view that title sheet, the fee charged is for viewing the title sheet only. Otherwise the search is charged for. There is no fee for a search that produces a nil result.)

Chancery and Judicial Registers

For a search in the Register of Deeds or Register of Judgements	£1.80
For a search against up to six names in the Register of Inhibitions	£1.80
For a search against a specified minute number	£1.80

(Note: A search includes a print disclosing relevant entries if requested within seven working days of the date of the original search.)

Land Register Reports New Fee

Land Register reports

Forms 10, 12, 14, P16 and P17	£28.50
Forms 11 and 13	£16.50
Form 10/P16 and Form 12/P17	£41.00

Miscellaneous Services New Fee

Miscellaneous services

Provision of a plain or duplicate copy deed	£8.00
Provision of a certified copy, office copy or official extract of deed	£15.00
Provision of extract from National Archives of Scotland	£5.00 plus NAS fee
For the handling of second copies requested at the same time as the first	£8.00
Provision of Land Register Archive Information from a deed or document in the archive, per deed	£8.00
Provision of a copy of minutes of Register of Inhibitions (per day)	£19.50
Information on sales by consideration	£450 per month for the whole of Scotland
Information on land values	£622 per month for the whole of Scotland
Information on transactions relating to a creditor or legal agent	£100 per month or per quarter
Data set of registration county boundaries	£100
Provision of minutes of General Register of Sasines	£252 per month
Report on postcode sectors	£105 per month or per quarter

Inhibitions

Part 5 of the Bankruptcy and Diligence etc (Scotland) Act 2007, which contains major reforms of the law of inhibition, was commenced on 22 April 2009: see the **Bankruptcy and Diligence etc (Scotland) Act 2007 (Commencement No 4, Savings and Transitionals) Order 2009, SSI 2009/67**. A minor amendment to part 5 was made by the **Bankruptcy and Diligence etc (Scotland) Act 2007 (Inhibition) Order 2009, SSI 2009/129**. A set of new forms for schedules of inhibition, notices of inhibition and so on is provided by the **Diligence (Scotland) Regulations, SSI 2009/68**, as modified by the **Diligence (Scotland) Amendment Regulations 2009, SSI 2009/396**.

The changes introduced by part 5 are largely technical in nature but include the abolition of the preference conferred by inhibition in insolvency proceedings and other processes: see *Conveyancing 2006* pp 137–38.

Work notices and maintenance plans

Important parts of the Housing (Scotland) Act 2006 were commenced on 1 April 2009 by the **Housing (Scotland) Act 2006 (Commencement No 7, Savings and Transitional Provisions) Order 2009, SSI 2009/122**. These include provisions on the new work notice and demolition notice (ss 30–34), the former replacing the repair notice, and also the provisions on the five-year maintenance plans which local authorities can impose in respect of buildings (in practice tenements) where the building is not being maintained to a reasonable standard (ss 42–51). For maintenance plans, see *Conveyancing 2005* pp 122–24. Maintenance plans require to be registered in the Land or Sasine Register (s 61), so that conveyancers will begin to encounter them.

The Scottish Government has been issuing *Advisory Guidance for Local Authorities* on implementation. For work and demolition notices (vol 2), see http://www.scotland.gov.uk/Publications/2009/03/25154921/0 and for maintenance plans (vol 3), see http://www.scotland.gov.uk/Publications/2009/03/25154634/0.

Community right to buy: new forms and new excluded land

New forms are provided in respect of the community right to buy, under part 2 of the Land Reform (Scotland) Act 2003, by the **Community Right to Buy (Prescribed Form of Application and Notices) (Scotland) Regulations 2009, SSI 2009/156**. This replaces the forms provided by the Community Right to Buy (Forms) (Scotland) Regulations 2004, SSI 2004/233 (for which see *Conveyancing 2004* p 34). The new forms are:

Schedule 1. Application to register or to re-register an interest in land.

Schedule 2. Notice where owner or creditor may be unknown.

Schedule 3. Notice by Ministers on whether community interest is to be registered or re-registered.

Schedule 4. Notice by owner or creditor of proposed transfer of land.

Schedule 5. Notices following receipt of a notice under section 48 of the Act.

Settlements of more that 10,000 people form 'excluded land' for the purposes of s 33 of the Land Reform (Scotland) Act 2003 and cannot be the subject of a community buy-out under part 2 of the Act. The **Community Right to Buy (Definition of Excluded Land) (Scotland) Order 2009, SSI 2009/207**, adds Armadale to the list (following population growth). It also establishes new boundaries for four settlement areas formed out of previously separate areas. These are:

Blackburn and Bathgate (formerly Bathgate)

Bonnybridge and Banknock (formerly Bonnybridge)

Falkirk and Hallglen (formerly Falkirk)

Whitburn and East Whitburn (formerly Whitburn).

The complete list of excluded land is now as set out in the schedule to the 2009 Order, namely:

Aberdeen; Alloa; Arbroath; Ardrossan; Armadale; Ayr; Blackburn and Bathgate; Bo'ness; Bonnybridge and Banknock; Broxburn; Buckhaven; Carluke; Carnoustie; Cowdenbeath; Cumbernauld; Dalkeith; Dumbarton; Dumfries; Dundee; Dunfermline; East Kilbride; Edinburgh; Elgin; Erskine; Falkirk and Hallglen; Forfar; Fraserburgh; Galashiels; Glasgow; Glenrothes; Greenock; Hamilton; Hawick; Helensburgh; Inverness; Inverurie; Irvine; Kilmarnock; Kilwinning; Kirkcaldy; Kirkintilloch; Largs; Larkhall; Linlithgow; Livingston; Montrose; Penicuik; Perth; Peterhead; St Andrews; Stirling; Stonehaven; Stranraer; Troon; Westhill (Aberdeenshire); Whitburn and East Whitburn.

The boundaries are given on official maps, for which see http://www.scotland.gov.uk/Topics/farmingrural/Rural/rural-land/right-to-buy/MappingTool.

New forms for crofting community right to buy

New forms are provided in respect of the crofting community right to buy, under part 3 of the Land Reform (Scotland) Act 2003, by the **Crofting Community Body (Prescribed Form of Application and Notice) (Scotland) Regulations 2009, SSI 2009/160**. This replaces the forms provided by the Crofting Community Body Form of Application for Consent to Buy Croft Land etc and Notice of Ministers' Decision (Scotland) Regulations 2004, SSI 2004/224 (for which see *Conveyancing 2004* p 35). The form in sch 1 is for applications by crofting community bodies to buy croft land or sporting interests. The notification of Ministers' decisions is to be given in the form prescribed in sch 2.

PART III
OTHER MATERIAL

OTHER MATERIAL

Registers of Scotland

Sin bin for applications

Registers of Scotland warn ((2009) 54 *Journal of the Law Society of Scotland* Jan/15) that:

> Acceptance of an application onto the application record only means that it meets basic requirements. It is not unusual to discover during title examination that further documentary evidence is needed, or that a deed requires to be returned for amendment. The application is then placed in 'standover' … Last financial year 14% of first registration applications, 8% for transfer of a part, and 9% for dealing with whole, went into standover.

A handy leaflet, *A Guide to Good Deeds* (available at http://www.ros.gov.uk/ pdfs/good_deeds_guide.pdf) provides a checklist of things to watch out for:

- Have the correct Forms 1, 2 and 3 etc been enclosed?
- Do any electronic forms have Unique Identifier Numbers?
- Are all documents and forms signed and dated?
- Have all the questions on pages 2, 3 and 4 of the registration forms been completed?
- If the transaction is dealing with a property that could be a matrimonial home, or a family home in terms of the Civil Partnership Act 2004, has all the evidence (eg affidavits etc) been submitted with the application?
- If the application is for first registration have all relevant prior titles been included?
- If the application is over already registered subjects, have the appropriate Land/ Charge Certificates been enclosed?
- Has all necessary evidence of change of name or of death been included?
- If a SDLT certificate is required is it included with the application?

Common areas after *PMP Plus*

The Keeper's policy on the description of common areas in developments, following the decision in *PMP Plus Ltd v Keeper of the Registers of Scotland* 2009

SLT (Lands Tr) 2, is set out in *Update 27* (available at http://www.ros.gov.uk/pdfs/update27.pdf). See **Commentary** p 122.

New information fees

New fees were prescribed by the Fees in the Registers of Scotland Amendment Order 2009, SSI 2009/171, and came into force on 31 May 2009. See p 59 above and, for background, *Update 25* (available at http://www.ros.gov.uk/pdfs/update25.pdf).

Scan and create

In the Land Register, application forms and accompanying deeds are now being scanned to capture information for use in the application record. See *Update 24* (available at http://www.ros.gov.uk/pdfs/update24.pdf). Instead of a physical case bag of paper documents moving from desk to desk as the application goes through the registration process, the electronic images go from person to person. This is significantly more efficient and also permits 'agile working' (including working from home). On completion of registration the scanned images go into the archive record. The overall idea is to speed up registration.

This admirable aim has caused some collateral damage. As the system works only if every application is accompanied by a form, the long-established practice of not insisting on a form for discharges if they accompany applications for registration of the purchaser's disposition has had to be abandoned: see *Conveyancing 2008* p 63. Further, it is necessary that the forms are completed in such a way that they can be read by the Optical Character Recognition technology. This means that only RoS-prescribed or RoS-licensed forms will do, that they must be completed in block capitals, and that all the information must be kept within the fields on the form.

Less obviously, but in the interests of the ominous-sounding 'dematerialisation' (which is surely something out of *Dr Who*), the new system has also led to the withdrawal of the practice of returning a duplicate form 4, which used to be annotated to show which deeds had been received. Its replacement – a 'streamlined acknowledgement by email or letter' – is not, apparently, always received. One disgruntled user (Eunice M McConnach) complained by letter to the *Journal of the Law Society of Scotland* (May/8) that:

> The electronic acknowledgements, when received, are woefully inadequate – there is no indication of how many or which deeds have been received for the application. If you exhibited it to a lender, they would rightly ask why it was evidence of the registration of their standard security – there would be no mention on the acknowledgement of either the lender (unless they are stated to be 'the applicant', in which case there would be no mention of the purchaser) or of the standard security.

She may not have been reassured by the reply from the Deputy Keeper (at p 8 of the June *Journal*), with its reference to 'our new IT infrastructure, which will equip us with the tools we need to deliver an excellent land registration system in the 21st century'.

£10m loss for Registers of Scotland

Predictably, the collapse in the property market has had a serious effect on Registers of Scotland's finances. An operating loss of £10.6 million is reported for the year ended 31 March 2009, compared with a profit of £10.8 million in 2008. This is a loss of getting on for £1 million a month. Revised projections show the deficit will continue until 2014, with losses of £22.4 million, £16 million, £21 million, £14 million and £13 million forecast for the coming years as a result of a reduction in fees and an expected drop in registering re-mortgages. The five-year deficit is £25 million higher than previously anticipated and will be covered by dipping into the organisation's reserves of £122.5 million, built up using past years' profits. See further the *Annual Report and Accounts 2008–09* (available at http://www.ros. gov.uk/public/publications/annual_reports.html).

Promotional truck

Registers of Scotland has purchased a promotional truck fitted with technology that will allow it to show the public the free property price search facilities and other general interest services. Details about where and when the truck will be used can be found at http://www.ros.gov.uk/public/news/events.html. (Disappointingly, when this link was consulted, it reported 'We currently have no public events'.)

New Keeper

Sheenagh Adams became Keeper of the Registers of Scotland on 1 July 2009, the first woman to hold this post. She has worked in Registers of Scotland since 2006 and was previously managing director. An interview can be found at (2009) 54 *Journal of the Law Society of Scotland* Aug/22. From now on all references to the Keeper will have to use the female form of personal pronoun.

ARTL

In the interview mentioned above, the new Keeper acknowledged that in relation to ARTL 'the takeup rate is slower than we had hoped'. The running total on the Registers of Scotland website showed that, as at the beginning of January 2010, around 22,000 applications had been submitted using ARTL. A year ago the figure was 13,000. No doubt the position will be helped by the glitzy official launch of ARTL at Dynamic Earth on 15 December 2009 (catch it in full at http://ros.gov. uk/launch/index.html). What symbolism was intended by the choice of venue is intriguingly unclear. A discussion of ARTL and risk management can be found at (2009) 54 *Journal of the Law Society of Scotland* Oct/42.

Home Owner and Debtor Protection (Scotland) Bill

This Bill was introduced to the Scottish Parliament on 1 October 2009 and passed on 11 February 2010. See **Commentary** p 179.

Fraud avoidance: some things to look out for

The Law Society's John Scott has provided a list of ten situations in which a conveyancer should be wary of the possibility of fraud: see (2009) 54 *Journal of the Law Society of Scotland* Jan/58. These are:

1. *Sales following a recent discharge.* If you didn't prepare the discharge you should check with the lender to make sure the loan has actually been redeemed.
2. *Back-to-back transactions.* Is there a genuine explanation? Of course the CML handbook will require you to tell the lender if the seller's title has not been registered for at least six months.
3. *Schemes designed to enhance loan-to-value.* These are often used by new-build developers as a marketing tool and can be quite legitimate. However they also originate from intermediaries with the aim of raising the level of the loan to 100% or more of the property's value. They can be complicated and may involve a 'finder's fee'. You should ensure (first) that you understand how the scheme works, and (secondly) that you report it to the lender. If you suspect fraudulent intent, remember your obligations to report to SOCA.
4. *Bogus sellers.* Make sure that your client is really the owner and has not stolen someone else's identity! A home visit is no longer a sufficient means of primary ID; you really need to see a passport or equivalent. Also check that the client's date of birth is consistent with appearance! [An example of this kind of fraud is *Frank Houlgate Investment Co Ltd v Biggart Baillie LLP* [2009] CSOH 165, discussed at pp 108–13 below.]
5. *Bogus purchasers.* It is absolutely essential to identify a client properly before an offer is submitted. Otherwise you risk exposure to serious criminal activity. You should also advise selling clients not to accept diverted mail for the purchaser before the date of entry.
6. *Stand-alone securities.* If you are preparing a security outwith a purchase, be wary if the client requests a specific recording date (as opposed to the date of drawdown).
7. *Stand-alone discharges.* If you are asked to record a discharge produced by the owner, check first with the lender that the loan has actually been redeemed.
8. *Prearranged private sales.* You should check that the transaction is genuine and not on unusual terms (particularly price).
9. *Sales with low-level marketing activity.* For example the seller requests no 'For Sale' signs, restricted viewing or no local advertising. Is there a good reason for this?
10. *Third party involvement in funds.* These can be on either side of the transaction, eg contributions to the price from relatives, or requests to pay sale proceeds to third parties. The former has money-laundering and conflict of interest implications. The latter should always be resisted.

Home reports

Home reports were introduced on 1 December 2008: see *Conveyancing 2008* pp 48–52. Their first anniversary led to a flurry of claims and counter-claims as to their effect and effectiveness: see eg the comments collected at http://www.scottishlawagents.org.uk/home_reports.html. Housing and Communities Minister Alex Neil claimed that the home report had been 'good news' for the

Scottish housing market while the Royal Institution of Chartered Surveyors said that the reports have tempted buyers back into the market (and in any event, in the words of Janette Wilson, 'have certainly saved the surveying profession from penury'). A detailed and reasoned defence of home reports was given by Lorne Crerar, who had chaired the relevant sub-group of the Housing Improvement Task Force: see (2009) 54 *Journal of the Law Society of Scotland* March/18. A survey of solicitors' views by Peter Nicholson, which appeared in the *Journal of the Law Society* for December 2009 (p 12), concluded that, while some solicitors have been won over, the majority view is that home reports 'act as a drag on the market by deterring people thinking of testing the level of interest in their house, are distrusted by many clients, and fall short of achieving their stated objectives'.

For the most part, indeed, the critics have remained unpersuaded. For example, David Borrowman, the managing partner at Caesar & Howie, wrote that:

> Sadly Home Reports were conceived in a Fantasy Land peopled by politicians, consumer 'champions' and surveyors, with a sprinkling of a few non-representative lawyers. ... Without wishing to be offensive I see from a recent press release that the proponents of Home Reports remain happily resident in Fantasy Land congratulating themselves on how they have fixed the house market – which they surely have.

Mr Borrowman blames home reports for the collapse in the property market. Designed to solve the (non-existent) problem of multiple surveys, they have led to a great increase in the number of such surveys (presumably due to sellers commissioning several to find the one with the highest valuation and most favourable terms or lenders demanding a survey of their own). Other aspects of the home report, says Mr Borrowman, have fared little better. 'Sellers and buyers alike treat Energy Performance Certificates ... with open contempt and see them as worthless', while 'some, and even most of the questions in the Property Questionnaire section are answered "don't know"'. No doubt the controversy will continue.

Combined Standard Clauses

After a period of negotiation between representatives of the Royal Faculty of Procurators in Glasgow and the Edinburgh Conveyancers Forum, and some input from professors of conveyancing (for details see p 56 of the September issue of the *Journal of the Law Society*), agreement was reached on the terms of new standard missives. Known as the 'Combined Standard Clauses' – the working title was the 'Harthill Missives' – these replace, from 1 October 2009, the separate but similar clauses which were in operation in Glasgow and Edinburgh. For details, see Ian Ferguson and Paul Carnan, 'The new Combined Standard Missive Clauses' (2009) 77 *Scottish Law Gazette* 89. Like other standard missives, the Combined Standard Clauses are available at http://www.lawscot.org.uk/Members_Information/convey_essens/stdmissives/. The big question now is whether other regions will also sign up, opening up the eventual prospect of all-Scotland clauses. On that topic (and others), see Stewart Brymer, 'The Combined Standard Clauses – a step in the right direction' (2009) 102 *Greens Property Law Bulletin* 1. A counter-blast, questioning the desirability of standard missives in the first place, is provided by Michael Smith, '"One size" is a dodgy fit' (2009) 54 *Journal of the Law Society of Scotland* Dec/54.

Rebate schemes and mortgage fraud

John Scott of the Law Society reports a device for obtaining 100% mortgages from unknowing lenders: see (2009) 54 *Journal of the Law Society of Scotland* Aug/54. He writes:

> How does a rebate scheme work? The purchaser offers a very full price, well above the seller's realistic expectations. At the same time the purchaser arranges a mortgage with a mainstream lender (on the basis of a questionable valuation), and signs a contract with a loan company for a facility to fund the gap between the mortgage and this price. Missives are concluded on the basis of the full price and the transaction proceeds as normal. At settlement the purchaser's solicitor sends the seller's agent a cheque for the full amount. Then the seller's agent pays back the deposit (and a fee) to the loan company in terms of an irrevocable mandate from the seller. This mandate removes any need for the company to have a postponed security over the property. The source of funding is not disclosed to the mortgage lender by the purchaser's agent, so that the lender is effectively induced to lend the whole of the net price received by the seller.

For a solicitor to participate in such a scheme, on either side, Mr Scott warns, is likely to breach professional duties and even to invite a criminal investigation.

Notices of potential liability for costs

A purchaser of a flat or other property has no liability for repairs already carried out but not paid for unless a notice of potential liability for costs was registered at least two weeks before settlement: see Title Conditions (Scotland) Act 2003 ss 10 and 10A and Tenements (Scotland) Act 2004 ss 12 and 13. For further information, see *Conveyancing 2004* pp 140–43. A parliamentary answer by John Swinney shows how often these notices are being used:

Notices of potential liability for costs

Financial year	Land Register	Sasine Register	Total
2005–06	1,166	61	1,227
2006–07	1,861	50	1,911
2007–08	2,019	77	2,096
2008–09	4,332	98	4,430

It will be seen that the number of notices doubled in 2008–09.

BSA standard mortgage instructions

On 1 January 2010 the Building Societies Association (www.bsa.org.uk) introduced a new set of mortgage instructions with the idea of preventing individual lenders having to write instructions of their own – other than to add specific requirements. The instructions have been introduced on a voluntary basis and it is for individual lenders to decide whether to adopt them. There are separate instructions for Scotland.

Environmental issues in the purchase of residential property

It is reported in the *Journal of the Law Society* for December 2009 (p 57) that:

> The Professional Practice and Conveyancing Committees have considered whether solicitors are under any duty to advise clients for whom they are acting in a purchase of residential property, in relation to environmental matters, and specifically as to whether an environmental report should be obtained. The committees' view is that conveyancing practitioners are not qualified to give advice in this connection and that they should accordingly include a clause in their standard terms of business indicating that environmental matters do not form part of their remit.

High hedges

In August 2009 the Scottish Government published a *Consultation on High Hedges and other Nuisance Vegetation* (available at http://www.scotland.gov.uk/Resource/Doc/281919/0085199.pdf). The paper explains (p 6) that:

> Two factors are likely to have exacerbated disputes between neighbours about high boundary hedges in recent years: the increased density of urban areas and the increased availability of low-cost, and often fast-growing hedges, which have sometimes not been properly maintained over the years.
>
> It is easy to see the attractions and benefits provided by a good hedge as a garden boundary. It can act as a useful barrier against weather, dust, noise and pollution; is relatively inexpensive, quick to establish and long-lasting, growing easily in a range of soil and weather conditions; and, in addition to offering privacy and security, can encourage wildlife and be a feature of beauty and interest in its own right.
>
> Problems can arise with hedges, however, if they are planted in unsuitable locations or become too large through a lack of maintenance. The Leyland cypress (*x Cupressocyparis leylandii*), for example, which has become increasingly popular as a hedging plant over the last four decades, grows at the rate of one metre per year and can reach heights of 30 metres if not trimmed two to three times per year.
>
> Owners may allow their hedge to grow unchecked because they genuinely value it and want to exercise their property rights, because of the time or cost associated with its maintenance, because it was an unwelcome inheritance from a previous owner of the property or – in some reported cases – because it becomes a tool or a matter of principle in disputes with their neighbours.
>
> The most commonly reported problems associated with high hedges and other types of nuisance vegetation are that they block light from gardens or house rooms, restrict views and risk damaging adjacent property. These, and the other impacts reported,

can lead to a general sense of oppression and a feeling that people's enjoyment of their homes and gardens has been spoiled. Neighbours of hedge owners feel that property rights are unfairly stacked in favour of the hedge owner.

Four options are suggested (p 14):

- Option 1: Do nothing – no Government action.
- Option 2: Promote existing remedies such as mediation.
- Option 3: Strengthen and supplement existing remedies with research, guidance and title conditions.
- Option 4: Provide a legislative solution by utilising or extending existing provisions or introducing new ones.

The consultation period closed on 13 November 2009.

Meanwhile a pressure group, Scothedge (www.scothedge.colwat.com), has contributed a piece to the November issue of the *Journal of the Law Society* (p 11). Scothedge campaigns 'on behalf of those suffering at the hands of uncaring growers of high trees and hedges'.

OFT study of property managers in Scotland

In February 2009 the OFT published a study on *Property Managers in Scotland* (available at http://www.oft.gov.uk/shared_oft/reports/comp_policy/oft1046. pdf). The study focuses mainly on tenements, which house some 36% of Scotland's population (and comprise around 780,000 households). But the study also has something to say about land maintenance services in respect of common areas in housing developments.

The OFT's press release opened with the announcement that 'the market is not working well for consumers in Scotland'. In summary, the key findings of the study were as follows (pp 5–6):

We found that most people – about 70 per cent – are happy with their property manager. The majority of respondents to our consumer survey said they found it easy to get repairs carried out, felt the services offered by property managers represented value for money and were of good quality. On the other hand, a substantial minority were less happy about the services provided. One illustration of this can be found among consumers that had made a complaint about their management firm: as many as two thirds were dissatisfied with the way their complaint was handled.

The relationship between the property manager and the owners in a shared property is defined by complex legislation, property deeds and agreements – many consumers do not understand their rights and obligations and are unsure about what they should expect from their property manager, or the standards of service that should apply. When consumers cannot easily and confidently identify the terms and conditions which apply to their relationship with a supplier, then the possibility of a breakdown of that relationship increases.

We found a very low level of switching in this market, even compared to some other markets such as banking, communications or energy where switching is either currently, or has historically been, low. In part this is due to the difficulties of coordinating the individual owners in a tenement block or property development to facilitate a switch, but it is also due to the problems these consumers have in understanding the processes involved in switching to another property manager.

There is very little evidence of active competition between property managers to encourage consumers to switch. We also found that some perceptions about the Code of Practice of the main trade association, the Property Managers Association of Scotland (PMAS), may have further dampened competition between property managers. We found evidence to suggest that some PMAS members believed that the PMAS Code of Practice prohibited members from approaching other members' customers with a view to encouraging them to switch from their current supplier of services. We are pleased to report that PMAS has confirmed to us that its code of practice should not be misinterpreted as discouraging competition and have written to their members to make it clear that the code of practice does not prohibit members from approaching other members' customers and that PMAS encourages healthy competition among its members for the benefit of consumers.

Owners in shared properties who have a complaint or are dissatisfied with their property manager have limited scope for redress. Even after using what complaint procedures do exist, typically the property managers' own complaints system, many are left with the issue either unresolved or with an unsatisfactory response and the only – unrealistic for many – recourse may be to the courts. There is no independent complaint or redress mechanism available to the owners of shared property in Scotland.

We also found that where consumers are organised and have a strategy for engaging with their property manager there are clear benefits. Consumers organised in an association or similar are better able to represent their collective interests effectively and assertively; property managers, acting with a clear mandate and instructions are more likely to be able to meet consumers' expectations.

In the light of these findings, the OFT makes four main recommendations (pp 6–9):

(1) The lack of effective competition in this market, difficulties with switching, and the complexity of the legal situation means that there is a need for an effective independent complaints and redress mechanism which is easily accessible to the owners of shared property. In order for this to work effectively, this scheme needs to operate within a framework which lays down minimum requirements for best practice so that complaints are assessed against clear standards. We recommend that these standards should provide for property managers to:

- set out in writing the details of the services they will provide and the relevant delivery standards
- encourage property owners to form an organised body (either a formal residents' association or limited company)
- the provision, as a matter of course, of a detailed financial breakdown and description of the services provided by the property manager and such supporting documentation as is appropriate (for example, invoices where appropriate)
- proactive explanations of how and why particular contractors have been appointed, demonstrating that the services being procured are charged at a competitive market rate

- automatically return floats to owners at the point of settlement of final bill, without consumers needing to request the return of the float
- have and operate a complaints procedure and to proactively make details of it available to consumers
- at a minimum follow Financial Services Authority (FSA) guidelines on disclosure of commission on insurance, whether FSA authorised or not
- in addition, there should be a mechanism to allow the audit of payments to contractors, either on a random basis or reactively in response to complaints, to reassure consumers that no improper payments are involved.

(2) To be effective in changing the nature of the market the standards and redress scheme needs to cover a large majority of Scottish property managers. The Scottish Government has put forward a proposal for a self-regulatory scheme that would bring together representatives of Consumer Focus Scotland, SFHA and PMAS but would be open to all engaged in property management. If such a voluntary scheme receives widespread backing, and includes the provision for an independent and robust complaint and redress mechanism, in the terms set out in the 'Recommendations' chapter of this report, this would be a big step toward solving the most serious problems.

(3) Given that there are benefits to a voluntary scheme, and there are indications such a scheme may be successful, this route should be attempted before considering statutory regulation. Nevertheless, given the low level of competition in the market, if self-regulation fails, there is a case for the introduction of statutory regulation … Given it is not certain industry support will be forthcoming, we recommend that if an effective scheme is not in place and operating successfully within two years, proposals for a statutory scheme should be brought forward and implemented.

(4) Our study has also shown that there is a need for clear advice and assistance to consumers on what is a complex area of law. In addition, the relationships between the owners of the shared property and between the owners of the shared property and the property manager can also be problematic, for a wide range of reasons not least because of communication, information or coordination difficulties. We therefore also recommend that the Scottish Government should work with local authorities to develop a centralised information, advice and mediation service for private sector property owners and all types of property managers providing services to private sector owners. We recommend that the advice service should be distinct from any self-regulatory scheme and more formal redress mechanism since its purpose would not be to resolve complaints or award redress, but to be a source of advice and guidance for all parties.

The OFT points out the similarities between the factoring of tenements and the provision of land maintenance services for open spaces, and recommends that those involved in the latter (often the same people) should be regulated in the same way (p 9).

In its response (http://www.scotland.gov.uk/News/Releases/2009/05/13143033), the Scottish Government broadly welcomed the OFT study. In the short term, at least, it will continue to promote a voluntary and industry-led accreditation scheme: see *Conveyancing 2008* p 70. As for recommendation (4), the Government view is that it is best to build on existing services provided by local authorities and by organisations such as Consumer Focus Scotland, Shelter, and Citizens' Advice Bureaux.

OFT study of home buying and selling

In February 2009 the Office of Fair Trading began work on a study of house buying and selling in the UK, including Scotland. The OFT explains the study in this way:

> The study will consider the consumer's experience of buying and/or selling a home from putting the property on the market, through making and receiving offers, up to completing the transaction. In particular it will look at:
>
> - How sellers decide how to bring their property to market, considering the different channels available (such as high street estate agents, internet property retailers, auction or through solicitors) and how service providers within these channels compete for business.
> - How agents bring together buyers and sellers; how efficiently this is achieved; and the scope for harm to either buyer or seller at this stage.
> - The role of agents and/or other service providers in moving the transaction from offer to completion (or exchange and conclusion of missives in Scotland).
> - Their relationships with other professional service providers, notably providers of surveys, searches, conveyancing, mortgage broking, Energy Performance Certificates (EPCs), Home Information Packs (HIPs) and, in Scotland, Home Reports (HRs).
>
> The main questions that the study will seek to answer are:
>
> - Has price competition improved since our market study of estate agency in 2004?
> - Are there barriers to innovation in this market?
> - What are the main risks to consumers in this sector?
> - Has consumer satisfaction improved since 2004?
> - Can more be done to improve confidence in this market?

Various consumer surveys have been carried out, and the OFT expects to report in early 2010. For further details, see www.oft.gov.uk/homes.

Review of the private rented sector

In March 2009 the Scottish Government published a major *Review of the Private Rented Sector* (http://www.scotland.gov.uk/Publications/2009/03/23153136/0). This is an overview report: the full *Key Findings and Policy Implications* report along with four volumes of research is available from www.scotland.gov.uk/ publications. The private rented sector (PRS) accommodates approximately 233,000 households. Landlords, the review finds, are largely individuals or couples investing for capital growth rather than rental income.

The flavour of the review can be given by some extracts from the executive summary:

The vast majority of tenants are satisfied with their landlord, agent and accommodation. … There are also around one in twenty households actively dissatisfied with their landlord and property and one in ten dissatisfied with their agent. The reasons for dissatisfaction were generally related to landlords and agents taking too long to deal with repairs or having poor standards of customer care, as well as minor and major repairs to the property not being satisfactorily undertaken. Problems with tenancy deposits were also given as a reason for dissatisfaction. …

There is evidence that a small minority of tenants are subject to poor standards of property and management and that rental affordability for particular groups is an issue. … There was evidence that around a quarter of tenants struggle to pay their rent in that they pay more than 25% of their income on rent, with one in three stating that they found it fairly or very difficult to meet rent payments. More than a quarter of households living in the private rented sector were also experiencing fuel poverty. … There was also some evidence of poor practice. Three percent of households did not have a written tenancy agreement; 7% said that they strongly agreed that they did not understand their tenant rights and 4% said they had problems finding out about their rights; 3% were very dissatisfied with their home; 2% had never had their gas serviced; and 5% felt that there was no point in taking action about a problem because they felt that nothing would be done. …

The tenancy regime appears to be operating satisfactorily. The short assured tenancy (SAT) is by far the most common rental contract in the PRS and is popular with both landlords and tenants. It offers a minimum six month contract between tenant and landlord, after which the tenancy can be renewed and either tenant or landlord can end the tenancy by giving appropriate notice. The tenancy regime has to suit a diverse range of tenants with some looking for long term, or even life-time accommodation, whilst others seek flexible temporary accommodation while they are students, forming new households, new migrants to an area, establishing careers or saving money to buy a home. … Length of minimum tenancy was by no means equal to length of stay. It was generally of benefit to both landlord and tenant to find a long term sustainable arrangement and, whilst 2 in 5 households had lived in their home for less than one year, a further 1 in 5 PRS households had lived in their home for more than 5 years. The review found that in most cases it was the tenant who decided to leave the property and end the tenancy rather than the landlord. …

A significant minority of tenancy deposits appear to be withheld, whether legitimately or not. A landlord can require a new tenant to pay a returnable deposit (of no more than two months' rent for an assured or short assured tenancy), all or part of which may be legitimately withheld at the end of the tenancy if the tenant has failed to meet his or her obligations, eg having caused damage or left bills unpaid … Where deposits are withheld, evidence suggests that around three quarters of tenants consider that the landlord (or agent) behaved unfairly in withholding the deposit. …

Some landlords have limited knowledge of housing law but are not interested in training. … It was also clear that tenants' awareness of specific initiatives remained quite low. Only 4 tenants in 10 had heard of landlord registration, 3 in 10 had heard of mediation as a means of resolving disputes between tenants and landlords and only 1 in 10 had heard of the Private Rented Housing Panel and the Repairing Standard. Of considerable concern was the finding that 1 in 3 households living in a House in Multiple Occupation (HMO) did not know whether the landlord had a licence.

Shelter and Consumer Focus Scotland published their own document on the PRS in December 2009: *Improving the private rented sector in Scotland for the benefit of consumers* (http://www.consumerfocus.org.uk/scotland/publications).

Ending the right to buy

Since its introduction 30 years ago, the right to buy has resulted in the sale, at a discount, of almost half a million homes for rent in Scotland. The Scottish Government now wishes to bring this to an end. A new Housing (Scotland) Bill was introduced to the Scottish Parliament on 13 January 2010, and s 129 of the Bill inserts a new 61ZA into the Housing (Scotland) Act 1987. This limits the right to buy to those who were tenants on the date that the provision came into force, and have continued to be tenants since. The effect is to exclude those who take up a Scottish secure tenancy for the first time after s 61ZA comes into force, and those who return to the social rented sector after a break. In explaining the change, Deputy First Minister Nicola Sturgeon said that 'building new homes for rent is pointless if we then simply sell them off under the Right to Buy. That is why I believe the Right to Buy has had its day'.

Claiming Lochaber for the MacDonalds of Keppoch

A petition (PE1297) by Ranald MacDonald of Keppoch, clan chief of the MacDonalds of Keppoch, calls on the Scottish Parliament to call on the Scottish Government to investigate the 'Dutchas/Duthchaich' or 'native title' system of land tenure. Mr MacDonald wishes to reclaim his clan territory – which he estimates as around 2,000 square miles at Lochaber – on the basis of 'the authentic and ancient laws of Ur Duthchas'. He continues:

> What I am seeking is further legislation or an extension to the existing Abolition of the Feudal System (Scotland) Act 2004 [*sic*] to correct the anomaly that exists and bring into line the same principles used in New Zealand, Australia and North America. Some of the lands that were usurped, 'stolen', from the indigenous peoples of those lands have been restored. The instrument used in each case was 'Native Title' and as already explained, Native Title is equivalent to Udal Title and Duthchaich Title.

Mr MacDonald gives further information on the clan website: http://macdonaldofkeppoch.org/news.php. 'Native title' has become big business in Australia and certain other former colonies, the most celebrated case being the decision of the High Court of Australia in *Mabo v Queensland (No 2)* [1992] HCA 23, (1992) 175 CLR 1.

At its meeting on 15 December 2009, the Public Petitions Committee agreed to write to the Scottish Government, Registers of Scotland, Law Society of Scotland, the Scottish Land Court and Andy Wightman seeking responses to the points raised in the petition and during the discussion. The discussion is not minuted.

Books

Alastair N Brown, *Money Laundering* (W Green; ISBN 9780414014459)

Kenneth S Gerber, *Commercial Leases in Scotland: a Practitioner's Guide* (W Green 2009; ISBN 9780414017283)

William M Gordon and Scott Wortley, *Scottish Land Law*, 3rd edn, vol 1 (W Green 2009; ISBN 9780414015548)

Somerled Notley, *Scottish Agricultural Law Handbook* (Avizandum Publishing Ltd 2009; ISBN 9781904968290)

Kenneth G C Reid and George L Gretton, *Conveyancing 2008* (Avizandum Publishing Ltd 2009; ISBN 9781904968115)

Robert Rennie, *Land Tenure and Tenements Legislation*, 3rd edn (W Green 2009; ISBN 9780414017870)

Jeremy Rowan-Robinson, *Compulsory Purchase and Compensation*, 3rd edn (W Green 2009; ISBN 9780414017528)

Articles

Ross Gilbert Anderson, 'A strange notice' (2009) 13 *Edinburgh Law Review* 194 (considering *Christie Owen and Davies plc v Campbell* 2009 SC 436)

Ross Gilbert Anderson and John MacLeod, 'Offside goals and interfering with play' 2009 SLT (News) 93 (considering *Gibson v Royal Bank of Scotland plc* 2009 SLT 444)

Richard Atkins, 'Performance review' (2009) 54 *Journal of the Law Society of Scotland* March/52 (discussing energy performance certificates)

Stewart Brymer, 'The Combined Standard Clauses – a step in the right direction' (2009) 102 *Greens Property Law Bulletin* 1

Graham Burnside, 'Islamic finance: a Scottish lead?' (2009) 54 *Journal of the Law Society of Scotland* Aug/56 (discussing a new Islamic mortgage in which the borrower holds the property in trust for both borrower and lender)

Malcolm M Combe, 'Access to land and to landownership' (2010) 14 *Edinburgh Law Review* 106

Lorne Crerar, 'Opportunity lost?' (2009) 54 *Journal of the Law Society of Scotland* March/18 (defending the introduction of home reports)

Andrew Duncan, 'Concluding missives in 2009? On your bike' (2009) 103 *Greens Property Law Bulletin* 5 (considering *Park Ptrs (No 2)* 2009 SLT 871)

Lesley-Anne Faichnie, 'Change to fair' (2009) 54 *Journal of the Law Society of Scotland* April/67 (considering responses to conditions in the commercial property sector)

Andrew Ferguson, 'Alienation and appropriation of common good land' 2009 SLT (News) 235

Ian Ferguson and Paul Carnan, 'The new Combined Standard Missive Clauses' (2009) 77 *Scottish Law Gazette* 89

Derek Flynn, 'Reforming crofting law' (2009) 77 *Scottish Law Gazette* 99

Alasdair G Fox, 'Variations and the three year rule' (2009) 54 *Journal of the Law Society of Scotland* March/42 (discussing reviews of agricultural rents)

Alasdair G Fox, 'Win some, lose some' (2009) 54 *Journal of the Law Society of Scotland* June/50 (considering new case law on agricultural leases)

Alasdair G Fox, 'Tackling improvements' (2009) 54 *Journal of the Law Society of Scotland* Dec/46 (considering *R & M Whiteford v Trustees for the Cowhill Trust* 29 July 2009, Land Ct)

William M Gordon, 'Servitudes abounding' (2009) 13 *Edinburgh Law Review* 519 (considering *Compugraphics International Ltd v Nikolic* [2009] CSOH 54)

Alan Henderson, 'What does the future hold for the UK's construction and commercial property markets?' (2009) 100 *Greens Property Law Bulletin* 1

Mark Higgins, 'Homing instinct' (2009) 54 *Journal of the Law Society of Scotland* Dec/16 (considering the Home Owner and Debtor Protection (Scotland) Bill)

Martin Hogg, 'The continuing confused saga of contract and error' (2009) 13 *Edinburgh Law Review* 286 (considering *Parvaiz v Thresher Wines Acquisitions Ltd* 2009 SC 151)

Graham Jackson, 'Energy performance certificates and leases' (2009) 99 *Greens Property Law Bulletin* 1

Gordon Junor, 'More parking (and other) problems' 2009 SLT (News) 83

Gordon Junor, '"Offside" heritable obligations and good faith' (2009) 99 *Greens Property Law Bulletin* 3

Gordon Junor, 'Can we get out of this deal?' (2009) 100 *Greens Property Law Bulletin* 5

Gordon Junor, 'Default and ejection – clarifying the position of the heritable creditor' (2009) 101 *Greens Property Law Bulletin* 6 (considering *Royal Bank of Scotland v Wilson* 2009 SLT 729)

Gordon Junor, '"Agreement to agree" – with all reasonable endeavours' (2009) 98 *Greens Property Law Bulletin* 4 (considering *R & D Construction Group Ltd v Hallam Land Management Ltd* [2009] CSOH 128)

Gordon Junor, 'Land Registration – The McCoach approach' (2009) 77 *Scottish Law Gazette* 117 (considering *McCoach v Keeper of the Registers of Scotland*, 19 Dec 2008, Lands Tr)

Gordon Junor, 'Servitudes: signs in the (un) fixed list!' 2009 *Juridical Review* 149 (considering *Romano v Standard Commercial Property Securities Ltd* 2008 SLT 859)

Jill Ley, 'Law out of step' (2009) 54 *Journal of the Law Society of Scotland* Oct/56 (considering *Park Ptr* [2009] CSOH 122)

John Logan, 'Risk: nip it in the bud' (2009) 54 *Journal of the Law Society of Scotland* April/25 (considering title insurance)

John A Lovett, 'Meditations on *Strathclyde*: controlling private land use restrictions at the crossroads of legal systems' (2008) 36 *Syracuse Journal of International Law and Commerce* 1 (considering *Strathclyde Joint Police Board v The Elderslie Estates Ltd* 2002 SLT (Lands Tr) 2)

Francis Lyall, 'Non-established church property in Scotland: a further case' (2010) 14 *Edinburgh Law Review* 113 (considering *Moderator of the General Assembly of the Free Church of Scotland v Interim Moderator of the Congregation of Strath Free Church of Scotland (Continuing) (No 2)* 2009 SLT 973)

Laura Macgregor, 'Acting on behalf of a non-existent principal' (2010) 14 *Edinburgh Law Review* 92 (considering *Halifax Life Ltd v DLA Piper LLP* [2009] CSOH 74)

Kenneth Mackay, 'Servitudes – new ground?' (2009) 54 *Journal of the Law Society of Scotland* Feb/50 (considering *Moncrieff v Jamieson* 2008 SC (HL) 1)

John MacLeod, 'Offside goals and induced breaches of contract' (2009) 13 *Edinburgh Law Review* 278

John MacLeod, 'Chalk dust in the law of inhibition' (2009) 13 *Edinburgh Law Review* 294 (considering *Park Ptrs* 2008 SLT 1026)

Douglas Milne, '"Can we keep the shop?" Invoking the Tenancy of Shops (Scotland) Act 1949' (2009) 98 *Greens Property Law Bulletin* 1

Peter Nicholson, 'Report card' (2009) 54 *Journal of the Law Society of Scotland* Dec/12 (considering responses to the home report)

Pamela O'Connor, 'Deferred and immediate indefeasibility: bijural ambiguity in registered land system titles' (2009) 13 *Edinburgh Law Review* 194

Gillian Orr, 'Lifting the stones' (2009) 54 *Journal of the Law Society of Scotland* Aug/52 (discussing contaminated land)

Donald B Reid, 'Rectification of deeds: part 1' (2009) 103 *Greens Property Law Bulletin* 1

Robert Rennie, 'Counting the cost in tenements' 2009 SLT (News) 137 (considering *PS Properties (2) Ltd v Calloway Homes Ltd* [2007] CSOH 162)

Robert Rennie, 'Marching towards equity – blindfolded' 2009 SLT (News) 187 (considering *Gibson v Royal Bank of Scotland plc* 2009 SLT 444)

Robert Rennie, 'Land registration and the decline of property law' (2010) 14 *Edinburgh Law Review* 62

Frances Sim, 'Challengeable transactions in challenging times' (2009) 101 *Greens Property Law Bulletin* 4 (considering gratuitous alienations etc in the context of insolvent property companies)

Euan Sinclair, 'Matrix evolutions' (2009) 54 *Journal of the Law Society of Scotland* May/24 (discussing the more restrictive approach to the factual matrix in the interpretation of contracts in Scotland)

Euan Sinclair, 'E-missives: it's time for delivery' (2009) 77 *Scottish Law Gazette* 114

Euan Sinclair, 'Never waste a good crisis' (2009) 54 *Journal of the Law Society of Scotland* Nov/56 (considering *Park Ptrs (No 2)* 2009 SLT 871)

Euan Sinclair, 'A new burden is born' (2009) 54 *Journal of the Law Society of Scotland* Dec/58 (discussing climate change burdens)

Michael Smith, '"One size" is a dodgy fit' (2009) 54 *Journal of the Law Society of Scotland* Dec/54 (questioning the value of standard missives)

Andrew J M Steven, 'Accessoriness and security over land' (2009) 13 *Edinburgh Law Review* 387

Ken Swinton, 'Destined to survive' (2009) 77 *Scottish Law Gazette* 56

Ken Swinton, 'Faxed missives – a walk in the park?' (2009) 77 *Scottish Law Gazette* 93 (considering *Park Ptrs (No 2)* 2009 SLT 871)

Andrew Todd, 'Drafting sub-leases of part' (2009) 98 *Greens Property Law Bulletin* 1

Andrew Todd, 'Examining titles: a reminder' (2009) 99 *Greens Property Law Bulletin* 7 (considering *McCoach v Keeper of the Registers of Scotland*, 19 Dec 2008, Lands Tr)

Peter Webster, 'Options for offside goals' (2009) 13 *Edinburgh Law Review* 524 (considering *Gibson v Royal Bank of Scotland plc* 2009 SLT 444)

Robbie Wishart and Paul Connolly, 'Discharging, terminating and ignoring real burdens with confidence: reminder list' (2009) 101 *Greens Property Law Bulletin* 1

⁍ PART IV ⁌
COMMENTARY

COMMENTARY

MISSIVES OF SALE

Missives by fax or pdf?

Introduction

Is it competent to conclude missives by fax? Or, what comes to the same thing but is more likely nowadays to be the question, is it competent to conclude missives by a pdf file attached to an email? In either case the missives are paper missives with a 'wet signature', and what is sent to the other side is not that piece of paper itself but an image of it. Of course, where fax or pdf is used, the practice is to mail the original, and so the answer to the question does not usually matter. It matters only when something happens between (i) the time when the addressee receives the fax/pdf and (ii) the time when the addressee receives the original by mail (whether the Post Office, courier or other). *Park Ptrs (No 2)* is an example.[1]

Missives were concluded for the sale of a property in Bothwell, Lanarkshire.[2] The Lord Ordinary (Temporary Judge M G Thomson QC) takes up the story:[3]

> On 31 August 2007, at about 14.50 hours, SM faxed to CBC a copy of an executed qualified acceptance still bearing the date 10 August 2007. Later that afternoon and during business hours CBC faxed to SM a copy of an executed final letter accepting the qualified acceptance. Thereafter, and prior to 17.00 hours on 31 August 2007, SM and CBC posted the original executed qualified acceptance and original executed final letter to each other by Legal Post. The original executed final letter from CBC reached the offices of SM after midnight on 31 August 2007. The original executed qualified acceptance from SM reached the offices of CBC on Monday 3 September 2007.

The question for the court was whether missives had been concluded by midnight on 31 August. That was because there was an inhibition against the sellers whose effective date was midnight, 31 August. The way the issue came before the court was that the sellers petitioned for the recall of the inhibition on

---

[1] [2009] CSOH 122, 2009 SLT 871.
[2] In fact the property was not owned by the sellers but rather held by them on long lease. But this is a detail that is not relevant to the case.
[3] Paragraph 3.

the ground that it came too late to affect the missives.[1] The inhibitor took the opposite view, namely that by midnight on 31 August missives had not yet been concluded. There was no dispute about the fact that missives had been concluded: the question was *when* they had been concluded. The issue was purely one about the competency of faxed missives. The 'postal acceptance rule' was not applicable on these facts, because it applies only to the final acceptance, and in this case the earlier missive was not received until after the date of the inhibition.[2]

The background law

The issue of missives by fax has been before the courts on two previous occasions. In *Merrick Homes Ltd v Duff*,[3] it was said (*obiter*) at first instance that missives can be concluded by fax but on appeal the court reserved its opinion on the point.[4] In *McIntosh v Alam*[5] it was held that missives can be concluded by fax. Academic opinion has not reached consensus on the matter.[6] The Requirements of Writing (Scotland) Act 1995 says that signed writing is needed to conclude missives, but it says nothing about how (or even whether) such signed writing has to be delivered to the other side, and the same was true of earlier legislation.

For ordinary contracts the question of delivery does not normally arise, because for ordinary contracts there are no requirements of form: they can be concluded orally, either face-to-face or by phone. They can even be concluded silently, for instance at the check-out queue at a supermarket. Obviously, therefore, they can be concluded by fax or email or text-message. Romantic young men can propose marriage by sky-writing or by tracing the big question in newly-fallen snow, and contracts could be concluded in the same way by romantic business people, if romantic business people exist. Or by telepathy, if telepathy exists. Of course, there can be exceptions. If Jack writes to Jill making an (unromantic) offer and the offer says that acceptance must be by signed letter delivered to him by a certain date, then a response by phone or even by fax would not work, for the acceptance would not have met the offer.[7] But whatever degree of formality is employed or insisted on, the need for communication is indispensable. The delivery of sheets of paper is often the means of communication that the parties

---

1 'The petitioners seek recall of that inhibition but in so far only as it relates to the subjects' (para 2). With respect we suggest that the petition was in the wrong terms. In such a case the petition should be for recall of the inhibition in relation to the *transaction*, not to the property: see G L Gretton, *The Law of Inhibition and Adjudication* (2nd edn 1996) p 60. But it seems that this issue was not raised, and it can be ignored for present purposes. It may be added that the sellers also sought recall on the ground of oppression: see *Park Ptrs* [2008] CSOH 121, 2008 SLT 1026, discussed in J MacLeod, 'Chalk dust in the law of inhibition' (2009) 13 *Edinburgh Law Review* 294. This issue was not dealt with in this particular phase of the litigation.

2 See para 21 of the Opinion. It may be added that the missives were sent not through the Post Office but through Legal Post. It is doubtful whether Legal Post is subject to the postal acceptance rule.

3 1996 GWD 9-508 (OH); 1996 SC 497 (IH).

4 'We should ... not be taken to be endorsing the view expressed by the Lord Ordinary where he indicates that an *obligatio literis* could be constituted by fax' (1996 SC 497 at 499).

5 1998 SLT (Sh Ct) 19.

6 The academic views are referenced in the case.

7 But see the exhibition of judicial generosity on this point in *Gibson v Royal Bank of Scotland plc* [2009] CSOH 14, 2009 SLT 444, 2009 SCLR 364 (Case (45) above).

choose, but that is a matter of choice, not a requirement of law. Or one could put it another way: in such cases delivery is needed, but all that means is the delivery of the message.

So that is the general rule for contracts. At the other side of the room, so to speak, is the case of a deed, such as a disposition. If the grantee has not received the deed, it is impossible to complete title. In such cases the issue is not normally whether the granter is 'bound'. Assuming (what is typically the case) that the deed is to implement a contract, such as missives, the granter is already bound anyway. Missives are different from ordinary contracts, because there are requirements of form, but also different from deeds, in that the missives do not need to be registered.

As a unilateral and written juridical act, a missive letter must probably be delivered if it is to bind the granter. But if delivery is needed, the question then arises as to whether that has to be actual delivery, or whether something less would suffice. That 'something less' could in principle take two forms. The first would be the sending of an image of the wet-signed paper, whether by fax or pdf or, indeed, by a photograph. The second would be for the sender to be deemed to hold the wet-signed paper on behalf of the other side.

The decision

In *Park Ptrs (No 2)* the Lord Ordinary held that missives had not been concluded by midnight 31 August. Thus he declined to follow *McIntosh v Alam*. But the Lord Ordinary did not go so far as to say that missives *cannot* be concluded by fax/ pdf. As for that question, he said:[1]

> The answer … depends upon the intention of the parties which may be derived either from a general practice among solicitors or from a specific agreement between the particular solicitors exchanging the particular missives.

By 'a general practice among solicitors' he did not mean, we think, a general practice of sending missives by fax/pdf, but rather a general practice of regarding such missives as binding. And he took the view that no such practice existed. For the Lord Ordinary, it came down to intention, and just as such intention might be (but in fact here could not be) based on general practice, so it could also be based on specific intention expressed in the faxed missive itself. He says:[2]

> It would … be open to the sender of any missive by fax to state thereon that from the time of transmission of the fax the sending solicitor would thereafter hold the missive which had been transmitted on behalf of the receiving solicitor, thereby achieving constructive delivery.

But that had not happened. The Lord Ordinary concluded that neither branch of the 'intention' test had been satisfied, ie that there was neither 'general practice'

---

1 Paragraph 23.
2 Paragraph 23.

nor 'specific agreement.' Hence missives had not been concluded by the time that the inhibition took effect.

Discussion

Before this case, it had been generally assumed that the answer to the question 'can you conclude missives by fax/pdf?' was either yes or no. The 'it depends' approach taken by the Lord Ordinary is a new development.

The two passages quoted above are not easy to reconcile. The first requires mutual intention: 'a specific agreement between the particular solicitors'. By contrast the second seems to say that such mutual intention is not necessary: all that is needed is a unilateral statement. Both, however, presuppose that *some* form of delivery is needed, and that mere communication is not enough.

The law about methods of delivery has developed mainly in connection with goods rather than documents, but with goods there can in some cases be constructive delivery through a 'possessory agreement'[1] in which both sides agree that the goods, though still in the hands of the transferor, are to be regarded as being held on behalf of the transferee. But this requires the agreement of *both* parties. It may be added that the courts have traditionally been reluctant to accept possessory agreements as being valid. In short, constructive delivery on the basis of a unilateral statement seems of doubtful competence, and even if there is mutual agreement its effect seems uncertain.

If constructive delivery of this type is possible, then logically it should not be necessary to send the fax/pdf at all. For if one side holds the wet-signed paper on behalf of the other side, that is all that is needed: constructive delivery has taken place.

So what is the law? We do not know, and we doubt whether anyone could give an answer with complete confidence. As already mentioned, the issue is not covered by the Requirements of Writing (Scotland) Act 1995 or by earlier legislation. The advent of fax machines brought the question into focus,[2] but *Park Ptrs* does not settle it. And it does not hold, as might at first appear, that actual delivery is required to produce a binding contract. The precise *ratio* of the decision is open to argument.

Practice?

The response of the Law Society's Conveyancing Committee has been that the fax/pdf should be followed up with the original 'as soon as possible'.[3] No doubt that was happening anyway.

---

1 The Latin, *constitutum possessorium*, tends to be used. For the whole subject see W M Gordon, *Studies in the Transfer of Property by Traditio* (1970); K G C Reid, *The Law of Property in Scotland* (1996) para 623 (W M Gordon); D L Carey Miller with D Irvine, *Corporeal Moveables in Scots Law* (2nd edn 2005) ch 8.
2 Fax arrived in law offices in the 1970s. But its history goes back further than one might think: according to Wikipedia it began to be used commercially as early as 1865: see http://en.wikipedia.org/wiki/Fax#History.
3 See (2009) 54 *Journal of the Law Society of Scotland* Dec/56.

We understand that, since *Park Ptrs*, there has been rather more use of hand delivery and delivery by courier, and also that some firms are taking up the suggestion made by the Lord Ordinary and including a clause saying that the missive whose image is being transmitted is held by the sender on behalf of the recipient, together with an undertaking to deliver it. Our information is that such clauses are (at least thus far) being employed more in commercial than in residential conveyancing. As we have said, we think that there must be some doubt as to whether such clauses are effective. There is always a danger in thinking that the law is clearer than in fact it is. *Dicta* by Outer House judges, however valuable, do not have the force of statute.

Law reform?

'Electronic missives' can mean two things. It can mean missives that use wet-signed sheets of paper, images of which are sent by fax or pdf. In that case, there still needs to be paper and there still needs to be ink. Or it can mean 'pure' e-missives, ie missives that need no paper and no ink. In pure e-missives what happens is simply that the missive is sent as an email, with an electronic signature.

It appears that the profession does want e-missives in one form or another[1] – though the distinction between the two types is not always recognised. There has been a suggestion by Euan Sinclair that 'the legal framework for electronic missives in fact already exists in section 1(2A) of the Requirements of Writing Act 1995'.[2] But as he notes, section 1(2A) is limited to the ARTL system. He adds that 'if ... any further technical changes to the 1995 Act are required, these can be speedily dealt with by an order under section 8 of the Electronic Communications Act 2000, which section expressly provides ministers with a power to change any primary legislation by order to facilitate electronic commerce'. Section 8 of the Electronic Communications Act 2000 was the means whereby the 1995 Act was amended so as to make ARTL possible. It could be used again. The Law Society also suggests that law reform may be needed.[3]

The Scottish Law Commission's new report on *Land Registration* recommends e-enablement for all conveyancing documents, including missives, though paper missives would continue to be competent.[4] What is recommended is the possibility of 'pure' e-missives, on the assumption that once this possibility is available, the idea of wet-signed paper followed by fax/pdf would be of little interest. And the Law Commission's draft bill provides, for the avoidance of doubt, that 'an electronic document may be delivered electronically'.[5]

---

1 See for example J Ley, 'Law out of step?' (2009) 54 *Journal of the Law Society of Scotland* Oct/56 and the references in the next footnote.
2 E Sinclair, 'Never waste a good crisis' (2009) 54 *Journal of the Law Society of Scotland* Nov/56. And see also E Sinclair, 'E-missives: it's time for delivery' (2009) 77 *Scottish Law Gazette* 114; A Duncan, 'Concluding missives in 2009? On your bike' (2009) 103 *Greens Property Law Bulletin* 5.
3 (2009) 54 *Journal of the Law Society of Scotland* Dec/56.
4 Scottish Law Commission, Report on *Land Registration* (Scot Law Com No 222 (2010), available at www.scotlawcom.gov.uk) pt 32.
5 Draft Land Registration (Scotland) Bill sch 5 para 20.

Grounds for rescission

McPhee v Black[1] was decided in 2008 but it came to our attention only in 2009, though an earlier stage in the proceedings was discussed in our 2006 volume.[2] The 2008 stage of the case was a proof. Though not destined to be a leading case, it is interesting as an example of what can happen when a buyer decides to back out of missives.

On 13 August 2004 Mr and Mrs Black concluded missives with Mr and Mrs McPhee to buy a substantial country property called 'The Cushats' at Sundrum in Ayrshire for £930,000 with entry at 10 December 2004. One of the clauses of the missives provided:

> In the event of the Title Deeds disclosing any matter materially prejudicial to the purchasers' interests then they will be entitled to resile from the bargain without expense but only by giving notice of the intention to do so in writing and that within ten working days from the date of receipt by you of the Title Deeds.

After examining the deeds the buyers' solicitors sent a letter, dated 13 October 2004, pulling out of the contract. The reasons given were:

1. The lack of exclusive access rights to the driveway and path leading to the Cushats. My clients have advised that had they known that access on the driveway and path were shared with a number of other users they would not have proceeded with the purchase.
2. The alternative access route described in your clients' title as 'the cart track' being blocked by a locked gate and being the subject of an ongoing dispute with the neighbouring proprietors. My clients do not wish to inherit any kind of disputes in respect of access.
3. The weight restrictions affecting the bridge and the implications these have in respect of access to the Cushats taking into account the points raised above.
4. The ongoing access dispute with Ms Sloan in respect of which our clients believe court action is being taken. Again, our clients do not wish to inherit any existing disputes with neighbour proprietors.
5. The potential boundary dispute to the north-west of your clients' title. My clients believe the occupational extent of your clients' title encroaches into that of the neighbouring High Walk Wood.
6. The existing boundary dispute with the proprietors of Barquey Wood to the south-east of the Cushats, being the subject of a requisition issued to your firm by the Keeper on 23 July 2004.
7. The discrepancy disclosed in the P16 Report submitted with your clients' application.

As to the last two points, it was in 2002 that the McPhees had bought the property that they were selling. This was a first registration, and no land certificate had yet been issued.

---

1 20 June 2008, Glasgow Sheriff Court.
2 *Conveyancing 2006* pp 4–5 and 98–99. We are grateful to Graeme Henderson for drawing the 2008 decision to our attention.

The sellers did not accept that the buyers were justified in resiling. Eventually, however, they remarketed the property and resold, at a lower price. They sued the Blacks for damages, namely the shortfall in the price, plus interest, plus certain incidentals such as additional legal expenses.

In the first phase of the case in 2006,[1] it was held that the word 'disclosed' meant that the buyers could found only on matters that they discovered from perusal of the deeds. Matters they discovered in other ways could not be founded on. It was also held that points (2) and (4) in the letter could not be founded on.[2] That left the other five points, and a 13-day proof took place in 2008 on the question of whether these justified the buyers in resiling.

Although accepting that the buyers did not back out for financial reasons, the sheriff (Alan R Mackenzie) found against them on all five points. As to point (1), two neighbouring properties had servitude rights along the driveway, but the sheriff considered that, given the nature of the property, this was not 'materially prejudicial'.[3]

As to point (3), there was a bridge in the driveway and one of the servitudes over the driveway stipulated a two-ton weight limit. The buyers wished to take horse boxes along the driveway and a horsebox with horse can weigh over two tons. It seems that this was in fact the main reason why the buyers got cold feet. The proof established that the buyers had been told by their solicitors that the weight limit applied to all users (and not just to those taking access by virtue of the servitude). The sheriff commented:[4]

> I accept that the defenders were shocked if not devastated in the light of this advice they had received and had this advice been correct as a matter of law, I am satisfied that viewed objectively the title deeds would have disclosed matter materially prejudicial to their interests. As the advice the defenders received was not correct, I am satisfied that the defenders were not entitled to withdraw from the missives when they did.

The way this is expressed might be criticised; what the buyers' solicitors did or did not advise their clients cannot, we suggest, be a ground for judging whether the sellers were bound to release the buyers from the deal. But the point could be re-expressed as being simply that the title deeds disclosed no weight limit that would bind the buyers. If the bridge was not strong enough for the intended use, that weakness was not something disclosed by the title deeds. Expressed in that way, the issue seems a narrow one. It might be argued that the buyers needed a strong bridge and the title deeds revealed that the bridge was not strong enough: hence the buyers were entitled to rescind. As against that it could be argued that the two-ton limit binding the neighbour did not necessarily mean that the bridge could not be used for vehicles over that weight. And perhaps it could be argued that the clause, in speaking of 'title deeds', must have been referring only to title matters, not matters of physical quality.

---

1 31 July 2006, Ayr Sheriff Court.
2 This was at an earlier stage of the litigation and we are not aware of the reasons.
3 Paragraph 100.
4 Paragraph 94.

As for point (5), the evidence indicated that the issue had not been *disclosed* by perusal of the deeds and so it could not be founded on.

With regard to point (7), little evidence was available (for instance the P16 was not produced) and accordingly the sheriff rejected this ground.

That left point (6). The area in dispute was 'approximately 200 by 15 yards'[1] ie about 2500 square metres. The sheriff described this as 'a very modest parcel of land in relation to the entire subjects' and held the issue to be non-material. We do not know the size of the entire subjects, and we do not know how the subjects of sale were described in the missives. But suppose that the overlap area was within the subjects of sale as defined by the missives. In that case the decision of the learned sheriff might be open to question.

In *Campbell v McCutcheon*[2] missives were concluded for the sale of a house in the centre of Milngavie. The description of the subjects of sale did not say (as nowadays one would normally expect) that the minerals were included only in so far as the seller had right thereto. When it turned out that the minerals did not belong to the seller, the buyer resiled. It was held in the Inner House that he was entitled to do so, even though in such a case the minerals must have been of 'modest' significance. On the other hand, *Campbell* could perhaps be distinguished on the basis that in that case the lack of title to the minerals was clear, whereas in *McPhee* the issue of possible overlap had arisen but the outcome was not yet clear.

Finally, after the letter of 13 October, the sellers' solicitors sent the property enquiry certificate to the buyers' solicitors, disclosing that the house was C-listed. The latter replied saying that this too was a good ground for resiling. The sheriff took the view that listed building status was not something that could be regarded as 'materially prejudicial'.

As so often with disputes of this type, one cannot help reflecting that the problems could have been avoided had the buyers seen the titles before conclusion of missives. That is not always possible, but usually it is. In the present case the offer to buy was dated 12 July and missives were not concluded until 13 August. One wonders why the titles could not have been available before then.

Agreements to agree

Is an 'agreement to agree' valid sometimes, always, never? The issue is not just a matter of esoteric academic discussion, but is of considerable practical importance. Contracts often have conditions about subsequent agreements being reached. If one looks at the authorities, the general rule is that an agreement to agree has no effect, but there are exceptions. No one quite knows what the exceptions are. In the two cases under discussion there were agreements to agree. In the first it was upheld and in the second it was not.

In *R & D Construction Group Ltd v Hallam Land Management Ltd*[3] Ms Kerr owned some land with development potential at Cleland (near Motherwell). For £7,000,

---

1 Paragraph 98.
2 1963 SC 505.
3 [2009] CSOH 128.

Ms Kerr granted Hallam Land Management a five-year option to acquire the land at 75% of its value. With that option in its pocket, Hallam then concluded missives to sell the land to R & D for a price of £571,314. The missives contained this clause (clause 4.1.10):

> The Missives shall be essentially conditional upon … the Seller [Hallam] agreeing a purchase price for the Subjects with the current proprietor [Ms Kerr] in terms wholly acceptable to the Seller (the Seller being required to use all reasonable endeavours in this regard).

The first part of this clause was to protect Hallam from the risk that the eventual price in the Kerr/Hallam contract might prove to be so high as to make the whole deal a loss-making one. The second part (the part in brackets) was to protect R & D from the risk that Hallam might use the first part of the clause as a get-out-of-jail-free card in relation to the contract with R & D.

Problems arose with the Kerr/Hallam contract, chiefly because they did not agree on the fair market value. The missives with R & D had a longstop date in them and eventually that longstop date passed without agreement between Hallam and Ms Kerr. R & D then sued to enforce its contract against Hallam. Hallam had two lines of defence. The first was that the contract was invalid. The second was that (*esto* the contract was valid) Hallam had in fact used all reasonable endeavours to reach agreement with Ms Kerr. The Lord Ordinary (Hodge) rejected the first defence but accepted the second. The interest of the case lies in the first defence.[1] For a summary of it we quote from para 32 of the Opinion:

> Mr Borland on behalf of the defenders submitted that the action was irrelevant as the 'reasonable endeavours' obligation in clause 4.1.10 of the purchase agreement was unenforceable. He advanced his submission on two grounds. First, he submitted that the clause amounted to an agreement to agree and was therefore unenforceable. He cited several cases in a long line of authority which supports the proposition that the courts cannot enforce such an agreement as there are not objective criteria which they can apply to give the provision sufficient certainty. Secondly, he argued that the object of the agreement, namely a price 'wholly acceptable' to Hallam, was also too vague and uncertain to have contractual force. Again, no objective criteria could be applied.

Clearly there is force in these arguments. Clause 4.1.10 could be read as saying that Hallam was to make reasonable endeavours to buy at the lowest possible price. That is something it hardly needed any urging to do. 'Wholly acceptable' is a subjective criterion: the Lord Ordinary accepted 'that by agreeing that the price had to be "wholly acceptable" to Hallam, the parties excluded any question of the reasonableness of what Hallam found acceptable or not acceptable'.[2]

Over the years there have been a good many reported cases in this area, cases that the Lord Ordinary discusses in his opinion. In broad terms, 'reasonable

---

1 As for the second, Hallam and Ms Kerr subsequently agreed a market value of £701,000, and Hallam paid her 75% of that = £525,750. Hallam then resold the property for £875,000, a gross profit of about £350,000.
2 Paragraph 47.

endeavours' clauses are valid if there exists some way of determining whether reasonable endeavours have been used. The Lord Ordinary commented:[1]

> If the courts are prepared to police an obligation to use reasonable endeavours to obtain a planning permission or an export licence, as Lord Ackner suggested in *Walford v Miles*,[2] or to use all reasonable endeavours to secure a planning agreement with a local authority (*Yewbelle Ltd v London Green Developments Ltd*)[3] the court should be able to police the negotiation of a price so long as the object of the negotiations can be objectively ascertained.

The Lord Ordinary went on to argue:[4]

> It is correct, as Mr Borland submitted, that the 'wholly acceptable' price is a subjective criterion but that does not mean that the court cannot ascertain it if there is evidence from which it may be inferred. Judges in criminal courts regularly direct juries that they are entitled to infer a person's state of mind from the circumstances and in particular from what he said or did. So also can a judge in a civil case. I do not think that the subjective nature of the object of the endeavours creates legal uncertainty. It is a question of fact.

This was, we think, a difficult case. The provision could have had at least three possible consequences. (i) It comes close to turning what is ostensibly a sale contract into an option to sell, ie a deal enforceable by Hallam but not by R & D. That, of course, would be perfectly valid, though a very surprising kind of deal for R & D to enter into, for it would be an option for which they were not paid. In the event neither party sought to assert this interpretation. (ii) It could have the consequence of making the contract unenforceable, as Hallam argued. (iii) It could have left the contract as a valid sale contract, which is what the Lord Ordinary held. This result, though formally distinct from (i), comes close to it in practice, because the task of proving that Hallam had not used reasonable endeavours to acquire the property from Ms Kerr on terms 'wholly satisfactory' to Hallam was never going to be an easy one.

Scottish Coal Company Ltd v Danish Forestry Co Ltd,[5] decided shortly after *R & D Construction Group*, had a different result: the contract was held to be unenforceable. Of course the facts were not quite the same, and so it is perfectly possible that both cases were correctly decided, and certainly the Lord Ordinary in the second case (Lord Glennie) does not say that the earlier case was wrong. Nevertheless there seems to be a certain tension between the two cases.

Danish Forestry Co Ltd (DFC) owned some land in Lanarkshire which it used (no surprises here) for growing trees. Scottish Coal Company Ltd (SCC) owned neighbouring land which it used (no surprises here either) for open-cast coal

---

1 Paragraph 46.
2 [1992] 2 AC 128.
3 [2008] 1 P & CR 17.
4 Paragraph 50.
5 [2009] CSOH 171, 2010 GWD 5-79.

mining. It turned out that there was plenty of coal underneath the forestry land. The two companies entered a contract under which SCC took an option to buy DFC's land.[1] If it exercised the option, it would make quarterly royalty payments to DFC. To secure these payments, the option agreement provided that SCC would grant to DFC a standard security over the land being acquired. Here is what the contract said:

> 10.1 The Company[2] shall grant in favour of Danish at the Settlement Date a Standard Security over the Option Area for (1) all sums due and which may become due by the Company to Danish in terms of this Agreement and (2) the performance of the Company's non-financial obligations in terms of this agreement. Danish agrees to enter into an agreement with the Company and/or the Company's bankers reasonably to regulate the relationship between the sums which will be recoverable under the Standard Security and the terms under which these sums will rank ahead of any other sums due by the Company to their bankers from time to time ('the Ranking Agreement'). ...

The idea was that SCC's bank (RBS) would also take a standard security over the property upon its acquisition by its customer. The option contract was thus saying that DFC agreed to agree with RBS.

A notice exercising the option was sent and in due course RBS submitted its proposed ranking agreement. This said: '[DFC] shall not without the prior written consent of [RBS] exercise any of its powers of enforcement over [the subjects] or otherwise have recourse to the same.' DFC was not happy with this. Impasse was reached. Eventually SCC raised this action to enforce the option contract. The defence was that the agreement to agree was unenforceable. The court agreed. The Lord Ordinary said:[3]

> In the absence of some objective criteria by reference to which to judge the reasonableness of the endeavours, such an obligation is unenforceable. ... And even if it were held to be enforceable, how would the court be able to stigmatise DFC's failure to enter into a Ranking Agreement as unreasonable when it was entitled, in negotiating with SC and RBS, to act in its own self-interest?

To repeat: we do not find it easy to reconcile this and the previous case.

Suspensive conditions and longstop dates

The story in outline

In *Mitchell v Caversham Management Ltd*[4] Mr and Mrs Mitchell owned a property in Market Street, Aberdeen, and on 27 February 2006 concluded missives to sell

---

1 It is a well-known phenomenon that cases, like buses, come together. For another case in which a mining company entered into an option with forest owners, see *Scottish Coal Company Ltd v Trs of Fim Timber Growth Fund III* [2009] CSOH 30, 2009 SCLR 630 (Case (67) above).

2 Scottish Coal Company Ltd.

3 Paragraph 66.

4 [2009] CSOH 26, 2009 GWD 29-465.

it to Caversham Management Ltd for £360,000. The buyer intended to develop the property, for which planning permission would be required. Clause 2 of the missives said:

> Entry and vacant possession shall be given within 45 days after the purification of the suspensive condition clause 4, or on such other date as the parties may mutually agree, when the price shall become payable and at least one key for all external locks will be delivered.

The relevant part of clause 4 said:

> The purchaser obtains planning permission/building warrants to convert the subjects into a minimum of eighteen residential units on reasonable terms of which he shall be the sole judge. He undertakes to submit the planning application by no later than 14 March 2006. In the event of his not obtaining planning permission by 30 June 2006, either party will be entitled to resile without penalty. In the event that the Local Authority have the application under consideration but have not made a decision, the purchaser will be permitted to extend this period by such time as it takes until the council have made their decision. The seller undertakes to cooperate with the application and not to object to the local authority.

The third and fourth sentences do not sit easily together. The third sentence says that if planning consent is not granted by 30 June, either party can walk away. But the fourth sentence says that whilst the buyer can walk away, the seller cannot (provided that the buyer opts for the extension and there is a pending application).

The buyer did not submit the planning application until on or about 24 May. This was just the beginning of a descent into muddle. It was obvious the planning permission could not be granted by 30 June, and on 21 June the buyer sent the Mitchells a letter proposing a variation to the missives:

1. With regard to clause 2 this will be amended that payment will be no later than 14 days after the purification of the amended suspensive clause and in any event the date of entry will be no later than 30 September 2006.
2. With regard to clause 4 the second sentence is deleted. The time for obtaining consent should be extended to 14 September 2006.

The Mitchells did not reply with a written acceptance but seem to have considered that 30 September was now a deadline. Matters dragged on, and on 18 August the buyer paid a deposit of £8,000. This was not covered by the missives or by any variation of missives or even letters: it was done on the basis of phone conversations on the previous day. In early October Mr Mitchell met the buyer's manager, Mr Keane, and told him the deal was over. On 24 October the buyer wrote to the Mitchells (i) withdrawing the unaccepted letter of 21 June and (ii) exercising the clause 4 option of extending the time until the planning authority had made its decision. The Mitchells, who by this time had agreed to sell the property to Mr Mitchell's brother, raised this action of declarator that the contract had come to an end.

The letter of 21 June: effective through personal bar?

The Mitchells argued that, whilst they had not formally accepted the letter of 21 June, it had become binding by 'statutory personal bar' under section 1(3) and (4) of the Requirements of Writing (Scotland) Act 1995. If that was the position, once 30 September had passed without the grant of planning permission, the deal was off. This argument was rejected by the court. For personal bar to operate the person concerned (the Mitchells) must have 'acted or refrained from acting in reliance on the contract ... with the knowledge and acquiescence of the other party to the contract' such that if the agreement is not binding then that person 'would be adversely affected to a material extent'. To bring themselves within the statutory provisions, the Mitchells argued:[1]

> (i) The pursuers had agreed to a further extension; (ii) the pursuers had refrained from seeking another purchaser; (iii) the pursuers had refrained from resiling sooner; (iv) the pursuers attending meetings with Mr Cohen[2] and Mr Keane;[3] (v) the pursuers instructing Mr Cohen to attend meetings with Mr Keane; and (vi) the pursuers generally had arranged their affairs on the basis that the transaction would settle by 30 September 2006.

But the argument failed, as arguments based on personal bar often do. The Lord Ordinary (Lord Bracadale) explained why:[4]

> In my opinion Mr Upton[5] is well founded in his submission that in order to satisfy the test in the 1995 Act it would not be sufficient that the defender knew generally that the pursuers were arranging their affairs in reliance on the fact that the contract had been varied. It seems to me that what is required is for the pursuers to be able to point to specific actings or examples of refraining from acting and that these must be known to and acquiesced in by the other party. These provisions provide relief from a failure to meet the general requirements as to written agreement. That would require a clear identification of the actings or refraining from acting. Further, the actings or refraining from acting require to be known about and acquiesced in by the other party. Accordingly, they should be capable of clear identification in order that the relevant knowledge and acquiescence of the other party may be ascertained.

Option exercised by phone?

One of the many puzzles is why the buyer did not exercise the time-extension option in clause 4 until late October, by which time the sellers had already said that they were pulling out. Whatever the answer may be, when the litigation took place the buyer argued that the phone conversations of 17 August had constituted the exercise of that option. This argument failed. The Lord Ordinary, after hearing evidence about what was and was not said in those conversations,

---

1 Quoted from para 18 of the Opinion.
2 For Mr Cohen, see below.
3 Mr Keane was the main figure behind Caversham Management Ltd.
4 Paragraph 23.
5 Counsel for the defender.

concluded that the buyer had not made out its case that the option had been exercised. A legal point that arose was whether such an option could be exercised orally:[1]

> Mr Upton submitted that clause 4(a) of the missives did not require the purchaser's option to extend time to be exercised in writing. The exercise of the option was not a variation of the contract but the implementation of that agreement. Accordingly, writing was not required by the Requirements of Writing Act 1995. The defender therefore did not need to prove that what was said on 17 August was succeeded by facts which met the criteria in sub-sections 1(3) and (4) of the 1995 Act. All that was necessary was a unilateral exercise of the option by the purchaser.

This argument was accepted by the Lord Ordinary, surely correctly,[2] though in the end it did not assist the defender.

Result

Although the sellers failed in their argument based on the letter of 21 June, the buyer failed in its argument based on the phone conversations of 17 August. That meant that once 30 June had passed the sellers could bail out at any time before the buyer exercised the time-extension option. And that is what happened: the sellers resiled in early October, ie before the buyer's letter of 24 October, which thus came too late. The notice of the sellers that they were pulling out appears to have happened orally, and it does not seem to have been a matter of debate whether it is competent to resile orally. Our view is that it is competent.[3]

Final comments

One remarkable aspect of the story has so far been left out. It is that the same solicitor acted for both sides.

Next, the case does not deal with the fate of the £8,000 that was paid on 18 August. Presumably it would fall to be repaid, either on the basis of an implied agreement to that effect or on the basis of the *condictio causa data causa non secuta*.

Lastly, this contract was fairly typical in one respect: sales to developers often contain clauses whereby the developer's obligation to go ahead is conditional upon obtaining planning permission. It may be wondered whether such contracts are sufficiently fair to sellers.[4] If a developer were to approach an owner and say 'I would like you to grant me an option over your land for six months and I will pay you nothing for it', that would be absurd. A developer who wants an option should pay for it. Yet contracts which take the form of missives of sale are often in effect just gratuitous options.

---

1 Paragraph 41 of the Opinion.
2 Cf *Stone v MacDonald* 1979 SC 363.
3 Cf W W McBryde, *The Law of Contract in Scotland* (3rd edn 2007) para 20-107.
4 See *Conveyancing 2003* pp 51–53.

Contracting for new burdens

In *Forbo-Nairn Ltd v Murrayfield Properties Ltd*[1] the pursuer concluded missives to sell land to the defender for £1 million. The missives called for a real burden to be inserted into the buyer's title, but the parties could not agree on its terms: hence the litigation. Clause 10.1 of the missives said:

> The Purchasers shall be prohibited in all time coming from developing the Subjects and/or the Adjoining Subjects (FE) for residential purposes. At settlement, the Purchasers and the Sellers shall execute and register or procure that there is executed and registered a Deed of Conditions in terms to be agreed between the parties (acting reasonably) which has the effect of validly inserting this restriction on use into the title of the Subjects ... In the context of this Clause 10.1 the term 'the Purchasers' shall have the meaning given it in the context of Clause 9.7.2.

Clause 9.7.2 said:

> The term 'the Purchasers' shall apply not only to the Purchasers ... but also to their nominees, any subsidiary or holding company of the Purchasers, designed as aforesaid, or any subsidiary or such holding company (as the term 'subsidiary' and 'holding company' are defined within s 736 of the Companies Act 1985), to any company or organisation that James Manclark residing at Monkrigg, Haddington, EH41 4LB has an interest in equating to greater than 5% of the issued share capital and also to the said James Manclark as an individual and his spouse, partner or any child.

The defender argued that the burden to be inserted in the title should apply only to the 'purchasers' as defined. That would not include singular successors. Accordingly the burden would be of little practical value to the pursuer. The pursuer argued that it was clear that the intention was that singular successors should be bound. The Lord Ordinary (Hodge) held that the approach of the pursuer was to be preferred. The defender reclaimed, and the Inner House adhered to the decision of the Lord Ordinary. The pursuer was perhaps fortunate to prevail.

Section 75 agreements

In 2002 the pursuer in *Cala Management Ltd v Messrs A & E Sorrie*[2] entered into two contracts with the defenders for land at Inverurie. One was an option to acquire certain land ('the option land') at 87.5% of its development value. The other was a contract to buy certain other land ('the purchase land') for £1.25 million, conditional on planning permission. The first contract had this clause:

> The Heritable Proprietors[3] will be obliged at the reasonable request of our clients to enter into such Agreements with the Local Planning, Roads or any other relevant Authority required as a pre-requisite to the grant of Planning Permission or any other necessary Consent in respect of the Option Area or any part or parts thereof.

---

1 [2009] CSOH 47, 2009 GWD 16-251 affd [2009] CSIH 94.
2 [2009] CSOH 79, 2009 GWD 40-687.
3 That is to say the defenders.

The second contract had a clause in almost the same words.

Aberdeenshire Council agreed to grant planning permission subject to a section 75 planning agreement. Such an agreement has to be granted by the proprietor and so the pursuer requested the defenders to sign. The defenders refused, and the pursuer raised this action to compel them to sign.

The Lord Ordinary (Drummond Young) held that the terms of the section 75 agreement were not reasonable from the standpoint of the defenders and accordingly the action was dismissed. The agreement would have imposed onerous obligations of a type not contemplated in the missives, not least because, in terms of the missives, the pursuer could acquire the land in tranches, with the result that the defenders could be lumbered with liability for land which was not for the time being, and might never be, acquired by the pursuer. For example the section 75 agreement included: (i) 'A Community Facilities Contribution to the Council' to be used by the Council towards the cost of providing nursery, primary and secondary school accommodation, community hall facilities, library provision, recreational facilities, public transport and waste facilities in order to serve the residential part of the development site, (ii) an obligation to pay a 'Percentage for Art Contribution', (iii) a 'Bus Subsidy', (iv) an obligation to construct roads, (v) an obligation sell some of the land to a registered social landlord 'for a consideration that is not to exceed the Affordable Housing Land Market Value', (vi) an obligation to landscape certain land and then to convey that land gratuitously to the Council or its nominees, together with payment of a lump sum to cover future upkeep, and (vii) an obligation to set aside some of the land as 'employment land' with an obligation to build roads and provide services.

In any event, as the Lord Ordinary pointed out:[1]

> It cannot be said … that obligations relating to the purchase land are necessary in order to obtain planning permission for the option land; the two areas are separated, and no reason was suggested that separate planning permission could not be granted for each area, each such planning permission being subject to its own section 75 agreement. In the circumstances I am unable to conclude that the section 75 agreement referred to in the letter of 10 November was 'required as a pre-requisite' of planning permission in respect of the option land. The section 75 agreement was negotiated by the pursuers, and it was their decision to structure the planning permission and relative agreement in this way.

So what should the developer have done? Apart from the problem caused by the existence of two separate contracts, which could be solved either by having a single contract or by more careful drafting, there is the problem that a section 75 agreement is inevitably going to be onerous. One possibility is suggested by the Lord Ordinary: 'the defenders' concerns could have been dealt with by an appropriate agreement between the parties containing suitable indemnities'.[2] As a practical point in this connection it might be worth noting that an indemnity

---

1 Paragraph 35.
2 Paragraph 46.

would not cover the risk that a developer might become insolvent, leaving the proprietor with the burden of the section 75 obligations.

SERVITUDES

Ancillary rights

A servitude may not be confined by its actual words; in certain circumstances an additional right – a so-called 'ancillary' right – can be implied. The test for ancillary rights was authoritatively laid down by the House of Lords in *Moncrieff v Jamieson*.[1] It has two limbs.[2] For a right to be implied it must be reasonably necessary to the use and enjoyment of the servitude, and it must also have been in the reasonable contemplation of the parties at the time when the servitude was created. The second requirement has the effect of reining in the first. It is true, as Lord Hope emphasised in *Moncrieff*, that a right may be within the parties' contemplation even if it is not in fact exercised at the time of the servitude's creation, for '[a]ctivities that may reasonably be expected to take place in the future may be taken into account as well as those that were taking place at the time of the grant'.[3] But parties – and especially the servient proprietor – cannot be taken to have contemplated activities for which there was no obvious need at the time of creation.

In *Moncrieff* the court managed to persuade itself – just – that a servitude right of way included, by implication, a right to park on the servient tenement, but only in the unusual circumstances of a remote rural property where the topography excluded any possibility of parking on the dominant tenement. *SP Distribution Ltd v Rafique*[4] is the first case on this point since *Moncrieff*. It concerned the basement flat at 2A Clarence Street in Edinburgh. As is normal in the Edinburgh New Town, the flat was reached by means of a flight of steps leading down from the pavement to a paved basement area. As is also normal, there were a number of cellars under the pavement. In 1966 three of these cellars were sold by the then owner of the basement flat to the South of Scotland Electricity Board. The disposition included the grant of:

> a heritable and irredeemable servitude right of access to and egress from the said cellars through and over the stairs leading from the corner of Clarence Street … and across the area in front of the said subjects …

The cellars were used by the SSEB to install an electricity sub-station three or four feet below the level of the door by which the cellars were entered. The height discrepancy gave rise to health and safety concerns, and in 1992 the SSEB, having

---

1 [2007] UKHL 42, 2008 SC (HL) 1. For background information, including plans and a video, see http://www.inksters.com/thelecture.aspx. The case has its own entry in Wikipedia: http://en.wikipedia.org/wiki/Moncrieff_v_Jamieson.
2 For a discussion, see *Conveyancing 2007* pp 111–17.
3 Paragraph 30.
4 2009 SCLR 891, 2010 SLT (Sh Ct) 8.

obtained planning permission, excavated a substantial part of the basement area and constructed a flight of four steps to allow access to the cellars at the appropriate level. Permission was not given by the then owner of the basement flat, but neither did he voice opposition to the works.

The ownership of the basement flat – and with it, the basement area – changed hands, and the new owner asked the electricity operator (by now SP Distribution Ltd) to remove the steps. In the ensuing litigation, the legal question was whether the installation of the steps was within the scope of the servitude. If 20 years had passed, the use of the steps would have been established by positive prescription, but although the steps had been in position for a number of years, the period for prescription had not yet elapsed. In the end the argument for SP Distribution Ltd was based on ancillary right. When the servitude was granted in 1966, it was argued, the grant had included by implication a right to use reasonable means, where necessary, to ensure the continued existence of the right of access. Given the subsequent concerns as to health and safety, that included a right to construct the steps.

At first instance the sheriff found for SP Distribution, but on appeal the sheriff principal[1] took a different view. As the sheriff principal pointed out, it was not enough to show that the steps were necessary for the servitude. *Moncrieff* presented an additional hurdle: the need for the steps must have been within the reasonable contemplation of the parties at the time of the grant in 1966. On the evidence, that hurdle could not be surmounted:[2]

> [I]n reaching the view that the implied right existed the sheriff does not appear to have approached the matter by examining what might have been in the minds of the parties and what might have been reasonable to infer as an implied right accompanying the express grant at the time it was made. What he appears to have done is to arrive at the view that by virtue of force of circumstances – perhaps including the impact of legislation [on health and safety] – the pursuers had no alternative but to create a stairwell to enable them to continue to use the cellars for a sub-station and has balanced that against the level of inconvenience and disadvantage to the defender. Whatever conclusion one can reach on those considerations, it is not in my view an appropriate manner in which to identify a right which could be implied into the agreement between the parties when it was originally made. As to the nature of what that implied right might be, when one removes from consideration the notion that the need to create a stairwell was brought about by statutory requirement,[3] for the pursuers to succeed one would have to come to the point of holding that they had a right to physically reconstruct the method of access to the cellars whenever they themselves considered it necessary.

There was, the sheriff principal concluded, no such right.[4]

---

1 Sheriff Principal E Bowen QC.
2 Paragraph 22.
3 A point which was not established in evidence.
4 Mention may also be made of another new decision, *Garson v McCleish* 2010 GWD 5-88 (Case (21) above), in which some consideration was given to ancillary rights (to improve a road) in the context of a servitude established by prescription. Self-evidently, the legal test must be different where prescription is involved, but the issue is not discussed.

What surprises in this case is not the fate of the argument that was made, but the fact that no argument seems to have been made on the more promising ground of personal bar. If a person carries out works on a neighbour's land without objection, that neighbour is usually taken to have acquiesced in the work and so is personally barred from requiring it to be undone. And it may be – although the law here is not clear – that where the works are obvious, the acquiescence extends even to successors such as the defender in the present action.[1] That argument was surely worth running.

So far, the doctrine of ancillary rights has fared no better in the English courts. In *Waterman v Boyle*[2] a mid-terraced house was reached by means of a private driveway over which there was a right of way coupled with an express right to park two cars. Parking for a further four vehicles was available at the rear of the house. As the parking spaces at the front were often in use, visitors took to parking on the driveway itself. The question was whether they were entitled to do so. In the Court of Appeal, Arden LJ emphasised that the facts of *Moncrieff v Jamieson* were 'quite exceptional' and hence 'far removed' from the facts of the present case.[3] Unlike in *Moncrieff*, the right of way 'could be substantially enjoyed without any further parking right'.[4] Further, 'where there is an express right attaching to the same property of a similar character to the right which is sought to be implied, it is most unlikely that the further right will arise by implication'.[5] In other words, the express right to park two cars was fatal to the argument that there was an implied right to park additional vehicles.

Taken together, *SP Distribution Ltd v Rafique* and *Waterman v Boyle* suggest a drawing back from the rather generous approach taken in *Moncrieff v Jamieson*. The doctrine of implied ancillary rights may be less far-reaching than initially appeared to be the case.

Servitude of overhang

Until recently, only around a dozen types of servitude were recognised in Scots law, and the list had remained unchanged since the eighteenth century. Suddenly, the position has become much more fluid. For this there are two main reasons. First, the Title Conditions (Scotland) Act 2003 abandoned the fixed list in the case of new servitudes provided they were created by registration.[6] Secondly, in 2007 the House of Lords in *Moncrieff v Jamieson*[7] recognised parking as a servitude and suggested that, even where the Title Conditions Act did not apply, there should be a greater willingness to accept new servitudes.[8] That suggestion was not immediately taken up. In *Romano v Standard Commercial Property Securities Ltd*,[9]

---

1 *Conveyancing 2005* pp 92–93; E C Reid and J W G Blackie, *Personal Bar* (2006) paras 6-56 – 6-63.
2 [2009] EWCA Civ 115.
3 Paragraph 34.
4 Paragraph 30.
5 Paragraph 31.
6 Title Conditions (Scotland) Act 2003 s 76.
7 [2007] UKHL 42, 2008 SC (HL) 1.
8 For a discussion, see *Conveyancing 2008* pp 108–10.
9 [2008] CSOH 105, 2008 SLT 859.

discussed in last year's volume,[1] Lord Carloway refused to allow a servitude of signage (ie a right to place a sign on property belonging to someone else). A new case, however, now takes a more indulgent line.

In *Compugraphics International Ltd v Nikolic*[2] a cumbersome set of pipes and ductwork ran along the outer wall of the pursuer's building and was supported by a series of metal posts fixed into the ground. As the wall marked the outer limit of the pursuer's property, it followed that the ductwork overhung, and was supported on, property which belonged to someone else – to the defender in the action. Although the case was ultimately decided on a different ground,[3] one of the issues between the parties was whether the ductwork, which had been in position for much longer than the 20 years needed for positive prescription, could be justified on the ground of servitude. If so, it was argued, that servitude would need to be a combination of support (in respect of the metal posts) and overhang (in respect of the ductwork).

There was no real difficulty as to the servitude of support (*oneris ferendi*), despite the claim on behalf of the defender that it was confined to building-by-building support and so could not apply to the support of a structure by posts on the ground.[4] The question of overhang (*projiciendi*) was more problematic. On the one hand it was clear that such a servitude existed both in Roman law and in the later civil law.[5] But on the other hand, as Lord Bracadale pointed out, the matter had 'not previously been the subject of a decision by a Scottish court'.[6] What was one to make of this silence? Did it mean that such a servitude was, by implication, rejected? Or was it merely that, although some cases had come close and indeed *Romano* could have been argued on that basis, the courts had yet to be presented with a chance to consider the issue? Lord Bracadale saw 'no reason in principle why the law of Scotland cannot recognise a servitude of overhang' but did not seek to justify that view with argument.[7] We would agree that overhang should be recognised, and would add that its obvious visual prominence means that there is no risk of someone buying the servient tenement in ignorance of the servitude – which is the standard reason for restricting the list of servitudes.[8]

The recognition of a new servitude is an important event, not least because it has retrospective effect. Admittedly, the decision in *Compugraphics* is, strictly

---

1 *Conveyancing 2008* pp 107–11.
2 [2009] CSOH 54, 2009 GWD 19-311. We take the facts from the court's opinion: there has not been a proof.
3 For which see pp 169–73 below.
4 The claim has rightly been described as 'rather desperate': W M Gordon, 'Servitudes abounding' (2009) 13 *Edinburgh Law Review* 519 at 522. Professor Gordon draws attention to *Digest* 8.2.33 which concerns support by pillars.
5 See W M Gordon, 'The struggle for recognition of new servitudes' (2009) 13 *Edinburgh Law Review* 139 at n 14. Gordon notes that the appropriate *Digest* text is 8.2.2 and not the text (8.2.17) mentioned in D J Cusine and R R M Paisley, *Servitudes and Rights of Way* (1998) para 3.22 n 18 and picked up in *Compugraphics* (at para 26).
6 Paragraph 28.
7 Paragraph 28.
8 Bell, *Principles* § 979 (note).

speaking, *obiter*, and in any event we understand that it has been appealed. But suddenly all the instances of overhang in the streets and gardens of Scotland look more secure than once they did.

Oddly, there was no need for the court in *Compugraphics* to be so adventurous. If one focuses on the purpose of the ductwork and not on the ductwork itself, one quickly realises that this is simply a pipeline servitude of the kind given express (and retrospective) recognition by section 77 of the Title Conditions (Scotland) Act 2003.[1] The servitude is the right to lead a substance in the form of gas, the ductwork merely the means by which such leading is achieved.

ACCESS RIGHTS AND COMMON PROPERTY

Common property, not servitude

From the point of view of those wishing rights to use a private road,[2] the right of common property is a much better legal arrangement than the right of servitude. A person who holds a mere servitude is confined to the terms, express or implied, of the grant, and must not increase the burden on the servient proprietor.[3] So a servitude for pedestrian use excludes the use of vehicles; a right of access to what was originally an open field cannot normally be used for the 200 houses which the dominant proprietor now proposes to build; and a servitude is extinguished by non-use for 20 years. Common property is different. It is a right of ownership and not merely a burden on the ownership of others. As such it is imprescriptible[4] and, by and large, unlimited. All that the law requires is that a *pro indiviso* owner use the property for 'ordinary' (as opposed to 'extraordinary') purposes, and does not exclude the use of other co-owners.[5] A road which is common property is thus virtually unrestricted as to type and volume of traffic.

These advantages are usefully brought home in *Gavin v Junor*, a case dating from 1992 but which has only just been reported.[6] The pursuer and defender were proprietors of different parts of what had once been Ballagan Estate in Strathblane. Access to each was by a private road which the parties owned in common (along with others). Subsequently, the defender acquired two additional areas of land, not part of the Estate, and used the road in order to gain access to them. If the defender's right had been one of servitude, it is clear that access could not have been taken in this way, because a servitude can only be used for the benefit of the

---

1 We owe this point to Professor Roderick Paisley. Section 77(1) reads: 'A right to lead a pipe, cable, wire or other such enclosed unit over or under land for any purpose may be constituted as a positive servitude.'

2 'Private' road is used here to mean a road over which there is no public right of passage. A road can also be 'private' in the sense that, whilst it is public as to right of use, it has not been taken over by the local authority for maintenance.

3 See eg D J Cusine and R R M Paisley, *Servitudes and Rights of Way* (1998) paras 12.148 ff.

4 Prescription and Limitation (Scotland) Act 1973 sch 3 para (a).

5 See generally K G C Reid, *The Law of Property in Scotland* (1996) paras 23–25.

6 2009 SLT (Sh Ct) 158 and 162.

actual dominant tenement.[1] But this was common property and not servitude. Nonetheless, the pursuer sought interdict against the defender's usage.

The pursuer's argument was simple. Common property could only be used for 'ordinary' purposes. But use for the benefit of land outside the original Estate was an 'extraordinary' purpose. Hence the defender's use was unlawful. This argument was rejected without difficulty, first by the sheriff,[2] and then on appeal by the sheriff principal.[3] It was indeed a hopeless argument. The 'ordinary' use of a road is, self-evidently, to take access. That was all that the defender was doing. In taking such access, there is no restriction to a particular property, as in the case of a servitude. As one who owned the road, the defender could use it to take access to whatever property he wanted.

Changing 'ordinary' use

The 'ordinary' use of common property is determined by two things. One is the nature of the property. The other is the history of its usage. The first considers the question: what is the normal and natural use of property of the type in question? The second asks: have alternative uses taken hold?[4] The relationship between these questions is raised by the facts of *Mason v Jones*.[5]

Originally a private access road served four houses, and was co-owned by the proprietors of each. Many years ago, in 1983, the owner of the house furthest from the public road ('Headways') acquired an alternative access, and proceeded, in effect, to incorporate the final stretch of the private road into his property. That stretch came to be separated from the rest of the road by a wall with a gate which, in time, became impassable. Shrubs were grown on both sides of the wall, and the owner of Headways erected a greenhouse. In 2005 new owners of Headways decided that they wanted the access reopened so – they said – that they could meet and visit neighbours, and to improve access for the emergency services. The immediate result was a collapse in neighbourly relations followed by litigation against the neighbours next door.

A key issue was whether access remained an 'ordinary' use of this stretch of road, and therefore one on which the owners of Headways could continue to insist. That in turn depended upon whether the recent history of actual usage – as a garden and paved area rather than as a means of access – could displace the original and primary use. The sheriff principal[6] thought that it could not. Authority in this area is sparse, but the court relied on a remark by Sheriff Principal R A Dunlop QC in *Apps v Sinclair*:[7] 'It is not suggested however that historic use may be relied upon to restrict a use which would otherwise be

---

1 The leading case, exactly in point, is *Irvine Knitters Ltd v North Ayrshire Co-operative Society Ltd* 1978 SC 109.
2 2009 SLT (Sh Ct) 158. The sheriff was G Crozier.
3 2009 SLT (Sh Ct) 162. The sheriff principal was T G Coutts QC.
4 K G C Reid, *The Law of Property in Scotland* (1998) para 24; W M Gordon and S Wortley, *Scottish Land Law* vol 1 (3rd edn 2009) para 15–19.
5 2009 GWD 9-152.
6 B A Lockhart.
7 2006 GWD 16-316 at para 22. The decision is discussed in *Conveyancing 2006* pp 10–11.

considered an ordinary use of the property.' That was taken to mean that the 'historic use' (ie the recent use as a garden) could not displace the 'ordinary' use of the road for access. The view expressed in *Apps* must, however, be taken in context. In that case there was no question of the road ceasing to be used for its primary purpose of access; the question was simply whether that primary purpose could be restricted by recent changes in use patterns. (It could not.) But in *Mason v Jones* the position may have been different and, if so, there seems no reason in principle why one 'ordinary' use of property (ie use for access) should not over time be wholly replaced by another (ie use as a garden).[1]

SOLICITORS

Usually when a conveyancing transaction leads to a claim against a firm of solicitors, the pursuer is the defender's client, or rather former client. But in 2009 there were two cases in which the pursuer was the client of the *other* side of the transaction.

In the ordinary case, when solicitors write 'on behalf of and as instructed by our clients' the clients do indeed exist, they are indeed who they say they are, and the solicitor has indeed been instructed by them. But what happens if something goes wrong? In two cases in 2009 one party to missives ended up suing, not the other party, but the other party's solicitors. The facts of the two cases are very different, but some of the issues are the same. And whilst the first case is of a type that is unlikely to crop up often, the second case may be something for conveyancers to worry about at 2 am.

The strange tale of Syndicate 227

Halifax Life Ltd v DLA Piper Scotland LLP[2] is one of the strangest conveyancing cases we have ever come across. On 29 May 2008 missives were concluded for the sale of property in West George Street, Glasgow, for £8.8 million. The seller was Halifax Life Ltd. Who were the buyers? They were identified in the missives as 'the Members of the 227 Syndicate'. There were, it seems, plans to set up such a syndicate but it did not exist at that time nor did it later come into existence. We do not know what sort of entity it was supposed to be.[3]

We do not know how the solicitors acting for the seller regarded the idea of a contract with 'the Members of the 227 Syndicate', or whether they thought they should check who this set of persons might be, or, if they did check, what the results of that check were. Nor do we know what steps were taken by the defender in this action, who acted for the 'buyers', to ensure that it had these clients, and to check their identity and that it had instructions from them. The

---

1 In fact the pursuer's action failed for other reasons.
2 [2009] CSOH 74, 2009 GWD 19-306.
3 Lloyd's syndicates have names such as 'Syndicate 234'. The Lloyd's website indicates that there is a Syndicate 227, so we conclude that whatever 'Syndicate 227' was meant to be, it was not a Lloyd's syndicate.

mystery, thick enough already, becomes yet thicker because (at least on the pursuer's pleadings) the actual solicitor who was acting for 'the Members of the 227 Syndicate' positively knew that the syndicate did not exist, for the simple reason that he was one of those who, had the syndicate ever come into being, would have been one of its members.

Since there was no syndicate there could be no members of the syndicate, and since there were no members of the syndicate the buyers did not exist.[1] In the absence of a buyer, the transaction could not proceed: no buyer, no sale. The seller remarketed the property and sold it for a substantially smaller sum. It now sought damages. But whom to sue? In the event, the seller sued DLA Piper (Scotland) LLP. It sought (i) declarator that the defender was personally liable to implement the contract, and damages for breach of that contract, and, in the alternative, (ii) damages for loss caused by negligent misrepresentation.

The Lord Ordinary (Hodge) considered the authorities on the 'non-existent principal' issue and concluded that an agent is bound by the contract only where it is known to the counterparty that no principal exists. Thus if A purports to act for Y in a contract with Z, and Z knows that A does not act for Y, then the contract is between A and Z. But in the present case there were no averments that the pursuer knew that there was no 'Syndicate 227'. So the pursuer's case that the defender was bound by the contract was dismissed. This is not the end of the story, however. The pursuer still had a case based on misrepresentation. There was also the possibility of a claim based on breach of warranty of authority. So the Lord Ordinary's decision is more a tactical victory for the defender than a substantive one, and the claim may well still have a future.[2]

Which Mr Cameron?

The story

The facts of *Frank Houlgate Investment Co Ltd v Biggart Baillie LLP*[3] were complex. In 2004 Mr Houlgate, the main shareholder of Frank Houlgate Investment Co Ltd (FHIC), was introduced to a man named John Cameron by investment advisers called St James's Place Partnership. Cameron persuaded FHIC to advance money for a business project. After advancing about £100,000, FHIC took the view that it would be unwise to advance further funds without security. Mr Cameron offered a standard security over some valuable land at Balbuthie in Fife. His solicitors were Biggart Baillie LLP (BB). FHIC was separately represented. A standard security was granted and registered in the Land Register. FHIC then advanced further sums.

---

1 Possibly the pursuer could have tried to argue that the persons who were intended to be members of the syndicate were the buyers. But this would have been a very long shot. In any case we do not know if those persons could have been identified. Even if they could have been identified there would have been the question of whether they had instructed DLA Piper Scotland LLP to make an offer on their behalf.

2 For further discussion of this case, see L Macgregor, 'Acting on behalf of a non-existent principal' (2010) 14 *Edinburgh Law Review* 92.

3 [2009] CSOH 165, 2010 GWD 4-71. We take the story from the Lord Ordinary's account of the pursuer's pleadings. No proof took place.

The Balbuthie property was indeed owned by John Cameron – but a different John Cameron. In December 2006 the owner of the Balbuthie property (John Bell Cameron) found out that the other Mr Cameron (John McGregor Cameron) had been passing himself off as the owner of Balbuthie in a different transaction[1] and at this point his solicitors contacted BB as solicitors for the other Mr Cameron. On 16 January 2007, John McGregor Cameron admitted to BB that he was a fraudster. BB did not inform FHIC of what it had learnt, and on 30 January 2007 FHIC advanced to the fraudster a further £100,000. The fraudster then instructed BB to draft a discharge of the standard security. That having been done, he then forged Mr Houlgate's signature and returned the discharge to BB.[2] BB presented the discharge to the Keeper, and it was registered in the Land Register.

Six months later, in July 2007, Mr Houlgate happened to be reading a Yorkshire evening newspaper. His eye fell on a story in which a Mr Cameron had been convicted of a fraud in England. He realised that this was the man to whom he had been lending money. By this stage FHIC had advanced about £380,000. In the present action it sued BB for this sum.[3]

Fraudsters often use false names. This one did not. His real name was John Cameron. His middle name was McGregor. The other Mr Cameron, the owner of the property at Balbuthie, was John Bell Cameron, and the Land Register showed that name in the proprietorship section of the Balbuthie title sheet. The standard security that the fraudster signed ran in the name of John Bell Cameron.

What about the fact, awkward for the fraudster, that the Balbuthie property was in the possession of John Bell Cameron? In the middle of 2006 Mr Houlgate was taken to see the property, but was told by the fraudster that the farmhouse was let to the Church of Scotland, and that neither the tenants nor the local community were at the time aware of the proposals for development.[4] No doubt the type of scam employed here is easier to pull off in a secured loan than it would be in a sale; in other words, Mr Cameron the fraudster would have found it hard to sell Balbuthie.

What did BB know?

Before this transaction, John McGregor Cameron had approached BB about a standard security over Balbuthie in connection with another loan, which, however, did not actually happen.[5] At this stage the solicitor who was acting obtained evidence of his client's identity by way of a passport photograph and verified that his full and correct name was John McGregor Cameron. Although he was aware that the title to Balbuthie was in the name of John Bell Cameron,

---

1 A loan by a company called Galen Finance Ltd.
2 Why the fraudster did this we do not know.
3 It may be that there was no stateable case in respect of the money advanced *before* the standard security was granted. So the figure of £380,000 may have been too high. But this issue seems not to have been raised in the case.
4 Paragraph 3.
5 This part of the story we take from the record rather than from the Lord Ordinary's Opinion.

he accepted the explanation of his client that this was his cousin and that they owned the property jointly. One wonders why. If the Land Register said the owner was John Bell Cameron but in fact the property was co-owned by John Bell Cameron and John McGregor Cameron, then the Register was inaccurate. Were steps taken to secure its rectification? As far as we can see, no such steps were taken. Moreover, if the property was co-owned by two persons, how could it be that a standard security could be validly granted by just one of them?

The legal analysis: the negligence case

The action was based on two grounds. The first was that the defender had been negligent. The second was that the defender had been in breach of an implied warranty of authority. In the event, neither ground was upheld. The main battleground seems to have been the first issue.

The negligence case was summed up by the Lord Ordinary (Drummond Young) thus:[1]

> The defenders had a duty to take reasonable care to confirm the identity of John M Cameron, and a duty to take reasonable care to confirm that John M Cameron was the registered title holder of Balbuthie Farm. They had a duty not to accept instructions from John M Cameron in respect of the constitution of a security over Balbuthie Farm without obtaining authority from the registered title holder of that property. It was reasonably foreseeable that the pursuers would rely upon the defenders as having established that John M Cameron was the registered title holder of the property, since only the registered title holder had the necessary capacity to execute the requisite security deed. It was the defenders' duty not to act in a transaction involving the granting of a security over property registered in the Land Register without being so instructed by the registered title holder. At least, it was the defenders' duty to advise the pursuers that it was acting for someone other than the registered title holder. It was further the defenders' duty, once they became aware that John M Cameron had no connection with the registered title holder and that his instructions in relation to the granting of a security over Balbuthie Farm had been fraudulent, to relay that information immediately to the pursuers and to warn them not to advance any further monies. It was the defenders' duty not to witness forged signatures on the standard security and deed of variation and then to pass those documents off as having been executed by the ex facie granter of those deeds.

So: can a solicitor owe a duty of care to someone who is not a client? The Lord Ordinary gives a valuable overview of the authorities. The general rule is that no duty of care is owed to non-clients. There can be exceptions. One is fraud:[2]

> If the solicitor becomes aware of dishonesty on the part of his client that amounts to a fraud on the other party to the transaction, he will plainly be under a duty to ensure that he does not further that fraud in any way. If he does anything in furtherance of the fraud, he will be liable to the other party to the transaction as a participant in the fraud. … If … the solicitor becomes aware of some fact that points towards a fraud on

1 Paragraph 7.
2 Paragraph 21.

the other party to the transaction, … he should refuse to act further in the transaction. In some cases the duty may go further, and require that the solicitor disclose the fraud to the other party; it is unnecessary to say more about that in the present case because the pursuers' case is not based on fraud or dishonesty. If the solicitor does continue to act, he becomes party to the fraud, and is liable accordingly.

An exception to the general rule also exists where the solicitor gives information to the non-client, taking on responsibility for its accuracy:[1]

> He must indicate expressly or impliedly that he is exercising professional skill in providing the advice or information; the other party to the transaction must rely on the advice or information as a matter for which the solicitor has assumed personal responsibility; and the solicitor must be aware that such reliance was likely.

But this is not an easy exception to establish:[2]

> It is significant that none of the reported cases dealing with the undertaking of responsibility has involved an implied representation rather than an express representation. … That is hardly surprising, because if the solicitor merely proceeds with a conveyancing or security transaction on behalf of his client it is highly unlikely that he could be taken to assume a specific responsibility towards the other party. On that ground alone, I am of opinion that this case does not involve any undertaking of responsibility.

The legal analysis: the breach of warranty case

So the pursuer failed on the negligence side of the action. The other ground was that the defender was liable for breach of warranty of authority.[3] The argument was that the defender had purported to act for John Bell Cameron of Balbuthie, but in fact had not acted for that gentleman. The Lord Ordinary dismisses this argument fairly shortly:[4]

> The representation that is averred is … that the defenders had authority to act for John M Cameron as registered title holder. The critical part is not the authority to act for John M Cameron; it is a matter of agreement that the defenders did in fact have authority to act on his behalf. The critical part of the representation relates to John M Cameron's capacity as registered title holder. In other words, the representation relates to the property owned by John M Cameron, or his title to that property, and not to authority to act for John M Cameron himself. In my opinion that does not fall within the principle of breach of warranty of authority. The matter can be tested by considering an example. A solicitor purports to enter into a contract on behalf of a client

---

1 Paragraph 20.
2 Paragraph 23.
3 For an English case from 2009 with comparable facts, in which the 'breach of warranty of authority' argument was also advanced, see *Excel Securities plc v Masood* 10 June 2009, QBD, unreported. Here the lender sought summary judgment against the fraudster's solicitor. The basis of the action was breach of warranty of authority. The application was refused. The action was still able to proceed, but the court expressed the view that the claim was likely to fail.
4 Paragraph 28.

for the sale of the client's house. The client has undoubtedly given him instructions for the sale, but it transpires that the client's title to the house is defective because the last registered proprietor was the client's mother and in her will she left the house equally between the client and his sister. When the defect comes to light, the client will be liable for breach of contract, but the solicitor will not be liable for breach of warranty of authority; the solicitor had authority to act for his client, and the problem is a defect in the client's title. I am accordingly of opinion that the pursuers have not stated a relevant case based on breach of warranty of authority.

It seems to us that this might not be the last word. In the example involving the will, the client asserts that the whole property belongs to him, whereas in fact he has only a half share. But he does not impersonate his sister, nor does he introduce into the transaction a female friend to impersonate his sister. Did the fraudster impersonate John Bell Cameron? It seems plausible to say that he did. Which Mr Cameron did BB represent itself as acting for? If the answer is 'the Mr Cameron of Balbuthie' then this is not a 'good client, bad title' case but a 'good title, bad client' case, and the breach of warranty of authority argument begins to look rather strong. Of course, if one characterises what John McGregor Cameron did as 'impersonation', then BB was, with the pursuer, a fellow victim of that impersonation. But that would not alter the fact that BB was acting without the instructions of the impersonated individual.

The case bears a relationship to the line of cases involving contracts for the sale (or HP) of goods in which the buyer is a fraudster and succeeds in taking the goods away on credit. Well-known cases from the Scottish law reports are *Morrisson v Robertson*[1] and *MacLeod v Kerr*.[2] In some of these cases the contract is held to be void but in others it is upheld. It is particularly likely to be upheld where the parties meet face to face. But in some face-to-face cases the contract has been held void. An example is *Hardman v Booth*[3] where Edward Gandell pretended to be Thomas Gandell, and a Mr Hardman contracted with him, face to face. It was held that the contract was void.[4] Much more recently, in *Shogun Finance Ltd v Hudson*,[5] a fraudster had a stolen driving licence and pretended to be the person named in it. He contracted for a car on HP. The contract was held to be void. Whether these cases (and others that might be cited) are all consistent with one another may be open to argument.

These cases suggest that a preliminary issue in *Houlgate* might have been: did FHIC enter into a valid contract with anyone? Given that the first tranche of the loan seems to have been advanced before the name 'Balbuthie' was mentioned, a good case could be made for saying that FHIC contracted with the man with whom Mr Houlgate, its director, had face-to-face dealings. If that is the right approach then the Lord Ordinary's rejection of the breach of warranty of authority

---

1 1908 SC 332.
2 1965 SC 253.
3 (1863) 1 H & C 803.
4 And see *Cundy v Lindsay* (1878) 3 App Cas 459. A fraudster called Blenkarn passed himself off as a trader called Blenkiron. The parties did not meet face to face. The contract was held to be void.
5 [2004] 1 AC 919.

argument looks right. However, matters are complicated by the fact that the loan contract may have been not with John McGregor Cameron but with a company he controlled called Securimax.[1]

If a law firm concludes missives without instructions, there is breach of warranty of authority. But this was not a sale, and it does not seem that BB actually purported to *contract* on behalf of Mr Cameron. That fact tends to weaken this side of the pursuer's case.

Implications for conveyancing practice?

At first sight this might seem rather a one-off case. But in fact any fraudster with a reasonably ordinary name could readily track down properties owned by persons of the same or similar name. And a fraudster with an unusual name could always change: James Moxdhtunlsidq would not be able to pull off Mr Cameron's scam – but he could if he changed his surname to Macdonald.

If the decision is right, is that perhaps an unacceptably large risk to clients such as FHIC? Does the conveyancing profession need to think whether change is needed? Is the law too undemanding? If, contrary to the decision, the warranty of authority argument is correct, the problem would be not so much that the law is too undemanding, but that it would perhaps be too demanding. The first leg of the pursuer's case was merely that BB owed to FHIC a duty to take reasonable care – something that few would object to. The second leg would (had it succeeded) have imposed an absolute liability, and perhaps absolute liability is too demanding a standard.

Returning to the first concern, that the law may be too undemanding, we offer no view here, but we do note that with the advent of registration of title, it could be argued that the Keeper's indemnity covers such risks. That is a subject that we consider elsewhere in this volume.[2]

REAL BURDENS

Mactaggart and pre-emptions

The law today is that a real burden must nominate and identify a benefited property, and the deed must then be dual registered, ie registered against both benefited and burdened properties. But this is new law, introduced by the Title Conditions (Scotland) Act 2003.[3] Before that Act there was no requirement that the benefited property be nominated, and often the law would do the conveyancer's

---

1 This is what the Lord Ordinary says at para 23. But the pleadings are not quite as clear as one would wish. No company is designed in the pleadings. And cond 2 of the record says: 'In the period between June and August 2004 the pursuer advanced the sum of £100,000 *to JMC* by way of investment in "Securimax"' (italics added). Similar language is used elsewhere in the pleadings. For example in cond 5 it is said: 'On 24 August 2006 … the pursuer advanced to JMC the total sum of £80,000.'
2 See p 127 below.
3 Title Conditions (Scotland) Act 2003 s 4(2)(c), (5).

work for him and imply which property or properties were to take the benefit. The rules, however, were highly complicated. Roughly speaking, they fell into two groups. The first was where burdens were imposed on two or more properties under a 'common scheme'. This could happen where a series of split-off writs imposed the same burdens on different properties, but it could also occur where a single conveyance was followed, later, by division of the burdened property. The second was where the granter disponed[1] land, imposing real burdens, but kept back other land which was adjoining or at least in the neighbourhood. In this second situation there was only one rule, the rule identified in *J A Mactaggart & Co v Harrower*.[2]

The Title Conditions Act swept away the first group of rules, replacing them – for pre-appointed day deeds only – with the tidied-up version now found in sections 52, 53 and 56 of the Act.[3] Unlovely and troublesome as these new rules may be, they are better than the rules they replace. The rule in *Mactaggart*, however, was left alone and continues to form part of the law. But the reprieve is temporary. Any enforcement rights which depend on that rule will be extinguished without replacement on 28 November 2014 unless they are preserved by registration of a notice of preservation under section 50 of the Act.[4] As there are tens of thousands of such rights, this mass culling is of some significance, and no doubt we will hear more of the rule in *Mactaggart* as the deadline approaches.

A difficulty with the rule is that it is rather vague and ill-formed. Essentially, it depends on just one case – the decision of the Second Division in *Mactaggart* in 1906 – and there has been little judicial guidance since.[5] *Braes v Keeper of the Registers of Scotland*,[6] an Outer House decision by Temporary Judge M G Thomson QC, is thus both welcome and timely.

From the *Mactaggart* case itself it seems that the rule is something like this: where (i) A dispones to B (ii) imposing real burdens but (iii) retaining other land in the neighbourhood which is capable of benefiting from the burdens, then (iv) in the absence of anything else in the disposition, that land is, by implication, the benefited property in the burdens. *Braes* – which concerned a right of pre-emption – now qualifies that rule in two important respects.

In the first place, the court distinguished pre-emptions from ordinary real burdens:[7]

> [T]he terms of a building restriction, in common with the terms of most real burdens, are apparent without needing to know the identity of the dominant tenement. The terms of most real burdens can be observed by the servient proprietor without

---

1 The rule did not apply where the lands were granted in feu: see Abolition of Feudal Tenure etc (Scotland) Act 2000 s 48. In such a case enforcement rights lay, by implication, with the superior.
2 (1906) 8 F 1101.
3 Title Conditions (Scotland) Act 2003 s 49(1).
4 Title Conditions (Scotland) Act 2003 s 49(2). The procedure is discussed in *Conveyancing 2004* pp 95–103.
5 For a review, see K G C Reid, *The Law of Property in Scotland* (1996) paras 403 and 404. To this must be added the decision in *Marsden v Craighelen Lawn Tennis and Squash Club* 1999 GWD 37-1820, discussed in *Conveyancing 1999* pp 59–61.
6 [2009] CSOH 176.
7 Paragraph 67.

knowledge of the identity of the party or parties entitled to enforce it.[1] A burden of pre-emption, however, is different. It cannot be observed by the servient proprietor without knowledge of the identity of the proprietor to whom the offer to purchase has to be made. In my opinion the decision in *J A Mactaggart & Co v Harrower* is not authority for a departure from the rule which requires the terms of the burden itself to be contained in the disposition.

That meant that the rule in *Mactaggart* could not apply to pre-emptions, and that a pre-emption would be valid only if the benefited property was expressly identified.

There is much to be said for this result. The law has always been strict as to the identification of the *burdened* property in a real burden. That it should be so indulgent to the *benefited* property as to allow its existence to be implied has long seemed an anomaly, and one which has only now been corrected by statute (albeit with prospective effect). Containing *Mactaggart* within strict limits thus seems correct as a matter of legal policy. Even if that were not so, however, it is hard to argue with the Temporary Judge's view that a person burdened by a pre-emption needs to know, from the deed itself, to whom the property is to be offered. It is both trite and proper that the full terms of a burden must appear from the four corners of the deed.[2]

The decision in *Braes* has important consequences. Pre-emptions in *feu* dispositions (except where preserved by notice) were abolished on the appointed day.[3] Now, following *Braes*, it seems that pre-emptions in *ordinary* dispositions fail as well except where a benefited property was expressly nominated. Not many pre-emptions in pre-appointed day deeds will survive this double attack. Of course, invalidity as a real burden does not prevent the pre-emption operating at a contractual level between the original parties. But once the first disponee has sold on, all subsequent owners take the property free from the pre-emption.[4]

There was also a secondary reason for the court's decision. The disposition in *Braes* had actually nominated a benefited property: the pre-emption was reserved in favour of 'me or my first successor as proprietor of Bordie Farm, Kincardine'. That in itself, the court said, excluded recourse to the rule in *Mactaggart* (even if otherwise permitted), for a benefited property could not be implied where one had already been expressed.[5] Presumably this is because an express nomination must be taken to be exhaustive: not only is there no need for an additional benefited property, but to imply one might be contrary to the parties' wishes. Again, there is nothing to quarrel with in this result. It seems worth noting, however, that the

---

1 One might, however, mention the case where a prohibition is qualified by a provision for obtaining the consent of a particular person.

2 K G C Reid, *The Law of Property in Scotland* (1996) para 388. See now Title Conditions (Scotland) Act 2003 s 4(2)(a).

3 Abolition of Feudal Tenure etc (Scotland) Act 2000 s 17(1). Provision for preservation of pre-emptions by notice was made by s 18A. In the event, only 642 such notices were registered.

4 They would do so anyway if the property had been offered back to the pre-emption holder and the offer refused: see Title Conditions (Scotland) Act 2003 s 84 (replacing Conveyancing (Scotland) Act 1938 s 9). But in practice there is often a failure to make the necessary formal offer: an informal inquiry by letter will not do.

5 Paragraph 69.

position is different in respect of common schemes (ie the first group described above); the fact that a benefited property is expressly nominated does not prevent the implication of further benefited properties under sections 52, 53 and 56 of the Title Conditions Act.[1]

In fact the express nomination in *Braes* was held to have failed.[2] There was no indication, either in the disposition or the prior titles, of what was meant by 'Bordie Farm', and even if extrinsic evidence could be used for identification, as surely it could, it seemed that only part of the farm would turn out to have been retained by the disponer. Hence, the court concluded, the pre-emption was invalid.

Mutuality principle

Before deeds of conditions became available, or at least in common use, split-off conveyances in developments often contained an obligation by the granter to impose like conditions in other grants in the same development. Indeed this was – indeed still is[3] – an indication of the existence of a common scheme of burdens and hence of mutual enforcement rights. But memories fade, especially where a development proceeds slowly or passes through the hands of more than one person. As a result, the developer or successor may forget to insert matching conditions. What then? What is the effect, if any, on the burdens which the developer remembered to impose?

This issue arose for decision in *Clarke v Grantham*.[4] The case concerned Pitlessie House in Fife which, in 2004, was sold in two lots. One lot comprised the House itself – a grade II listed building dating from 1737[5] – and the other some outbuildings which had been converted into a second house ('the Maltings'). Between the two was an open courtyard. The Maltings was sold first. In the disposition it was provided that:

> our disponees shall be prohibited from parking vehicles on the area cross hatched [ie the part of the courtyard which was being conveyed] with the exception of setting down temporarily and we hereby bind ourselves to insert a similar condition in any future deeds, transmissions or investitures of or relating to the retained subjects under pain of nullity.

The burden was declared to be for the benefit of the House.

In the event, the disposition of the House, granted the following year, failed to include the corresponding burden. According to the Lands Tribunal, this meant

---

1 Scottish Law Commission, Report on *Real Burdens* (Scot Law Com No 181 (2000), available at www.scotlawcom.gov.uk) para 11.71.
2 Compare *Perth and Kinross Council v Chapman*, 13 Aug 2009, Lands Tr (Case (27) above), where the description of the benefited property was held to be sufficient.
3 Title Conditions (Scotland) Act 2003 s 52(1).
4 2009 GWD 38-645. The full opinion can be found at http://www.lands-tribunal-scotland.org.uk/decisions/LTS.TC.2008.49.html. The Lands Tribunal comprised J N Wright QC and K M Barclay FRICS.
5 Now run as a guest house: see http://www.pitlessiehouse.com/.

that the original burden on the Maltings was not enforceable due, it seems, to the mutuality principle:[1]

> [T]he failure to make the second purchaser similarly bound removes the basis for enforcement of this parking restriction by that purchaser. Whatever any party might have thought had been intended, the provision for insertion of a similar obligation in the title of the House clearly establishes the basis of the obligation, which was undertaken on the basis that a similar obligation would be imposed on the purchaser of the House. This makes it an obligation of a mutual nature so that it cannot be enforced where, as here, the counterpart has not been performed, the scheme has not been followed through and the owner of the House is not similarly bound.

No authority is cited for this view, and indeed there is none. It seems to be based on a confusion. Professor McBryde states the mutuality principle as follows: 'A party who is in breach of obligations cannot enforce performance by the other party.'[2] But in *Clarke* the breach was by the developer and not by the potential enforcer of the burden, ie the purchaser of the House. For that breach the developer was, in principle, liable in damages.[3] The purchaser, however, was innocent of the breach and free from the obligation which, but for that breach, would have been hers. That is not to say that the mutuality principle cannot apply to real burdens: where, for example, the houses in a development are subject to the same burdens, an owner who is in breach of a particular burden is disabled from enforcing that burden against anyone else.[4] But the principle requires the potential enforcer to be herself in breach. That was not the case with the purchaser of the House in *Clarke*.

The Tribunal did not go so far as to say that the burden was extinguished. 'Conceivably', the Tribunal said,[5] 'an adequate basis for enforcement might be restored if the respondent or a subsequent owner of the House were prepared to undertake a similar condition.' The basis for this approach is that the mutuality principle does not extinguish rights, but merely suspends their enforceability.

Interpretation

As no real burden looks as well drafted in hindsight as it did at the time it was first produced, one way of trying to escape from its grip is to say that the wording is too vague for the burden to be enforceable. In this enterprise courts have often been willing accomplices, showing a perhaps unwholesome enthusiasm for striking down apparently blameless provisions.[6] On this point the Title Conditions Act has tried to recover some ground, section 14 providing that:

---

1 Paragraph 35.
2 W W McBryde, *The Law of Contract in Scotland* (3rd edn 2007) para 20–47.
3 An example is *Leith School Board v Rattray's Trs* 1918 SC 94.
4 K G C Reid, *The Law of Property in Scotland* (1996) para 435.
5 Paragraph 35.
6 K G C Reid, *The Law of Property in Scotland* (1996) paras 415–22; W M Gordon, *Scottish Land Law* (2nd edn 1999) paras 22–41 ff; G L Gretton and K G C Reid, *Conveyancing* (3rd edn 2004) para 13–20.

Real burdens shall be construed in the same manner as other provisions of deeds which relate to land and are intended for registration.

The purpose of this odd-sounding provision is to bring real burdens into line with other rights found in deeds, such as servitudes, so that, while burdens should continue to be interpreted *contra proferentem* and in favour of freedom, they should no longer be singled out for unpleasant treatment.

Issues of interpretation cropped up in *Clarke v Grantham*.[1] As will be recalled, the burden there began: 'our disponees shall be prohibited from parking vehicles on the area cross hatched with the exception of setting down temporarily'. It was argued for the burdened proprietor that the word 'temporarily' had no clear meaning and introduced a fatal uncertainty into the provision. Although section 14 was not cited,[2] the Lands Tribunal – surely correctly – had no difficulty in rejecting this submission:[3]

> It seems to us, however, that that expression, 'prohibited from parking vehicles ... with the exception of setting down temporarily', has a tolerably clear meaning. ... The exact time duration of 'temporarily' might be a matter of dispute in particular cases, but that does not make the meaning of the word unclear. Given the variety of circumstances, it is difficult to envisage this qualification of the prohibition being expressed any more precisely, except perhaps by some arbitrary time duration which would inevitably often not meet the case.

Interest to enforce

It has always been the law that a person seeking to enforce a real burden must show interest as well as title. The innovation in the Title Conditions Act was the attempt at a definition. In terms of section 8(3) of the Act a person has interest if:

> in the circumstances of any case, failure to comply with the real burden is resulting in, or will result in, material detriment to the value or enjoyment of the person's ownership of, or right in, the benefited property.

Quite properly, this definition focuses on the circumstances of the particular case. As Sheriff Principal R A Dunlop QC explained in *Barker v Lewis*:[4]

> Much will depend on the nature of the burden and its breach, the nature of the neighbourhood, including issues of proximity of burdened and benefited properties, and no doubt other circumstances particular to the case under consideration – the

---

1 2009 GWD 38-645, discussed in the previous section.
2 It did, however, apply, notwithstanding that the burden was created before the appointed day: see Title Conditions (Scotland) Act 2003 s 119(4), (10).
3 Paragraph 34. Similarly, in another case from 2009 – *Perth and Kinross Council v Chapman* 13 Aug 2009 (Case (27) above) – the Tribunal had no difficulty in dismissing the argument that a condition from 1945 was invalid because it was described as a 'servitude' and not, as it ought to have been, as a 'real burden'.
4 2008 SLT (Sh Ct) 17 at para 27. For a discussion of this decision, see *Conveyancing 2008* pp 92–95.

question being whether in those circumstances the detriment, viewed objectively, is of sufficient significance or import to persuade the court that it is proper to allow the benefited proprietor to enforce the burden.

In *Barker* itself the pursuers were held to have had no interest to prevent an immediate neighbour from conducting a bed-and-breakfast business – a rather surprising result and one which suggests a quite high threshold for interest. *Clarke v Grantham*[1] is now a second decision on this topic.

The issue came about in an odd way. A courtyard which separated two houses was owned, in separate parts, by the proprietors of both. One of these parts was subject to a prohibition on parking; the other was not. As the burdened proprietors did not actually use their part of the courtyard for parking, there was no 'failure to comply with the real burden' and hence no question of interest to enforce arose. Nonetheless, the Lands Tribunal was willing to offer a hypothetical view. As in *Barker v Lewis*, but with more obvious justification, the conclusion was that interest would be lacking:[2]

[W]e are satisfied on the evidence but also with the benefit of our own inspection that an owner of the House who herself is entitled to and does use the courtyard for parking will not suffer any significant disadvantage, either in terms of any effect on value or in terms of enjoyment of her ownership of the House, from parking (as opposed to passing traffic) in the prohibited area. There was no professional or objective evidence of any such effect, and, particularly in the light of our own inspection of the locus, we do not accept the respondent's evidence on this. Quite simply, if, as is not in dispute, cars are regularly parked on the side of the courtyard nearer the House, we do not consider that parking in the prohibited area could have any significant effect, far less sufficiently significant effect, on the value or enjoyment of the House.

The Tribunal thought that the position might, however, be different if the benefited proprietor ceased to use her own part of the courtyard for parking.

Discharging community burdens

Where they regulate housing estates or blocks of flats, real burdens are typically 'community burdens', that is to say, burdens which apply to the whole 'community' and which are mutually enforceable amongst its members.[3] Because of the potentially large numbers of enforcers, variation or discharge of community burdens by voluntary deed is often difficult or impossible. Certainly a standard minute of waiver – a deed signed by all owners of all houses in the development[4] – is likely to be a non-starter. Some modest help, however, is provided by the Title Conditions (Scotland) Act 2003. Section 35 allows community burdens to be varied or discharged for a particular unit or units if the deed is signed by the owner of the unit or units in question and by the owners of all other units within four

---

1 2009 GWD 38-645, discussed in the two previous sections.
2 Paragraph 39.
3 Title Conditions (Scotland) Act 2003 s 25.
4 Title Conditions (Scotland) Act 2003 s 15.

metres (but disregarding roads of less than 20 metres in width). An alternative, under section 33, is to have a deed signed by the owners of a majority of units in the development (or by a manager acting for that majority). This can be used either to release individual units or for the benefit of the entire development.[1] Whichever method is used, those owners of units who have not signed the deed must be notified of its terms and allowed eight weeks to object.[2] An objection is made by a formal application to the Lands Tribunal for preservation of the burden or burdens.[3] If no such application is made, the deed is endorsed by the Tribunal to that effect and may then be registered.[4]

Fleeman v Lyon[5] marks the first occasion on which an objection to a discharge was taken to the length of a Lands Tribunal hearing. It also serves as a useful warning as to how not to go about preparing a deed under the provisions for community burdens.

With only six houses, the estate in *Fleeman* was well suited to using the new procedures. The houses, which were in Slockavullin, Argyll, comprised three groups of semi-detached bungalows. One of those bungalows ('Kairos') occupied a site twice the size of any other, and one which was suitable for the construction of a second house. But this was contrary to clause (first) of the deed of conditions of 1982. This read:

> Each of the said plots shall be used only for the purpose of a single private dwelling-house for the residents of one household. No buildings other than one private dwellinghouse with relative garage and offices in connection therewith shall be erected on any plot and the buildings on any plot shall not be used as an hotel, public house or other place for the sale of exciseable liquor, restaurant, shop, place of trade or manufacture or for any other purpose which might constitute a nuisance to the neighbourhood. The parking or keeping of any caravan or tents in any part of the said development is prohibited. No livestock other than dogs or cats as domestic pets shall be kept in any dwellinghouse or on any plot. The erection or display of any notice boards or advertisements other than the name of the dwellinghouse is prohibited. Each plot so far as not built upon shall be laid out and properly maintained as garden ground or amenity ground in connection with the dwellinghouse erected thereon. Each purchaser will require to maintain any landscaping implemented by the builders for a period of ten years. No trees on plots are to be felled or removed without the written consent of Argyll & Bute District Council Planning Authority and any tree removed shall be replaced with a species to be agreed with the said Authority. Any landscaping which is a condition of the planning consent issued by the said District Council will be undertaken by the Builders and maintained by the purchaser to the satisfaction of the said District Council.

---

1 In *Fleeman v Lyon* 2009 GWD 32-539, the Lands Tribunal doubted (at para 21) whether s 33 envisaged variation or discharge in respect only of single units, but the doubt seems misplaced.
2 Title Conditions (Scotland) Act 2003 ss 34, 36.
3 Title Conditions (Scotland) Act 2003 ss 34(3), 37.
4 There must also be a sworn statement that intimation has been properly carried out: see s 37(4).
5 2009 GWD 32-530. The Lands Tribunal comprised J N Wright QC and K M Barclay FRICS. The full text of the decision can be found at http://www.lands-tribunal-scotland.org.uk/decisions/LTS. TC.2008.60.html.

Faced with this condition, the owners of Kairos sought to have it discharged by invoking the majority provisions of section 33. A deed was drawn up and signed by the owners of four of the houses. The only people not to sign – apart from the owners of 'Kairos' itself[1] – were the owners of the adjacent semi-detached house ('Bruach'). With hindsight, the deed was over-ambitious. Instead of releasing Kairos from clause (first) only so far as necessary (ie only for the purposes of building the particular house in question), the deed disapplied clause (first) in its entirety. Not only would this mean that anything at all could now be built on Kairos, but it also removed other restrictions which had nothing to do with building – for example, the prohibition on the sale of exciseable liquor.

Unhappy with the proposed new house, one of the owners of Bruach applied to the Lands Tribunal for preservation of clause (first). For the most part, such an application proceeds in the same way as any other to the Tribunal in respect of real burdens. In particular, the Tribunal is directed to decide the application by reference to the various factors set out in section 100. But there are three important differences.

First, the onus of proof is on the person seeking to retain the burden and not, as usual, on the person seeking to have it discharged. This is the same reverse onus as also obtains in applications for renewal of burdens following a notice of termination under the 'sunset' rule for burdens which are more than 100 years old.[2]

Secondly, instead of deliberating on the reasonableness of the application, the Tribunal is directed to determine whether the proposed variation or discharge is in the best interests of all the owners of units in the community (taken as a group) or alternatively is unfairly prejudicial to one or more of those owners.[3] Where, as in the present case, there is only a single objector, the Tribunal will naturally focus on the question of unfair prejudice, and is thus involved in the kind of balancing of interests which is familiar from standard applications.

The third difference had not previously been noticed. Drawing attention to the wording of its powers under section 90(1), the Tribunal pointed out that whereas, in the normal case, it is empowered to 'vary' as well as to discharge or, as the case may be, to renew, in the case of an application to preserve – the present case – there was no power to vary.[4] It was thus 'all or nothing': the Tribunal could either preserve the burdens (by granting the application) or discharge them (by refusing it). What it could not do – as it quite often does in other cases[5] – is to discharge the burdens but only to a certain extent. There was, the Tribunal thought, a reason

---

1 Although they could have signed to make up the majority: see Title Conditions (Scotland) Act 2003 s 33(3).

2 Title Conditions (Scotland) Act 2003 s 20. For a discussion, see *Council for Music in Hospitals v Trustees for Richard Gerard Associates* 2008 SLT (Lands Tr) 17 at para 28.

3 Title Conditions (Scotland) Act 2003 s 98.

4 See also Title Conditions (Scotland) Act 2003 s 34(3) ('preservation, unvaried'). Not having received detailed submissions on this question, the Tribunal formally noted that it 'might require further consideration on the basis of fuller submissions in another case' (para 29). But the Tribunal's decision on this point seems correct.

5 'Rather than refusing applications, we commonly allow applications subject to conditions such as for example maximum heights of buildings': *Gibb v Kerr* 2009 GWD 38-646 at para 38.

for this difference. A section 33 deed can affect all of the units in a community and not merely (as in the present case) a single unit. In such a case it is unlikely that all the units would be represented in proceedings before the Tribunal. It would be wrong, therefore, for the Tribunal to make an order which was not foreshadowed in the deed itself.[1]

It was this third difference which proved crucial in *Fleeman*. While the Tribunal would have been minded to vary clause (first) to allow the building of the proposed new house – for the effect on Bruach would, the Tribunal thought, have been rather small[2] – it was not prepared to countenance a complete discharge:[3]

> Clearly this building restriction does substantially impede the Kairos owners' enjoyment, in the legal sense, of their property. However, it is an amenity (as well as a community) burden which may well in some situations particularly benefit the immediate neighbours. It is not a particularly old burden, and no change of circumstances is suggested. It gives Bruach, as well as the other houses, an important benefit of control. Whatever we think of the current proposals, the effect of simply removing that control would be that Bruach would be left with no right to object to any building proposal.
>
> Additionally, as we have already mentioned, the provision as it stands in the majority agreement would discharge the whole of Clause (First) as regards Kairos. That is unfair to Bruach, as it potentially exposes Bruach to, for example, some business use of Kairos involving pedestrian traffic through Bruach and other potentially disturbing uses. We are sure that this was not what was intended, but that is the agreement which is before us and which we require to consider on an 'all or nothing' basis.

In those circumstances the Tribunal felt bound to grant the application for preservation.

Where does this leave the owners of Kairos? A more modestly framed deed would have led to success before the Lands Tribunal. As it is, they will now have to start again. However, the Tribunal's remarks on their building plans were, and were no doubt intended to be, helpful. The owners of Bruach now know that a targeted proposal is likely to gain the Tribunal's approval (whether this comes in response to a revised deed or to a simple application by the owners of Kairos for a variation).[4] The way thus seems open for agreement between the parties.

LAND REGISTRATION

PMP Plus: the aftermath

Introduction

The Scottish courts decide quite a few property law cases every year. In a sense they are all important, but it is rare for a really major case to come along, and when that happens it is usually a decision of the Inner House or even the House

---

1 Paragraph 26.
2 Paragraph 46.
3 Paragraphs 43, 44.
4 Although the Tribunal quite properly emphasised (at para 48) that 'we cannot of course bind the Tribunal in any future application'.

of Lords (or Supreme Court as from 2009), cases such as *Sharp v Thomson*[1] or *Burnett's Tr v Grainger*.[2] *PMP Plus Ltd v Keeper of the Registers of Scotland*[3] was only a decision of the Lands Tribunal and yet it is one of these landmark cases. And in some ways it is even more important than the House of Lords decisions just mentioned. Famous cases often deal with situations that do not often arise in practice. Academics may be fascinated by them but for practitioners they are not particularly important. One could spend many years in practice and never come across the types of facts that so troubled the courts in *Sharp v Thomson* or *Burnett's Tr v Grainger*. The same could not be said of *PMP Plus*.

The facts of that case are everyday facts. In brief, what was held was that a conveyance of a *pro indiviso* share of an area that cannot be identified at the time of the conveyance is a nullity. In *PMP Plus* the split-off dispositions purported to convey:

> … a pro indiviso share with all the proprietors of all other dwellinghouses and flatted dwellinghouses erected or to be erected on the Development known as Festival Park, Glasgow being the whole development of the subjects registered in the Land Register of Scotland under Title Number GLA69039 (hereinafter referred to as 'the Greater Development') in and to those parts of the Greater Development which on completion thereof shall not have been exclusively alienated to purchasers of dwellinghouses or flatted dwellinghouses, which said parts comprise or shall comprise inter alia the boundary walls, quay wall and jetty, walkways, railings, fences, hedges and other walls enclosing the Greater Development, footpaths, sewers, drains, water supply pipes, electric mains, underbridge, car parking areas, parking area accesses, lay-bys, any embankments and access steps, the entrance drives, service roads, pathways, ornamental garden ground, play areas and other areas of open space and others so far as these serve and are common to all dwellinghouses, flatted dwellinghouses or others erected on the Greater Development (hereinafter referred to as 'the said common parts') …

That was held to be invalid. It is not possible to transfer something that cannot be identified with reasonable certainty at the time of the transfer.

We dealt with the case last year.[4] Since then there have been two developments to note. One is a further decision in the litigation on whether the 'offside goals' rule might apply. The Lands Tribunal held that it did not apply.[5] Since this was effectively a decision in absence, its significance is limited. The other, and much more important, development has been the Keeper's statement of how common areas in developments will be handled in future. The statement appeared in July 2009 and is called 'Creation, Identification, and Transfer of Rights in Common Area in Developments'.[6]

---

1 1997 SC (HL) 66.
2 2004 SC (HL) 19.
3 2009 SLT (Lands Tr) 2.
4 *Conveyancing 2008* pp 133–49.
5 *PMP Plus Ltd v Keeper of the Registers of Scotland (No 2)*, 19 March 2009, Lands Tribunal (Case (54) above).
6 *Update 27* (available at http://www.ros.gov.uk/pdfs/update27.pdf). A brief notice appeared at (2009) 54 *Journal of the Law Society of Scotland* Aug/17.

The Keeper's new policy

The Keeper's new policy took effect as from 3 August 2009. In the first place, something should be said about what does *not* change. There is no change to the way the Keeper handles dealings with properties that *already* have this type of 'together with' clause in the title. For example, suppose that in 2002 Jack bought a house in Fife, and the disposition purported to convey a *pro indiviso* share in an indeterminate common area, and the disposition was duly registered in the Land Register. Now (ie after 3 August 2009) Jack sells the property to Jill. The disposition will be registered in the same way as it would have been before 3 August 2009. In other words, Jill will have, on the face of the Register, a *pro indiviso* right to a common area. Indemnity will not be excluded on the ground that there may be *PMP*-based doubts about the title to the common area.

Although the Keeper's statement does not expressly address the point, we understand that there will also be no change in the way the Keeper deals with cases where a property held on a Sasine title comes in for first registration and the title has a 'together with' clause which refers to a *pro indiviso* share of a common area dependent on what was, at the time of the deed, a future uncertain event. For example, take Jack's case and change the county from Fife to Sutherland, where the Land Register was not introduced until 2003. The split-off disposition to him will have been recorded in the Register of Sasines. When, in 2010, he sells to Jill, that will trigger a first registration. Assuming that the title is in other respects acceptable, we understand that the 'together with' clause will appear in Jill's title sheet, and will do so without exclusion of indemnity.

Another thing that does not change is the way that split-off dispositions will be handled in respect of new developments where the first split-off deeds had already been registered by 3 August 2009. The Keeper takes the view that deeds within one and the same development should be dealt with on the same footing. Hence there is a 'run-off' period for new developments. Put another way, the new policy affects only such developments where the first split-offs happen after 3 August 2009.

Unless one of these exceptions applies, the new policy operates as from 3 August 2009. The new policy is, to quote the Keeper's words, that 'the Keeper will only reflect in Land Register title sheets the terms of the conveyancing in relation to common areas where the identification of common areas does not depend on a future uncertain event'. That does not quite say that the common area must be shown on a plan. What it does mean is that if the description of the common area is merely verbal, it will be rejected if it appears that the area is not already, at the time of the deed, identifiable on the ground. Thus if the sort of description quoted above were to appear in a disposition in a new development, it would fall foul of the new policy. What would be the consequence? The consequence would not be that the deed as a whole would be rejected. It would be that the deed would be accepted (assuming of course that it was valid in other respects) but the title sheet would not include a share in the common area in the property section.

That leaves the possibility of a split-off deed that (i) does not include a plan of the common area but (ii) does not suggest that the common area is to be determined by a 'future uncertain event'. The Keeper's policy is to accept such deeds, but:

> The Keeper … notes the comments of the Lands Tribunal that in the context of land registration the concept of a description without reference to extraneous material is well understood and might well be thought to be a central feature of a map-based registration system. In the PMP case the Tribunal did not require to decide whether such a description was necessarily ineffective or restricted in effect. However, applicants may wish to consider the Tribunal's comments.

In other words, it might turn out that registration in this type of case would be ineffective.

Practice

Where buying for a client, and the common area is to be described by reference to a future uncertain event, it is relevant to know whether the development is an 'existing development' or not. An 'existing development' is one in which the first split-off disposition was registered before 3 August 2009.[1] Since the way the Keeper treats the deed varies according to whether the development is 'existing' or not, it may be worth asking the developer's solicitors.

Assuming the development is 'existing', the Keeper will register the disposition without exclusion of indemnity,[2] and will include the 'together with' clause in the property section of the title sheet. That is less comforting than appears. The client's title to the share in the common area may be void. Moreover, it is far from certain that the Keeper's indemnity would apply to the share in the common area – even though there is no express exclusion of indemnity.[3]

Could a buyer refuse to settle on the ground that the disposition would not be validly conveying part of what the purchaser has contracted to buy, namely the share in the common area? In principle the answer would seem to be affirmative.[4]

In the case of a *new* development (ie one in which the first split-offs happen after 3 August 2009), the Keeper will not include the share of the common area in the title sheet, if the common area can be determined only by a 'future uncertain event'. How developers and purchasers will respond remains unclear. At the moment there are few new developments, but that is a situation that will not last. So what are the options?

---

1 At least, that is the deemed registration date. Dispositions can sit in the Keeper's in-tray for some time. But assuming that the application is eventually accepted, the deemed date of registration is the date of receipt of the application.
2 Assuming that the application is satisfactory in other respects.
3 On this see *Conveyancing 2008* p 143.
4 See eg *Campbell v McCutcheon* 1963 SC 505. That would probably be true even if the missives say 'you must pay the full price regardless of title defects' because such a clause would, we think, be invalid under the Unfair Terms in Consumer Contracts Regulations 1999, SI 1999/2083. See *Conveyancing 2008* p 84.

(a) The ostrich approach: carry on as before. That seems out of the question, though it may take further time before everyone realises that.

(b) Finalise the estate layout before the first sale. That would mean that the common areas could be mapped and a plan attached to each split-off disposition. This is perfect for buyers, but developers may not like it because it would deprive them of flexibility.

(c) At the end of the development have a second round of dispositions to each of the owners in the estate, giving each a *pro indiviso* share in the common area, which by this stage can be mapped. This might be workable in a small development of say half-a-dozen houses but the larger the development, the less workable it becomes.

(d) At the end of the development, dispone the common areas, which can by now be mapped, to an entity that represents the residents. This might be a community body or, if the Development Management Scheme is in use, the residents' association.[1] Or it might be the local authority – if the local authority will play ball. This is an approach that is sometimes adopted anyway. One difficulty concerns upkeep. Suppose that the common areas are disponed by the developer to XYZ Ltd, the idea being that the various owners in the development will collectively pay XYZ Ltd for the upkeep. That cannot be done merely through an initial contract, because whilst such a contract would bind the first generation of buyers it would not bind their singular successors. So real burdens are needed. But are real burdens for this purpose valid? The point is uncertain.[2]

The Scottish Law Commission's report on land registration

This important report was published in February 2010[3] and will be covered in next year's volume. Three points, however, may be mentioned here by way of a preview.

Ascertainment deeds

The Commission offers a new way of tackling the *PMP* issue.[4] It would only be an option, so that if it proved unpopular it would simply be ignored. In this new option, a developer would, at the end of the development, simply lodge a plan with the Keeper, showing the common area. On that happening, each of the properties on the estate would automatically acquire a *pro indiviso* share in that area. The Commission calls such a plan an 'ascertainment plan', because it would ascertain the previously unascertained area.

---

1 For the Development Management Scheme, see p 130. In the DMS the residents' association has legal personality and so can own heritable property.
2 See *Conveyancing 2008* p 144.
3 Scottish Law Commission, Report on *Land Registration* (Scot Law Com No 222 (2010), available at www.scotlawcom.gov.uk).
4 Report on *Land Registration* pt 6. The *PMP* issue was discussed in the previous section.

Advance notices

Next, the Commission recommends the introduction of 'advance notices' to protect grantees of deeds.[1] An advance notice would be lodged with the Keeper and would last 35 days – the 'protected period'. So long as the acquirer's deed is registered within the protected period, the acquirer would have nothing to fear from adverse entries in that period, either in the Land Register or in the Register of Inhibitions. The system would make letters of obligation redundant. It would be an optional system: if people did not like it they would not have to use it, and could carry on with letters of obligation.

Electronic deeds and missives

At the moment some types of deed can be in electronic form. But many cannot, such as, for example, split-off dispositions. Nor can missives. Even where a deed can be in electronic form, it has to be used in the ARTL system. The Commission recommends that all conveyancing documents, including missives, should be capable of being in electronic form.[2]

The *Houlgate* case

Elsewhere[3] we discuss the remarkable case of *Frank Houlgate Investment Co Ltd v Biggart Baillie LLP*.[4] In that case John M Cameron signed a standard security over property at Balbuthie in Fife, being property that was owned by John B Cameron. The creditor in the security was Frank Houlgate Investment Co Ltd. The security was registered in the Land Register. So at this stage the title sheet showed the Houlgate security in the C section. Later, John M Cameron forged a deed of discharge, and this too was registered. So now the C section of the title sheet was blank once again.

The company sued Biggart Baillie LLP for its loss. But was there also the possibility of recourse against the Keeper? This is not a straightforward question – indeed questions turning on inaccuracies in the Land Register are seldom straightforward. First, suppose that before the forged discharge John B Cameron (the true owner) had noticed the problem, had pointed out to the Keeper that the security was signed by a fraudster, and asked the Keeper to rectify the Register by deleting the security. What would have happened? Presumably the Keeper would have agreed. It is true that the Keeper is normally forbidden to rectify the Register against the interests of a 'proprietor in possession'[5] but the company was not a proprietor in possession.[6] Had rectification taken place, the company (unless 'careless') would presumably have been entitled to indemnity from the

---

1 Report pt 14.
2 Report pt 32. For missives by fax under current law, see *Park Ptrs (No 2)* [2009] CSOH 122, 2009 SLT 871, discussed at p 85 above.
3 See p 108.
4 [2009] CSOH 165, 2010 GWD 4-71.
5 Land Registration (Scotland) Act 1979 s 9(3)(a).
6 Cf *Kaur v Singh* 1999 SC 180.

Keeper.[1] So the company would have been protected by the land registration system. The Keeper would have been subrogated to the company's claims against third parties,[2] so it might have been the Keeper who ended up suing Biggart Baillie LLP.

But that is not what happened. The forged deed of discharge meant that the security no longer appeared on the title sheet of John B Cameron, the true owner. The Register was now accurate again. So where does that leave the company? As far as we can see, it leaves the company with no claim against the Keeper. So it rather looks as if the company's indemnity in relation to the standard security has vanished into thin air. If that is correct, it is an odd result.[3]

Non-statutory liability for the Keeper?

Section 12, and to some extent also section 13, of the Land Registration (Scotland) Act 1979 establish a framework whereby the Keeper can be obliged to pay compensation. *Braes v Keeper of the Registers of Scotland*[4] is unusual in that the pursuer's claim against the Keeper was based on common law, and no claim was made under section 12.

In 1982 Mr Braes disponed some property to the National Coal Board, reserving a right of pre-emption. Later the property was acquired by Scottish Coal Company Ltd who later transferred it to Scottish Coal (Deep Mine) Company Ltd. Neither of these transfers triggered the pre-emption right because they came under the 'subsidiary company' exception in the pre-emption. Later the property was sold to M & D Russell (Haulage) Ltd. The first registration of the property appears to have taken place when the property was acquired by Scottish Coal Company Ltd. The right of pre-emption was omitted from the title sheet. Mr Braes' solicitors wrote to the Keeper to point this out, and received the following reply, dated 30 September 2004:

> I refer to your letter of 17 September.
>
> I am very sorry that the Keeper omitted the right of pre-emption from FFE12758. The right does not apply to disposals to Coal Industry Estates Limited or other subsidiary companies of the National Coal Board, but does apply to a disposal to any other party. The Keeper should therefore have shown the right of pre-emption in the Burdens Section of FFE12758 until he had the appropriate evidence to remove it.
>
> In terms of Section 12 (1)(d) of the Land Registration (Scotland) Act 1979, your client is entitled to be indemnified by the Keeper for any loss he has suffered as a result of an error or omission in a Land Certificate. Any claim should be properly quantified and vouched for.
>
> The subjects have now been purchased by M & D Russell (Haulage) Limited. In terms of Section 9(3) of the 1979 Act, the Keeper can only rectify an inaccuracy in the register in limited circumstances if such rectification would prejudice a proprietor in possession. Section 9(3)(ii) permits rectification where there is agreement by the parties

---

1 Land Registration (Scotland) Act 1979 s 12(1)(a). For carelessness, see s 12(3)(n).
2 Land Registration (Scotland) Act 1979 s 13.
3 Under the Scottish Law Commission's recommendations (above), that result would not ensue.
4 [2009] CSOH 176.

concerned. If you wish, I will write to the agents for M & D Russell (Haulage) Limited to ask if they will permit the addition of the right of pre-emption in the Burdens Section of FFE12758. Of course, even if they agree, the right will not take affect until M & D Russell (Haulage) Limited come to dispose of the subjects.

A letter of 3 August 2005 confirmed this:

The Keeper will indemnify your client for any loss directly attributable to the omission of the right of pre-emption from the title sheet. The Keeper will also meet your reasonable legal costs to quantify any such loss. Should a determination of quantum be required in this case, I advise that the Keeper may instruct the District Valuer to carry out a valuation survey on his behalf. ...

But for Mr Braes, there was a problem. As he stated in his pleadings:

Even had the defender 'rectified' the Land Register so as to include the right of pre-emption in Title Sheet FFE12758, this would not have had retroactive effect, would not have given the pursuer Title to the Subjects (as he would have had, had the right of pre-emption been on the Land Register at the time of the proposed sale by SCDM to M & DRH) and would not have enabled him to work the colliery waste situated within the Subjects and, thereafter, develop the Subjects.

Likewise, even if the Keeper had, instead of rectifying, paid the pursuer compensation under section 12(1)(b), that too would have been of limited value. The reason is that the compensation would have been tied to the result on non-rectification. Hence the 1979 Act did not sufficiently protect the pursuer. The problem lay in the unusual nature of the burden: its value existed at a particular moment in time – the time of the sale to M & D Russell (Haulage) Ltd.

Mr Braes therefore raised an action for £1,389,860.35 in damages based on non-statutory grounds. The figure needs explanation. As we understand it, the pursuer's position was that the sale of the property was at a price of £40,000, which was far below the true value. In other words, had he been able to exercise the pre-emption he would have been able to step in and snap the property up at the bargain price of £40,000. The benefit of the low price would have gone to him rather than to M & D Russell (Haulage) Ltd. The pursuer's case was based partly on a general common law duty of care, and partly on the basis that the Keeper's letters constituted a promise to pay, or, at least, that they personally barred the Keeper from denying a duty to compensate.

For reasons we discuss elsewhere,[1] it was held that the pre-emption right was not a valid real burden anyway, so that its omission by the Keeper was not an error. This sank the pursuer's argument based on duty of care and would equally have sunk any claim based on section 12 of the 1979 Act. Although the case based on the Keeper's letters survived in theory, at best there was no more than a promise to compensate for loss, and since the pre-emption right was not a valid burden anyway there was no loss for which compensation was due. The

---

1 See pp 113–16.

court did, however, allow a proof before answer on whether the Keeper should compensate the pursuer for expenses.

One of the Keeper's defences was that the ordinary rules of promise and personal bar should not be applied to the Keeper in a land registration case. This defence was rejected.[1] Another was that, given the statutory scheme, the Keeper could not be liable in negligence. This too was rejected, but the Lord Ordinary (Temporary Judge M G Thomson QC) accepted 'counsel for the Keeper's criticism that the pursuer has not relevantly pled the specifics of the claimed negligence'.[2] The overall approach on both points seems sound. We see no reason why the Keeper should not, as a matter of principle, be capable of becoming liable to pay compensation outwith the framework of the statutory scheme, albeit that in practice such claims will usually be hard to make stick.

DEVELOPMENT MANAGEMENT SCHEME

The Development Management Scheme has arrived! The Title Conditions (Scotland) Act 2003 (Development Management Scheme) Order 2009, SI 2009/729, provides the final piece in the jigsaw of reforms initiated by the Abolition of Feudal Tenure etc (Scotland) Act 2000, the Title Conditions (Scotland) Act 2003, and the Tenements (Scotland) Act 2004. The Order came into force – and hence the Development Management Scheme ('DMS') became available for use – on 1 June 2009. It has been a long wait. Because the owners' association in the DMS is a body corporate, it was thought to be beyond the powers of the Scottish Parliament and Executive to make provision for it.[3] Hence it was necessary for a statutory instrument to be made by the UK Government under section 104 of the Scotland Act 1998. Why it has taken five years for this to happen has never been explained.

The DMS originated with a draft prepared by the Scottish Law Commission in its Report on *Real Burdens*, published in 2000.[4] Part 8 of the Report – readily available on the Law Commission's website[5] – contains a detailed discussion of the provisions and much useful information. Our account is necessarily much briefer.

What is the DMS?

The DMS is a model statutory scheme for the management and maintenance of developments such as housing estates and tenements. Unlike its cousin, the

---

1 Paragraph 83.
2 Paragraph 89.
3 See para 3.3 of the official Explanatory Memorandum.
4 Scot Law Com No 181. The DMS is set out in sch 3 of the draft Bill appended to that Report (pp 426–44). An earlier version still can be found as Management Scheme B in the Scottish Law Commission's Report on the *Law of the Tenement* (Scot Law Com No 162 (1998)).
5 www.scotlaw.com.gov.uk. The Report is number 181.

Tenement Management Scheme ('TMS'),[1] it is an opt-in scheme. That means that the DMS applies only if you want it to apply. Furthermore, with the exception of part 2, which contains mandatory provisions about the owners' association, it is freely variable.[2] So the DMS can be applied as enacted or in whatever form a developer chooses. This is done by registering a deed known as a deed of application.[3]

The availability of the DMS increases, in an important way, the range of options available for the management and maintenance of developments. Take the case, first, of a development comprising villas and other non-flatted property. Hitherto the only mechanism available has been real burdens – so-called 'community burdens'[4] – imposed, in practice, by a deed of conditions. Now the DMS offers an alternative. It can do everything which a deed of conditions can do but, as we will see later, it can also do some extra things. And the DMS can be applied either as enacted or as tailored for the development in question.

Next, consider the case of a block of flats. Apart from the DMS there are two other options. One is to make no provision at all, in which case the TMS will apply in full.[5] The other is to use a deed of conditions, in which case the TMS will still apply to the extent (if at all) that the deed of conditions does not provide. In other words, the TMS operates as a kind of safety net, filling in any gaps in the deed of conditions. If the DMS applies, however, the TMS does not.[6] This is because the DMS is more extensive than the TMS and no safety net is needed. So for tenements, the only way of being sure to exclude the TMS is to use the DMS.

Finally, there is the case of a development which includes *both* blocks of flats *and also* villas. The choice here is between the DMS and a deed of conditions. The former provides a complete system of regulation and so excludes the TMS. The latter is still subject to the TMS but in respect of the blocks of flats only.

These choices can be summarised in tabular form:

Developments without blocks of flats

Action	Governance of development
Deed of conditions	The community burdens in the deed
Deed of application without variations	DMS as enacted
Deed of application with variations	DMS with stipulated variations

---

1 For which see Tenements (Scotland) Act 2004 sch 1.
2 Title Conditions (Scotland) Act 2003 (Development Management Scheme) Order 2009, SI 2009/729, art 6.
3 Title Conditions (Scotland) Act 2003 s 71, discussed further below.
4 'Community burdens' are real burdens imposed on a group of properties and mutually enforceable amongst the owners of those properties: see Title Conditions (Scotland) Act 2003 s 25.
5 Tenements (Scotland) Act 2004 s 4. For a discussion, see *Conveyancing 2004* pp 127 ff.
6 Tenements (Scotland) Act 2004 s 4(2).

Developments comprising blocks of flats (only)

Action	Governance of development
Do nothing	TMS
Deed of conditions	The community burdens in the deed + TMS
Deed of application without variations	DMS as enacted
Deed of application with variations	DMS with stipulated variations

Developments comprising blocks of flats and other types of property

Action	Governance of development
Deed of conditions	The community burdens in the deed + (for the flats only) the TMS
Deed of application without variations	DMS as enacted
Deed of application with variations	DMS with variations

Joining

As an opt-in scheme, the DMS only applies if it is brought into operation by registration of the appropriate deed, known as a 'deed of application'.[1] This must be granted by or on behalf of the owner of the land. As with deeds of conditions, a deed of application takes effect – and so the DMS becomes live – immediately on registration unless provision is made for a later date. In theory the DMS could be used for developments which already exist and have been sold on, but this would require the agreement of all the owners. In practice, therefore, its main use will be for new developments, where only a single person – the developer – has to execute the deed.

No particular form has to be used for a deed of application. But the following information *must* be included in order to fill certain blanks in the DMS itself:[2]

- the name of the owners' association;
- the name and address of the first person who is to manage the development;
- definitions of –
  (a) the development
  (b) the scheme property and
  (c) unit.

---

1 Title Conditions (Scotland) Act 2003 s 71(1).
2 Title Conditions (Scotland) Act 2003 s 71(2).

The name of the association is to be inserted in rule 2.2 of the DMS, and the details of the first manager in rule 7.1. The former must take the form either of 'The Owners' Association ...' or 'the ... Owners' Association'.[1]

The three definitions are to appear in rule 1, beside the other definitions in that rule. 'The development' is the land to which the DMS is to apply,[2] while the 'scheme property' is that part of the development – for example, landscaped areas, roads, parking bays and other parts owned or used in common – which is to be managed and maintained under the scheme. There is thus an implicit distinction between (i) the parts of the development that are to be maintained by everyone, or at least by groups of owners and (ii) the parts – in other words, individual properties – which are the sole responsibility of individual owners. Where the development comprises or includes flatted property, it will be necessary to include under 'scheme property' those parts of the tenement building which are to be maintained in common. But in case of accidental omissions, a list of strategic parts – roof, external walls, foundations and the like – is automatically deemed to be scheme property.[3] This list is identical to the default meaning of 'scheme property' in the TMS.[4] 'Unit', the final term requiring to be defined, means the individual properties – villas, flats and the like – which are, or are intended to be, in separate ownership.[5]

A style of deed of application for a mixed development of villas, townhouses and flats might look like this:[6]

WE, ARDUOUS DEVELOPMENTS LIMITED, a company incorporated in Scotland under number SC 0987654321 and having our registered office at Five Eldon Crescent, Glasgow, hereby provide as follows:

1. This deed is granted under section 71 of the Title Conditions (Scotland) Act 2003.

2. The development management scheme shall apply to the development (as hereinafter defined).

3. In the development management scheme as so applied –

    (a) for the purposes of rule 1 –

    'the development' is ALL and WHOLE the subjects lying to the north of Dewar Road, Glasgow and registered under title number GLA987654321;

    'scheme property' means (a) the recreational areas, roads, parking spaces and others being the subjects outlined in red on the plan annexed and signed as relative hereto, and (b) in respect of each of the four blocks of flats –

---

1 2009 Order art 6(3). The same provision is made in s 71(2)(b) of the Title Conditions (Scotland) Act 2003 except that, oddly, the apostrophe is omitted. The apostrophe is used throughout the DMS itself.

2 2009 Order art 2.

3 2009 Order art 20(2).

4 TMS rules 1.2 and 1.3.

5 2009 Order art 2.

6 Another possibility, favoured by the Property Standardisation Group, is to incorporate the deed of application as part of an otherwise standard deed of conditions: see http://www.psglegal.co.uk/.

(i) the ground on which the block is built;
(ii) its foundations;
(iii) its external walls (but excluding windows);
(iv) its entrance passageway and stairs (but excluding doors); and
(v) its roof;
'unit' means any villa, townhouse or flatted dwellinghouse.
(b) for the purposes of rule 2.2, the association is known as the Dalrymple Park Owners' Association.
(c) for the purposes of rule 7.1, the first manager is James Sibelius McWhirter, 43 Greenock Palace Road, Glasgow G449 8HQ.

4. Rule 19.1 is varied so as to read –

'The service charge imposed under this scheme is to be divided into (a) four parts corresponding to the cost of maintaining the scheme property in each of the four blocks of flats and (b) one further part corresponding to all remaining costs. The service charge in respect of each part mentioned in (a) is divided equally among the units in the block of flats in question. The service charge in respect of (b) is divided equally among all the units in the development. This rule is subject to rule 19.2.'

5. At the end of rule 22 there is added –

[*Here insert an additional part, Part 5: Amenity Conditions, setting out use restrictions in respect of the individual units and the common areas.*]

IN WITNESS WHEREOF

A few words of explanation may be helpful. Clause 1 is formal and not strictly necessary. Clauses 2 and 3 contain mandatory information. Clause 4 is the only actual change to the text of the DMS. Rule 19.1 in its 'normal' form provides that the service charge is to be divided equally among all units. Quite often that will not be a satisfactory rule. For example, if the units are very different in size and value, it may be necessary to express liability in terms of different percentages. The change made in the present case is to take account of the fact that the scheme property includes certain parts of the blocks of flats as well as common recreational areas. It ensures that only the owners of flats in the block in question are responsible for the cost of repairs. Finally, clause 5 enables the insertion of a new part for amenity conditions of the kind that are usually found in deeds of conditions but are not included in the default version of the DMS, which is only concerned with management and maintenance. We return to this subject later.

DMS: the Scheme in full

The DMS is set out in schedule 1 of the Title Conditions (Scotland) Act 2003 (Development Management Scheme) Order 2009. It is easy to find, and to download: see http://www.opsi.gov.uk/si/si2009/uksi_20090729_en_1. The full terms of the DMS are as follows:

DEVELOPMENT MANAGEMENT SCHEME
PART 1
INTERPRETATION
RULE 1 – INTERPRETATION

1 Definitions

In this scheme, unless the context otherwise requires–

'the Act' means the Title Conditions (Scotland) Act 2003;

'advisory committee' means any such committee formed in pursuance of rule 15.1;

'association' means the owners' association of the development established under article 4 of the Development Management Scheme Order;

'deed of disapplication' means a deed granted pursuant to section 73 of the Act;

'deed of variation' means a deed of variation or discharge granted pursuant to article 7 or 8 of the Development Management Scheme Order;

'the development' is [*specify the extent of the development*];

'the Development Management Scheme Order' means the Title Conditions (Scotland) Act 2003 (Development Management Scheme) Order 2009;

'general meeting' means an annual or other general meeting of the association;

'maintenance' includes repairs or replacement, cleaning, painting and other routine works, gardening and the day to day running of property; but does not include demolition, alteration or improvement unless reasonably incidental to the maintenance;

'manager' means the person appointed to be manager of the association;

'member' means a member of the association in accordance with rule 2.3;

'owner' has the meaning given in article 18 of the Development Management Scheme Order;

'regulations' means regulations made under rule 3.6;

'reserve fund' means money held on behalf of the association to meet the cost of long term maintenance, improvement or alteration of scheme property or to meet such other expenses of the association as the association may determine;

'scheme property' means [*describe the property which is subject to maintenance under the scheme*];

'service charge' means the contribution to association funds payable in accordance with Part 4 of this scheme and includes additional service charge; and

'unit' means [*specify the individual properties forming the development*].

PART 2
THE OWNERS' ASSOCIATION
RULE 2 – ESTABLISHMENT, STATUS ETC.

2.1 Establishment

The association is established on the day on which this scheme takes effect.

2.2 Status

The association is a body corporate to be known as [*specify the name of the owners' association*].

2.3 Members of the association

The members are the persons who, for the time being, are the owners of the units to which this scheme applies and has taken effect; and where two or more persons own a unit both (or all) of them are members.

2.4 Address of association

The address of the association is that of–
> (a) the development; and
> (b) the manager,

or either of them.

RULE 3 – FUNCTION, POWERS AND ENFORCEMENT

3.1 Function of association

The function of the association is to manage the development for the benefit of the members.

3.2 Powers of the association

The association has, subject to rule 3.3, power to do anything necessary for or in connection with the carrying out of the function mentioned in rule 3.1 and in particular may–
> (a) own, or acquire ownership of, any part of the development;
> (b) carry out maintenance, improvements or alterations to, or demolition of, the scheme property;
> (c) enter into a contract of insurance in respect of the development or any part of it (and for that purpose the association is deemed to have an insurable interest);
> (d) purchase, or otherwise acquire or obtain the use of, moveable property;
> (e) require owners of units to contribute by way of service charge to association funds;
> (f) open and maintain an account with any bank or building society;
> (g) invest any money held by the association;
> (h) borrow money; or
> (i) engage employees or appoint agents.

3.3 Prohibited activities

The association shall not have power to–
> (a) acquire land outwith the development;
> (b) carry on any trade whether or not for profit; or
> (c) make regulations other than in accordance with rule 3.6.

3.4 Scheme to be binding

This scheme is binding on the association, the manager and the members as are any regulations which have taken effect; and a rule, or any such regulation, in the form of an obligation to refrain from doing something is binding on–

(a) a tenant of property affected by the rule or regulation; or

(b) any other person having the use of such property.

3.5 Enforcement of scheme

The association may enforce–

(a) the provisions of this scheme and any regulations which have taken effect; and

(b) any obligation owed by any person to the association.

3.6 Regulations

The association may, at a general meeting–

(a) make regulations as to the use of recreational facilities which are part of the scheme property; and

(b) revoke or amend regulations made under paragraph (a),

but any such regulation, revocation or amendment takes effect only after a copy of it has been delivered or sent to each member.

RULE 4 – THE MANAGER

4.1 Association to have manager

The association is to have a manager who, subject to any other provision of this scheme, is a person (whether or not a member) appointed by the association at a general meeting.

4.2 Power to remove manager

The association may at a general meeting remove the manager from office before the expiry of that person's term of office.

4.3 Validity of actings of manager

Any actings of the manager are valid notwithstanding any defect in that person's appointment.

4.4 Manager to be agent

The manager is an agent of the association.

4.5 Exercise of powers

Subject to this scheme, any power conferred on the association under or by virtue of this scheme is exercisable by–

(a) the manager; or

(b) the association at a general meeting.

4.6 Duties owed to association and members

Any duty imposed on the manager under or by virtue of this scheme is owed to the association and to the members.

4.7 Manager to comply with directions

The manager must, in so far as it is reasonably practicable to do so, comply with any direction given by the association at a general meeting as respects the exercise by the manager of–

(a) powers conferred; or

(b) duties imposed,

on the association or on the manager.

4.8 Information about management

Any member may require the manager to allow that member to inspect a copy of any document, other than any correspondence with another member, which relates to the management of the development; and if the document is in the manager's possession or it is reasonably practicable for the manager to obtain a copy of it the manager must comply with the requirement.

4.9 Notice to manager on sale etc of unit

Any member who sells or otherwise disposes of a unit must, before the date on which the person to whom the unit is to be sold (or otherwise transferred) will be entitled to take entry, send a notice to the manager stating, to the extent to which the information is known by that member–

(a) the entry date and the name and address of that person;

(b) the name and address of the solicitor or other agent acting for that person in the acquisition of the unit; and

(c) an address at which the member may be contacted after that date.

RULE 5 – EXECUTION OF DOCUMENTS

5 Execution of documents by association

A document is signed by the association if signed on behalf of the association by–

(a) the manager; or

(b) a person nominated for the purpose by the association at a general meeting,

provided that the manager or person acts within actual or ostensible authority to bind the association.

RULE 6 – WINDING UP

6.1 Commencement of winding up

The manager must commence the winding up of the association on the day on which this scheme ceases to apply as respects the development.

6.2 Distribution of funds

The manager must, as soon as practicable after the commencement of the winding up, use any association funds to pay any debts of the association; and thereafter must distribute in accordance with this scheme any remaining funds among those who were, on the date when the winding up commenced, owners of units.

6.3 Final accounts

The manager must–

(a) prepare the final accounts of the association showing how the winding up was conducted and the funds were disposed of; and

(b) not later than six months after the commencement of the winding up, send a copy of those accounts to the owner of every unit.

6.4 Automatic dissolution of association

Subject to rule 6.5, the association is dissolved at the end of the period of six months beginning with the commencement of the winding up.

6.5 Delayed dissolution

At any time before the end of the period of six months mentioned in rule 6.4, the members may determine that the association is to continue for such period as they may specify; and if they so determine it is dissolved at the end of the period so specified.

PART 3

MANAGEMENT

RULE 7 – APPOINTMENT OF MANAGER

7.1 First manager

The first manager is [*complete name and address of manager*] and–
- (a) acts as manager until the first annual general meeting is held;
- (b) is entitled to reasonable remuneration; and
- (c) is eligible for reappointment.

7.2 Appointment of manager

The association–
- (a) at the first annual general meeting; and
- (b) where the manager's period of office expires or a vacancy occurs, at any subsequent general meeting,

is to appoint a person to be manager on such terms and conditions as the association may decide.

7.3 Certificate of appointment

Not later than one month after the date of a general meeting at which a person is appointed to be manager–
- (a) that person; and
- (b) on behalf of the association, a member,

must sign a certificate recording the making, and the period, of the appointment.

RULE 8 – DUTIES OF MANAGER

8 Duties of manager

The manager must manage the development for the benefit of the members and in particular must–
- (a) from time to time carry out inspections of the scheme property;
- (b) arrange for the carrying out of maintenance to scheme property;
- (c) fix the financial year of the association;
- (d) keep, as respects the association, proper financial records and prepare the accounts of the association for each financial year;
- (e) implement any decision made by the association at a general meeting;
- (f) in so far as it is reasonable to do so, enforce–

(i) any obligation owed by any person to the association; and

(ii) the provisions of the scheme and of any regulations which have taken effect;

(g) if there are regulations, keep a copy of them (taking account of revocations and amendments); and

(h) keep a record of the name and address of each member

RULE 9 – CALLING OF GENERAL MEETINGS

9.1 First annual general meeting

The first annual general meeting must be called by the manager and held not later than twelve months after the day on which, in accordance with rule 2.1, the association is established.

9.2 Annual general meetings

The manager must call an annual general meeting each year; and a meeting so called must be held no more than fifteen months after the date on which the previous annual general meeting was held.

9.3 Other general meetings

The manager may call a general meeting at any time and must call a general meeting if–

(a) a revised draft budget requires to be considered;

(b) required to call that meeting by members holding not less than twenty five per cent. of the total number of votes allocated; or

(c) so required by a majority of the members of the advisory committee.

9.4 Calling of meeting

Not later than fourteen days before the date fixed for a general meeting the manager must call the meeting by sending to each member–

(a) a notice stating–

(i) the date and time fixed for the meeting and the place where it is to be held; and

(ii) the business to be transacted at the meeting; and

(b) if the meeting is an annual general meeting, copies of the draft budget and (except in the case of the first annual general meeting) the accounts of the association for the last financial year.

9.5 Validity of proceedings

Any inadvertent failure to comply with rule 9.4 as respects any member does not affect the validity of proceedings at a general meeting.

9.6 Member's right to call meeting in certain circumstances

Any member may call a general meeting if–

(a) the manager fails to call a general meeting–

(i) in a case where paragraph (b) or (c) of rule 9.3 applies, not later than fourteen days after being required to do so as mentioned in those paragraphs; or

    (ii) in any other case, in accordance with this scheme; or

(b) the association does not have a manager.

9.7 Procedure where member calls meeting

Where under rule 9.6 a general meeting is called by a member–

(a) any rule imposing a procedural or other duty on the manager in relation to general meetings (other than the duty imposed by rule 9.4(b)) applies as if it imposed the duty on the member; and

(b) if there is a manager, the member must send that person a notice stating the date and time fixed for the meeting, the business to be transacted at it and the place where it is to be held.

RULE 10 – GENERAL MEETING QUORUM

10.1 Number required for quorum

A quorum is–

(a) where there are no more than thirty units in the development, members present or represented holding fifty per cent. of the total number of votes allocated;

(b) where there are more than thirty such units, members present or represented holding thirty five per cent. of the total number of votes allocated.

10.2 Quorum necessary for meeting to begin

A general meeting is not to begin unless there is a quorum; and if there is still no quorum twenty minutes after the time fixed for a general meeting then–

(a) the meeting is to be postponed until such date, being not less than fourteen nor more than twenty eight days later, as may be specified by the manager (or, if the manager is not present or if there is no manager, by a majority of the members present or represented); and

(b) the manager (or any member) must send to each member a notice stating the date and time fixed for the postponed meeting and the place where it is to be held.

10.3 No quorum at postponed meeting

A meeting may be postponed only once; and if at a postponed meeting the provisions in rule 10.2 as respects a quorum are not satisfied, then the members who are present or represented are to be deemed a quorum.

10.4 Quorum need not be maintained

If a general meeting has begun, it may continue even if the number of members present or represented ceases to be a quorum.

RULE 11 – GENERAL MEETINGS: VOTING

11.1 Allocation and exercise of votes

For the purpose of voting on any proposal at a general meeting one vote is allocated to each unit; and any right to vote is exercisable by the owner of that unit or by someone (not being the manager) nominated in writing by the owner to vote.

11.2 Exercise of vote where two or more persons own unit

If a unit is owned by two or more persons the vote allocated to that unit may be exercised by either (or any) of them; but if those persons disagree as to how the vote should be cast then no vote is counted for that unit.

11.3 Decision by majority

Except where this scheme otherwise provides, a decision is made by the association at a general meeting by majority vote of all the votes cast.

11.4 Method of voting

Voting on any proposal is by show of hands; but the convener may determine that voting on a particular proposal is to be by ballot.

RULE 12 – GENERAL METINGS: FURTHER PROVISIONS

12.1 Election of convener

The members present or represented at a general meeting are to elect one of their number or the manager to be convener of the meeting; and on being so elected the convener is to take charge of the organisation of the business of the meeting.

12.2 Additional business

Any member present or represented at a general meeting may nominate additional business to be transacted at that meeting.

12.3 Manager to attend and keep record of business transacted

Except where unable to do so because of illness or for some other good reason, the manager must attend each general meeting and–
  (a) keep a record of the business transacted; and
  (b) not later than twenty one days after the date of the meeting, send a copy of the record of business to each member,
and where the manager does not attend the convener is to nominate a person present to carry out the manager's duties under paragraphs (a) and (b) of this rule in respect of the meeting.

RULE 13 – SPECIAL MAJORITY DECISIONS

13.1 Special majority required

The association may–
  (a) make a payment out of any reserve fund which it has formed; or
  (b) use any money held on behalf of the association to carry out improvements or alterations to, or demolition of, scheme property (not being improvements, alterations or demolition reasonably incidental to maintenance),
but only after the association have, at a general meeting, by majority vote of all the votes allocated, determined to do so.

13.2 Consent of owner to be given where not common property

Where scheme property is not the common property of the members (or not the common property of members who between them own two or more units) a determination under rule 13.1 for the purposes of paragraph (b) of that rule may be implemented only if the owner of the property consents in writing to the improvements, alterations or demolition in question.

RULE 14 – EMERGENCY WORK

14.1 Power to instruct etc

Any member may instruct or carry out emergency work.

14.2 Reimbursement of member

The association must reimburse any member who pays for emergency work.

14. Meaning of 'emergency work'

'Emergency work' means work which requires to be carried out to scheme property–
  (a) to prevent damage to any part of that or any other property; or
  (b) in the interests of health or safety,
in circumstances in which it is not practicable to consult the manager before carrying out the work.

RULE 15 – ADVISORY COMMITTEE

15.1 Power to elect advisory committee

The association may at a general meeting elect such number of the members as it may specify to form an advisory committee whose function is to provide the manager with advice relating to the manager's–
  (a) exercise of powers; and
  (b) fulfilment of duties,
under or by virtue of this scheme.

15.2 Manager to consult advisory committee

Where an advisory committee is formed, the manager is from time to time to seek advice from the committee.

RULE 16 – VARIATION

16.1 Deeds of variation under article 7

The manager may, on behalf of the association and after consulting the advisory committee (if any), grant a deed of variation under article 7 of the Development Management Scheme Order, and at the first general meeting after the granting of the deed the manager must then report that it has been so granted.

16.2 Deeds of variation under article 8 and deeds of disapplication

The manager may, on behalf of the association, grant a deed of variation under article 8 of the Development Management Scheme Order or a deed of disapplication but only after the association has, at a general meeting, by majority of all the votes allocated, determined to do so.

17 Distribution of funds on winding up

Where funds are distributed under rule 6.2 the basis of distribution is that each unit receives one share.

PART 4
FINANCIAL MATTERS

RULE 18 – ANNUAL BUDGET

18.1 Duty of manager to prepare annual budget

Before each annual general meeting the manager must prepare, and submit for consideration at that meeting, a draft budget for the new financial year.

18.2 Content of draft budget

A draft budget is to set out–

- (a) the total service charge and the date (or dates) on which the service charge will be due for payment;
- (b) an estimate of any other funds which the association is likely to receive and the source of those funds;
- (c) an estimate of the expenditure of the association; and
- (d) the amount (if any) to be deposited in a reserve fund.

18.3 Consideration of draft budget by association

The association may at a general meeting–

- (a) approve the draft budget subject to such variations as it may specify; or
- (b) reject the budget and direct the manager to prepare a revised draft budget for consideration by the association at a general meeting to be called by the manager and to take place not later than two months after the date of the meeting at which the budget is rejected.

18.4 Rejected budget – payment of service charge

Where the budget is rejected the service charge exigible under the budget last approved is, until a new budget is approved, to continue to be exigible and is to be due for payment on the anniversary (or anniversaries) of the date (or dates) on which it was originally due for payment.

18.5 Revised draft budget

At a general meeting at which a revised draft budget is considered, the association may approve or reject the budget as mentioned in rule 18.3(a) and (b).

RULE 19 – SERVICE CHARGE

19.1 Amount of service charge

Except where rule 19.2 applies, the amount of any service charge imposed under this scheme is the same as respects each unit.

19.2 Service charge exemption

The association may at a general meeting decide as respects a particular owner and in relation to a particular payment that no service charge (or a service charge of a reduced amount) is payable.

19.3 Manager to collect service charge

When the draft budget has been approved in accordance with this scheme, the manager–

    (a) must send to each owner a notice requiring payment, on the date (or dates) specified in the budget, of the amount of the service charge so specified; and

    (b) may send to each owner at any time a notice–

        (i) requiring payment, on the date (or dates) stated in the notice, of an additional amount of service charge determined under rule 20.1; and

        (ii) explaining why the additional amount is payable,

and each owner is liable for that amount accordingly.

19.4 Redistribution of share of costs

Where an owner is liable for a service charge but the service charge cannot be recovered (for example because the estate of that owner has been sequestrated, or that owner cannot, by reasonable inquiry, be identified or found) then that service charge is to be shared equally among the other owners or, if they so decide, is to be met out of any reserve fund; but that owner remains liable for the service charge.

19.5 Interest payable on overdue service charge

Where any service charge (or part of it) remains outstanding not less than twenty eight days after it became due for payment, the manager may send a notice to the owner concerned requiring that person to pay interest on the sum outstanding at such reasonable rate and from such date as the manager may specify in the notice.

19.6 Interpretation of rule 19

In rule 19 references to 'owner' are references to an owner of a unit.

RULE 20 – ADDITIONAL SERVICE CHARGE

20.1 Additional service charge

The manager may from time to time determine that an additional service charge, limited as is mentioned in rule 20.2, is payable by the members to enable the association to meet any expenses that are due (or soon to become due) and which could not be met otherwise than out of the reserve fund.

20.2 Limit on amount of additional service charge

In any financial year the total amount of any additional service charge determined under rule 20.1 is not to exceed twenty five per cent. of the total service charge for that year as set out in the budget approved by the association; but in calculating that percentage no account is to be taken of any additional service charge payable in respect of the cost of emergency work (as defined in rule 14.3).

20.3 Supplementary budget

If in any financial year the manager considers that any additional service charge exceeding the percentage mentioned in rule 20.2 should be payable, the manager must prepare and submit to the association at a general meeting a draft supplementary budget setting out the amount of the additional service charge and the date (or dates) on which the charge will be due for payment; and rules 18.3, 18.4 and 19.3(a) apply as respects that draft supplementary budget as they apply as respects a draft budget and revised draft budget.

RULE 21 – FUNDS

21.1 Association funds

Any association funds must be–

  (a) held in the name of the association; and
  (b) subject to rule 21.2, deposited by the manager in a bank or building society account.

21.2 Special treatment of certain funds

The manager must ensure that any association funds which are likely to be held for some time are–

  (a) deposited in an account which is interest bearing; or
  (b) invested in such other way as the association may at a general meeting decide.

21.3 Reserve fund

The manager must ensure that any association funds forming a reserve fund are kept separately from other association funds.

RULE 22 – SENDING

22.1 Sending

Where a rule requires that a thing be sent–

  (a) to a person it shall suffice, for the purposes of that rule, that the thing be sent to an agent of the person;
  (b) to a member and that member cannot by reasonable inquiry be identified or found, it shall suffice, for the purposes of that rule, that the thing be sent to the member's unit addressed to 'The Owner' (or using some other such expression, as for example 'The Proprietor').

22.2 Method of sending

Any reference to a thing being sent shall be construed as a reference to its being–

  (a) posted;
  (b) delivered; or
  (c) transmitted by electronic means.

22.3 Date of sending

A thing posted shall be taken to be sent on the day of posting; and a thing transmitted by electronic means, to be sent on the day of transmission.

DMS: a summary

In preparing the DMS, every effort was made to achieve clarity both of layout and of language. 'It is drafted', said the Scottish Law Commission, 'in as simple a style as is consistent with legal certainty. The intention is that the scheme should be no harder to use than the rules of a golf club, and that the owners should be able to operate it with the minimum of legal or other professional assistance.'[1] That view may be optimistic. Nonetheless, the DMS is much easier to read, and much more succinct, than the average deed of conditions. For the most part it can be left to speak for itself. This account of the content of the DMS is accordingly rather brief.

The DMS has two principal aims. One is to provide a robust management structure, which acknowledges that owners are often too busy or lethargic to play an active role and that professional help will often be the best solution. The other is to provide for regular maintenance and for the building up of a reserve fund to deal with major repairs.

Management is organised around an owners' association and a manager. The former is a body corporate, ie a juristic person.[2] But it is not a company. It thus has the advantages of incorporation but without the disadvantages, and so avoids the mistake made by the equivalent scheme in England and Wales ('Commonhold') where the association is a company limited by guarantee.[3] In Scotland property owners are liberated from the need to carry around copies of the Companies Act 2006. Unlike a company, an owners' association is not registered anywhere, and there are no publicity requirements. All owners of units (ie the individual properties) are automatically association members for as long as they remain owners.[4] The association meets once a year in annual general meeting and can meet more often in certain circumstances.[5] The DMS makes provision in respect of the conduct of meetings and of voting.[6] The association has residual power, and can appoint or dismiss the manager and tell him or her what to do.[7] But the day-to-day running of the development is in the hands of the manager, who is thus the key figure in the DMS.[8]

The manager can be an individual or a juristic person such as a company or partnership. Although it is possible for one of the owners to act as manager, it is envisaged that in most cases the manager will be a professional.[9] As we have seen, the first manager is nominated in the deed of application,[10] and serves until the first annual general meeting, when he will either be reappointed or replaced.[11] It is up to the association to determine, at a general meeting, for how long a manager should be appointed and on what terms.[12]

The manager's duties are listed in rule 8, and fall into four broad categories. First, he must keep the state of the scheme property under review and carry out

1 Scottish Law Commission, Report on *Real Burdens* para 8.5.
2 2009 Order art 4(2). For the powers of the association, see DMS rule 3.2.
3 Commonhold and Leasehold Reform Act 2002 s 34. This is but one aspect of the very considerable complexity of Commonhold which no doubt explains why, so far, it has been virtually unused.
4 DMS rule 2.3.
5 DMS rule 9.
6 DMS rules 10–12.
7 DMS rules 4.2, 4.7 and 7.2.
8 DMS rules 4.4 and 4.5.
9 DMS rule 4.1.
10 Title Conditions (Scotland) Act 2003 s 71(2)(c).
11 DMS rule 7.1.
12 DMS rule 7.2.

routine maintenance.[1] This is done without the permission of the association, but improvements or alterations require the agreement of a majority of all owners.[2]

Secondly, he must organise and attend the annual general meeting and any other general meetings which become necessary or are requisitioned by the members,[3] and he must implement any decisions which a meeting makes.[4]

Thirdly, he must prepare accounts for the year just ended and propose a budget for the year to come.[5] The budget, which must be approved at a general meeting,[6] sets out the annual service charge and explains how it is to be spent.[7] This can include a contribution to a reserve (or sinking) fund which accumulates money for major repairs.[8]

Finally, the manager must interact with members in various ways. He maintains a record of names and addresses, and is notified when a unit changes hands.[9] He collects the service charge in the proportions set out in the DMS,[10] where the default rule (which can and no doubt often will be varied in the deed of application) is that each owner pays the same.[11] The manager can collect up to 25% more by way of service charge than was agreed in the annual budget;[12] if yet more is needed he must obtain approval for a supplementary budget at a general meeting.[13] The manager also has the task of enforcing the rules of the DMS against individual members.[14] Unless, however, an appropriate addition has been made to the scheme,[15] individual members cannot enforce the DMS against each other. That is an important difference from the position under a conventional deed of conditions.

The manager acts alone: the DMS is careful to avoid the inertia of management by committee. But the members at a general meeting can, if they wish, set up a committee to advise the manager.[16] While, however, the manager must listen to such advice, he does not have to take it. Only a general meeting can tell the manager what to do (or not to do).

The Scottish Law Commission's Guide

In its Report on *Real Burdens* the Scottish Law Commission included a guide, written in non-technical language, which is intended to be given to owners who

---

1 DMS rule 8(a), (b).
2 DMS rule 13.1.
3 DMS rules 9.1–9.4.
4 DMS rule 8(e).
5 DMS rules 8(d) and 18.1.
6 If it is rejected, there is provision in rules 18.3–18.5 for a revised budget.
7 DMS rule 18.2.
8 Use of the reserve fund for this purpose requires the approval of a majority of all owners: see rule 13.1.
9 DMS rules 4.9 and 8(h).
10 DMS rules 19.3–19.6.
11 DMS rule 19.1.
12 DMS rules 20.1 and 20.2.
13 DMS rule 20.3.
14 DMS rule 8(f).
15 2009 Order art 10(1).
16 DMS rule 15.

live in a development regulated by the DMS.[1] A client-friendly way of doing this would be to reproduce the DMS with the relevant part of the guide after each rule. Due to a number of small changes which have now been made to the Commission's version of the DMS, the guide has become slightly out of date, but we have made the necessary revisions. Obviously, the guide would have to be further adjusted to take account of any changes to the DMS made in the deed of application. As revised, the guide reads as follows:

GUIDE TO THE DEVELOPMENT MANAGEMENT SCHEME

The Scheme comprises a set of rules for running the development. It is divided into four parts and consists of 22 rules which are explained more fully below.

PART 1

Part 1 consists of a single rule (rule 1) which explains the meaning of some of the words used in the Scheme.

Rule 1

'The development' is the total area covered by the Scheme. A 'unit' is an individual property belonging to one of the owners. 'Scheme property' is that part of the development which is managed and maintained in common.

PART 2

Under the Scheme the development is managed by an association of all the owners. Part 2 describes how the owners' association works. Part 2 is not very important for the day-to-day running of the development, and some of the rules are technical in nature.

Rule 2

The owners' association comes into being at the same time as the Scheme itself (rule 2.1). All owners of units (ie of individual properties) are members, for as long as they remain owners. If a unit belongs to two people (such as a husband and wife) both are members (rule 2.3).

Rule 3

Rule 3 sets out the functions and powers of the association. The association's main function is to manage the development for the benefit of the members (rule 3.1). A general meeting of the association can make regulations for the use of any recreational facilities (rule 3.6). The association is restricted to the functions and powers listed in rule 3, and any other activities would be invalid.

Rule 4

The members can meet together in a general meeting. A general meeting of members is the governing body of the association and can make decisions on any matter on

---

1 See Report pp 438–42.

which the association has power to act (rule 4.5(b)). (Those matters are listed in rule 3.) Rules 9 to 12 give further information about general meetings.

The day-to-day running of the association, and of the development, is in the hands of a manager. The manager can be an ordinary person or a firm or company. A member can be manager (rule 4.1). Rule 7 gives further details. The first manager of the development, however, is the person named in rule 7.1. The duties of a manager are set out in rule 8.

The general meeting of members has ultimate authority over the manager. The manager must do what he is told by the general meeting (rule 4.7). The general meeting can also dismiss the manager (rule 4.2). However, in some cases dismissal may be a breach of the contract made with the manager and may lead to a claim for damages against the association.

Rule 4.8 gives members access to documents concerning the management of the development.

Rule 4.9 requires a person who is selling or disposing of a unit to give certain information to the manager.

Rule 5

This explains how the association signs documents (such as contracts).

Rule 6

A general meeting of members can decide that the Scheme should no longer apply (rule 16.2). In that case the association needs to be wound up. This involves a number of technical steps which are set out in rule 6 and in rule 17.

PART 3

Part 3 of the Scheme describes the day-to-day running of the development.

Rule 7

The person named in rule 7.1 as the first manager holds office only until the first annual general meeting. From that point on it is up to the members to appoint their own manager, at a general meeting (rule 7.2). All owners are members (rule 2.3). The first manager can be re-appointed, if the members so wish (rule 7.2(c)). It is up to the members to decide how long a manager should be appointed for and how much he should be paid. It is unwise to appoint someone as manager unless he has already indicated willingness to act. Rule 4 has some further provisions about appointments.

Rule 8

This rule sets out the main duties of the manager. Some other duties can be found in other parts of the Scheme. In practice the manager's most important task is usually to arrange a proper programme of maintenance. The manager can be told what to do by a general meeting of members (rules 4.7 and 8(e)), but otherwise he is free to decide himself what maintenance needs to be done. However, he is restricted in what he can spend by the budgeting arrangements described in part 4 of the Scheme.

Rule 9

Members must meet once a year for an annual general meeting (rule 9.2). Normally they will not meet more often than this. But if the need arises an extra meeting can be arranged at the instance of the manager or of a number of members (rule 9.3). It is up to the manager to organise the meeting although, if he fails to do so, any member can step in and call the meeting instead (rules 9.6 and 9.7).

Rule 9.4 lists certain documents that the manger must send to all members at least 14 days before the general meeting. These include a draft agenda, although members may add further items to the agenda at the meeting itself (rule 12.2).

Rule 10

A meeting cannot begin unless a certain number of the members or their representatives (see rule 11.1) are present. This is known as a quorum. The quorum is based on the number of votes held by the members present (or represented). There is one vote per unit (rule 11.1), and normally a quorum is 50% of the votes (rule 10.1(a)). (The meaning of 'unit' is given in rule 1.) So if there are 20 units in a development, a quorum is reached when members for 10 of the units are either present at the meeting or are represented there by someone else. However, if the development has more than 30 units, a quorum is only 35% of the votes (rule 10.1(b)). A quorum is required only for the start of the meeting, and the meeting can continue even if some members leave before the end (rule 10.4).

Rules 10.2 and 10.3 make special provision for where there is no quorum at the start of a meeting.

Rule 11

The main business at an annual general meeting will often be approval of the draft budget for the following year (see rule 18). Other decisions may also need to be made. Even after a decision has been made, it can be challenged by any member who did not support it. This is done by making an application to the sheriff court within 28 days of the meeting (or notification of the decision if the member was not at the meeting). Further details are given in article 14 of the Title Conditions (Scotland) Act 2003 (Development Management Scheme) Order 2009.

Except in the special cases mentioned in rules 13.1 and 16.2, decisions are reached by a simple majority of the votes actually cast at the meeting (rule 11.3). There is one vote per unit (rule 11.1), and the vote is exercised by the owner of the unit or (if a unit is owned by more than one person) by any of the owners (rule 11.2). (The meaning of 'unit' is given in rule 1.) An owner can give written authority to someone else (but not the manager) to vote for him (rule 11.1).

Rule 12

Rule 12 explains who is to be convener at a general meeting. The meeting must be attended by the manager, and it is up to him to keep a record of all decisions reached and other business transacted. A copy must then be sent to all members within 21 days (rule 12.3).

Rule 13

Usually decisions at a general meeting are taken by a majority of the votes *cast* (rule 11.3). But in the two cases listed in rule 13.1 (and in a third mentioned in rule 16.2), a decision requires a majority of the votes *allocated*. Each unit is allocated one vote (rule 11.1). So in a development of 20 units, a majority of the votes allocated would be 11 votes.

The two cases are:

- *A decision to use money from any reserve fund.* A reserve (or 'sinking') fund is money put away for long-term expenditure of various kinds (rule 1). Sometimes a part of the service charge is ear-marked as a contribution to the reserve fund (rule 18.2(d)). Not all developments have reserve funds, but members can decide at a general meeting to set one up.
- *A decision to carry out improvements, alterations, or demolition.* These are relatively unusual activities. *Ordinary* maintenance can be carried out by the manager without the need for a decision by members (rule 8(b)). (The meaning of 'maintenance' is given in rule 1.)

Rule 14

This rule allows a member to carry out work to scheme property in an emergency, where there is no time to consult the manager. (The meaning of 'scheme property' is given in rule 1.) The association reimburses the cost of the work.

Rule 15

This rule allows a general meeting of members to set up a committee to give advice to the manager. Such a committee is consultative only. The manager must listen but he need not take the advice. Only a general meeting of members can tell the manager what to do (rule 4.7). However, a majority of members of the advisory committee can insist on calling a general meeting (rule 9.3(c)).

Rule 16

Sometimes it may be necessary to alter the Scheme. If the alteration is to affect one unit only, the manager can sign the appropriate legal deed without special permission (rule 16.1). But he must consult the advisory committee (if there is one) and report the alteration to the next general meeting. The deed must also be signed by the owner of the unit in question and by a close neighbour (Title Conditions (Scotland) Act 2003 (Development Management Scheme) Order 2009 article 7).

Alterations affecting the whole development require the approval of a general meeting, by a majority of all the votes allocated (rule 16.2). The necessary legal deed is then signed by the manager. The same procedure applies for a decision to bring the Scheme to an end. A member who is unhappy about either decision can apply to the Lands Tribunal to have the legal deed set aside. The application must be made within eight weeks of the member being sent a copy of the deed. Further details are given in article 9 of the Title Conditions (Scotland) Act 2003 (Development Management Scheme) Order 2009 (alteration) and in section 74 of the Title Conditions (Scotland) Act 2003 (termination).

Rule 17

Rule 17 explains how surplus assets are to be distributed in the event of the association being wound up under rule 6.

PART 4

Part 4 describes the process of annual budgets, and the collection of service charge.

Rule 18

The association has a financial year, which is fixed by the manager (rule 8(c)). Each financial year the manager must prepare a draft budget which is then sent to members not later than 14 days before the annual general meeting (rules 9.4(b) and 18.1). The budget sets out the projected expenditure of the association for the year, and explains how that expenditure is to be met (rule 18.2). Usually expenditure is met by levying a service charge on the members. The draft budget must state the amount of the service charge and when it is to be collected. At the annual general meeting members vote on the draft budget. If they are not willing to approve it they can either amend it, or reject it altogether and require the manager to produce a new budget (rule 18.3).

Rule 19

Once a draft budget is approved, the manager will ask the members to pay the agreed service charge on the agreed dates. Each unit pays the same amount of service charge (rule 19.1). (The meaning of 'unit' is given in rule 1.) However, a general meeting of members has discretion to alter this rule in particular cases (rule 19.2).

   Where two or more people own a unit (such as a husband and wife), both are members of the association and either can be made to pay the full amount for that unit. (The details are given in section 11(5) (as applied by section 72) of the Title Conditions (Scotland) Act 2003.)

   No one need pay anything until a notice is received from the manager. The notice sets out the amount due and the date (or dates) on which it is to be paid (rule 19.3). If a member pays late the manager has a discretion to charge interest (rule 19.5).

   Rule 19.4 deals with the situation where a member is unable to pay.

Rule 20

Normally the manager will levy the exact amount of service charge agreed in the annual budget. But he has a discretion to ask for up to 25% more (rules 20.1 and 20.2). This gives a certain amount of flexibility and recognises the fact that it is difficult to predict future expenditure. However, the manager cannot go beyond the 25% figure without preparing a supplementary budget and submitting that budget for approval at a new general meeting (rule 20.3).

Rule 21

Rule 21 controls the way in which the manager is to invest association funds.

Rule 22

This rule sets out ways in which documents can be sent to members.

DMS rules as quasi community burdens

The DMS rules are not real burdens. Yet they bear a close legal and functional resemblance to that type of real burden known as the community burden[1] and are governed by many of the same statutory provisions, either directly (because the relevant sections of the Title Conditions Act are declared to apply)[2] or indirectly (because the relevant sections are lightly adapted and written out in the Title

---

1 Community burdens are real burdens which govern a 'community' such as a housing estate or tenement and are mutually enforceable within that community. See Title Conditions (Scotland) Act 2003 s 25.

2 Title Conditions (Scotland) Act 2003 s 72 read with 2009 Order art 5.

Conditions (Scotland) Act 2003 (Development Management Scheme) Order 2009). So, for example, DMS rules are subject to the same or similar provisions as real burdens in relation to content, liability, interpretation, variation or discharge by voluntary deed or by the Lands Tribunal, and extinction by acquiescence and negative prescription. Take the case of variation and discharge. A community burden can be varied or discharged for the whole community either by a deed granted by the owners of a majority of units (or by a manager acting on behalf of that majority) or by the Lands Tribunal on application by the owners of a quarter of the units.[1] Comparable provisions apply to DMS rules. A deed which varies or discharges a rule for the whole development must be approved by an absolute majority of owners at a general meeting and then signed by the manager,[2] while the owners of a quarter of the units can make a direct application to the Lands Tribunal.[3]

Adding amenity provisions

In practice a developer is likely to want to add amenity provisions – provisions preventing or controlling business use, or the parking of commercial vehicles, or the keeping of cats, dogs, dragons etc – to the rules on management and maintenance already contained in the DMS. If so, the developer faces two choices.

The first is whether to constitute the provisions as community burdens or as DMS rules. Either can readily be done. It would be an easy thing to add a group of community burdens to the deed of application, thus resulting in what would be in effect a combined deed of application and deed of conditions.[4] Or the amenity provisions could simply be added to the DMS itself in the form of a new group of rules constituting a new part (part 5) of the scheme.

If the developer elects for the latter course – and this will usually be simpler and more elegant – then there is a further choice to be made. As it stands, all enforcement in the DMS lies in the hands of the manager, and – unlike with community burdens – there can be no neighbour-to-neighbour enforcement.[5] But neighbour enforcement rights can be added if that is what is wanted.[6] Enforcement by the manager only may be thought to have certain advantages. It avoids the embarrassment of suing one's neighbour; enforcement is at the expense of the association and not of an individual owner; and – of particular significance given the case law on this topic[7] – there is no need to show interest to enforce. This final point requires emphasis. Many provisions in a deed of conditions are not, in reality, enforceable because no owner would ever be able to show the requisite

---

1 Title Conditions (Scotland) Act 2003 ss 33, 91.

2 2009 Order art 8; DMS rule 16.2.

3 2009 Order art 23.

4 This is the approach taken by the Property Standardisation Group: see http://www.psglegal. co.uk/.

5 DMS rule 8(f).

6 2009 Order art 10(1).

7 As to which see, most recently, *Clarke v Grantham* 2009 GWD 38-645, discussed at pp 116–19 ff above.

interest. By contrast, a manager requires no interest under the DMS and all DMS provisions are potentially enforceable. If neighbour enforcement rights are added to the DMS, there is a statutory requirement of interest to enforce,[1] but the rules remain enforceable by the manager even without interest.

Leaving

Developments crumble and may eventually have to be demolished. For that reason among others it may become necessary to bring the DMS to an end. Leaving is much like joining: with the agreement of an absolute majority of owners at a general meeting, the manager signs and registers a deed known as a deed of disapplication.[2] This can be challenged within eight weeks in the Lands Tribunal by disaffected members.[3] Otherwise the DMS comes to an end, normally on registration of the deed, and the manager must then wind up the owners' association and distribute any surplus funds to the members.[4] The association itself is automatically dissolved six months after the DMS ceases to apply.[5]

The case for the DMS

With the arrival of the DMS it will be necessary for solicitors acting for developers to decide whether to persevere with deeds of conditions and community burdens or whether to move into the new world of the DMS. In our view, there are a number of distinct advantages in the latter course.

First, the DMS is impressive as to form. It is clearly laid out, easy to read, and has been written with considerable care by professional parliamentary draftsmen. It is infinitely more attractive than the labyrinthine intricacies of many deeds of conditions. Could conveyancers do better? The evidence suggests: not usually.

Secondly, the DMS is also impressive as to content. The development is managed through an attractive blend of democracy and dictatorship: rapid day-to-day decisions by a manager with full executive power, but subject to the ultimate control of the members at a general meeting. There is provision for annual budgets, making financial planning unusually orderly. And there is the possibility of saving for major repairs by means of a reserve fund.

Thirdly, the DMS achieves something which a deed of conditions cannot: the owners' association is a juristic person. The convenience is obvious. The association can hold property – including heritable property such as 'common' areas – in its own name.[6] Through the agency of its manager[7] it can open bank

---

1 2009 Order art 10(2), (3).
2 Title Conditions (Scotland) Act 2003 s 73; DMS rule 16.2.
3 Title Conditions (Scotland) Act 2003 ss 74, 90(1)(d).
4 DMS rules 6.1–6.3. The default position is that each member receives the same amount: see rule 17.
5 DMS rule 6.4, but subject to rule 6.5.
6 The extent of the association's powers is set out in DMS rules 3.2 and 3.3. For example, while it can own any part of the development, it cannot acquire other land. The reason we put 'common' in inverted commas is that if title is vested in the association, it is not technically held in common by the various owners.
7 DMS rule 4.4.

accounts, borrow money, make investments, enter into contracts and enforce obligations owed to it. And a properly clear distinction becomes possible between the association on the one hand and the owners who from time to time comprise its members on the other.

Finally, there are various advantages of a technical nature. The ability to enforce DMS rules without the need to show interest to enforce has already been mentioned. A second advantage is the ability to make unregistered but binding rules for the use of any recreational facility in the development[1] – something which is not possible under a deed of conditions (even where, in a spirit of hopefulness, express provision for this is made, as it sometimes is).[2] A third is that, as with tenements,[3] the sheriff court has a general supervisory jurisdiction over the DMS and is empowered to resolve disputes.[4]

PUBLIC ROADS AND PUBLIC RIGHTS

'Listing' and public rights of passage

Why can the public use some roads but not others? And how does one tell *which* roads are 'public' (in this sense) and which are not? For conveyancers the rule of thumb is usually whether the road has been adopted, because a road that has been taken over by the local authority for maintenance may reasonably be assumed to be subject to public rights.[5] So on buying a property for a client it is simply a matter of checking the council's list of roads and then drawing the obvious conclusion. Though no doubt sensible as a matter of practice, however, this is open to question as a matter of law. A road does not become open to the public *because* it is adopted. Rather the position is that a road cannot be adopted *unless* it is open to the public. Public rights over roads are thus a cause of adoption and not a consequence. Adoption by itself confers no rights whatsoever.

This is clear enough from the legislation. Section 16 of the Roads (Scotland) Act 1984 says that an authority must adopt a road if requested to do so by the requisite number of frontagers (normally a majority) and if the road is of a sufficient standard. But only a 'road' is capable of being adopted, and 'road' is defined, in section 151(1), to mean 'any way (other than a waterway) over which there is a public right of passage'. A public right of passage must therefore be in existence *before* the road is adopted.

At one level this justifies the conveyancer's assumption; for if a road must be subject to public rights before it is adopted, it follows that checking whether it has been adopted is a good way of finding out whether there is a public right

---

1 DMS rule 3.6. By rule 8(g) the manager must keep a copy.
2 *Conveyancing 2002* p 67.
3 Tenements (Scotland) Act 2004 s 6.
4 2009 Order art 15.
5 A note on terminology. Roads are commonly said to be 'adopted' or 'taken over' by the local authority. These mean the same thing. Neither is used by the Roads (Scotland) Act 1984, which speaks of 'listing' a road.

to use it. Indeed in a new case, *Hamilton v Nairn*,[1] Lord Glennie appears to go further. If we understand him correctly,[2] he says that if a road is listed, then such listing is 'conclusive': 'the fact that it is listed confirms that there is a public right of passage over the road and verge'.[3] The only way in which the public right can be challenged, he suggests, is by having the road delisted – which in practice is likely to require an application for judicial review of the Council's original decision to list. Lord Glennie's remarks are *obiter*.[4] We doubt whether they can be correct. No doubt as a matter of evidence the fact that a road has been listed is a strong indication that a public right of passage exists, and exists, indeed, over the whole road, verges and all.[5] But listing does not of itself create a public right of passage, and so it is hard to see how it can be regarded as 'conclusive' of the existence of such a right.

Just occasionally the listing of a road is challenged, and twice in the last ten years the basis of the challenge has been the absence of a public right of passage. The first case was *MacKinnon v Argyll and Bute Council*,[6] decided in 2000. The other was an important new case, *Hamilton v Dumfries and Galloway Council (No 2)*,[7] with which this section of commentary is mainly concerned. As the road in *Hamilton* was the only means of access to a housing estate, it may well be that houses changed hands on the basis that, the road being listed, the public rights were secure. That, as we will see, was far from being the case.

Legal basis of public rights

We return to the question with which we began: why can the public use some roads and not others? What, in other words, is the legal basis of public rights over roads? On this fundamental and apparently simple[8] question there is remarkably little authority. In 1904 James Ferguson wrote an enormously long book on *The Law of Roads, Streets and Rights of Way, Bridges and Ferries in Scotland* – some 600, often uninviting, pages – without really getting round to giving an answer. The courts, on the whole, have been equally reticent, while the treatment in the institutional writers is patchy and, inevitably for a subject of this kind, hopelessly out of date. In the absence of authority, confusion has reigned. Partly this is a matter of history: some public roads have existed for so

---

1 [2009] CSOH 163, 2010 GWD 1-11.
2 Our hesitation is because, on one reading, Lord Glennie is only advancing the more modest (but still questionable) view that, if there is a public right of passage and a road is then listed, the public right must be taken to extend over the whole road (including the verge) as listed. The definition of 'road' in the Roads (Scotland) Act 1984 s 151(1), he says (para 14), 'does not contemplate that there may be a public right of passage over part only of a road'.
3 Paragraphs 15, 17.
4 This is because, on the evidence, he found that a common law right of access had been established in respect of the verge by possession for the prescriptive period: see para 17.
5 *Hamilton v Nairn* was a case about verges.
6 2001 SLT 1275. For a discussion, see *Conveyancing 2000* pp 49–51.
7 [2009] CSIH 13, 2009 SC 277, 2009 SLT 337, 2009 SCLR 392. The opinion of the court was given by Lord Reed.
8 As Lord Reed notes in *Hamilton* (at para 45), the words 'public right of passage' 'do not at first sight give rise to any difficulty'.

many years – centuries indeed[1] – that their origin is conjectural and the legal basis of public use obscure.[2] The institutional writers saw public roads as part of the *regalia* – as a feudal equivalent of the *res publicae* of Roman law.[3] Partly also the confusion is one of terminology. Terms like 'highway', 'public right of way' and 'public right of passage' (the term in the definition of 'road' in the 1984 Act) are used indiscriminately and, often, interchangeably. A further and persistent confusion is whether 'highway' refers to the right (ie of passage) or the thing (ie the road) over which the right is taken. Arguing, probably correctly, for the former usage, Lord Brougham, in the leading case of *Galbreath v Armour*,[4] warned that:

> [W]e are not to take 'highway' to mean that, which it is often used to mean, by the ordinary confusion of language in common parlance, where, in this case, as in many others, you confound the thing with the use of the thing. You talk of a 'reading', and sometimes confound it with a book. You talk of a 'drawing', and sometimes confound it with the paper upon which the drawing has been made.

Finally, there is an entirely natural confusion about 'public'. For on one classification a road is 'public' if it is available for public use; on another – the classification used in the Roads Act itself[5] – a road is 'public' if it has been adopted for maintenance by the local authority. It is important to keep these meanings apart. A road which is 'public' in the second sense is, as we have seen, almost always 'public' in the first; the reverse, however, is not true, for a road which is public as to use can be private as to maintenance.[6] In the *Hamilton* case Lord Reed, following Rankine,[7] calls such roads 'public rights of way (in the narrow sense)'.[8]

Against this unpromising background, it is an act of courage to embark on a restatement of the law. So it must have been tempting for the Extra Division in *Hamilton* to avoid the larger issues altogether and to decide the case on a narrow question of statutory interpretation. We should be grateful that it did not do so. In an impressive display of learning and reasoning, Lord Reed sorts through the debris to produce a convincing account of where the law now stands. The court's decision thus provides a secure basis for future development.

The facts of *Hamilton v Dumfries and Galloway Council*

The facts of *Hamilton* show that questions of the kind just discussed are not matters of merely theoretical interest. A small housing estate in Collin in Dumfriesshire,

---

1 Some roads can be traced back to Roman times, such as Dere Street in the Borders. Some others are pre-Roman.
2 For brief historical sketches, see eg J Ferguson, *The Law of Roads, Streets and Rights of Way, Bridges and Ferries in Scotland* (1904) pp 1–3; D J Cusine and R R M Paisley, *Servitudes and Rights of Way* (1998) para 18.02.
3 See eg Erskine, *Inst* 2.6.1; Hume, *Lectures* IV, 238–39.
4 (1845) 4 Bell's App 374 at 389.
5 Roads (Scotland) Act 1984 s 151(1) (definition of 'public road').
6 Moreover, the *solum* of a road may be in private ownership or public ownership.
7 J Rankine, *The Law of Landownership in Scotland* (4th edn 1909) p 329.
8 Paragraphs 36, 54.

known as Townhead Park, was completed in 1999. The only means of access to the public road was by a section of a different road which, formerly on the Council's list of public roads, had since been stopped up and thereafter deleted from the list.[1] In 2001 Mr Hamilton, the petitioner, acquired land that included the stopped-up road. When he sought to charge for vehicular use,[2] the Council searched for a solution which would allow access without payment of money. One possibility would have been compulsory purchase, but that could not be done without compensation. Instead the Council re-adopted the road, thus returning it to the list of public roads. The precise thinking involved is not clear, but the view may have been taken – although, as we have seen, it is not supported by the legislation – that if a road was 'public' in the sense of being adopted, then it became a road to which the public had an irrevocable right of access.

Mr Hamilton sought judicial review of the Council's decision. In a preliminary skirmish, he founded on the requirement that, under section 16 of the 1984 Act, an application for adoption must be made either by a majority of frontagers or by such number of frontagers as together own land which includes not less than half of the boundary fronting or abutting the road. In the present case, the application only complied with this definition if the frontagers were taken to include the owners of two houses which were adjacent to the road. These houses, however, were separated from the road by a pavement, and while the pavement was included in their respective titles, the grant turned out to be *a non domino*. By an unlucky chance, the period for positive prescription was not completed until 2 June 2005, which was a week after the date on which the road was adopted. The court accepted that, for this reason, the adoption was flawed and fell to be reduced,[3] and this view was confirmed in the Inner House.[4]

By the time that this decision was reached, prescription had of course long since run, so that it would be possible for the Council to embark once again on the process of adoption. To make sure that this did not happen, Mr Hamilton sought declarator that the road was not now a 'road' within the 1984 Act and so could not be adopted.[5] At first instance, Lady Smith rejected this argument.[6] In her view, the 'public right of passage' mentioned in the statutory definition of road indicated a right which could fall short of a full public right of way, for

---

1 It should be noted that a road can be delisted (ie 'unadopted') without also being stopped up (ie extinguished as a public right of passage). Why the local authority did both we do not know. Had it merely delisted the road, the ensuing problems would never have happened. A delisted road does not cease to be subject to a public right of passage and so can always be relisted. But stopping-up has irrevocable consequences. See further A Faulds et al, *Scottish Roads Law* (2nd edn 2008) p 60.

2 As for non-vehicular use, that would be likely to be protected under the 'right to roam' provisions in part 1 of the Land Reform (Scotland) Act 2003.

3 [2007] CSOH 96, 2007 GWD 20-347.

4 [2007] CSIH 75, 2007 GWD 34-582.

5 The various procedural stages are set out in 2009 SC 277 at paras 16–22. In fact, the question now raised had already been considered by Lord Kingarth at an earlier stage of the proceedings: see [2006] CSOH 210. He concluded that the disputed section was a 'road' because a public right of passage could be established either by the owner's permission or tolerance, or alternatively by possession which fell short of the 20 years required for (proper) public rights of way.

6 [2008] CSOH 65, 2008 SLT 531.

which 20 years' prescriptive possession was needed. In the present case there
had been use by the public for a number of years and that, said Lady Smith,
was enough. The phase of the case now under discussion is the appeal against
that decision.

Three methods of constitution

In considering the appeal, the first task which the Extra Division set itself was
to embark on a detailed consideration of the authorities, and in particular of
those from the nineteenth century. As those authorities showed, a right of
highway or public right of way – the terms were interchangeable – was usually
created by positive prescription. In the modern law, indeed, this was the
subject of a dedicated statutory provision: section 3(3) of the Prescription and
Limitation (Scotland) Act 1973, which requires possession for 20 years. But there
were two further methods of creation.[1] One was grant by the road's owner,
whether express or, more usually, implied. The other was creation by what
an English writer on this topic from the early nineteenth century called 'that
all-powerful instrument, an Act of Parliament'.[2] There was no fourth method
of creation.

How did these methods relate to the 'public right of passage' required by the
definition of 'road' in the 1984 Act? The Extra Division held, surely correctly, that
the statutory words 'would, according to their ordinary meaning, refer to any
way which any member of the public is entitled, as a matter of right, to use for
the purpose of passage'.[3] Far from being a new statutory right, with more lenient
rules of constitution, a public right of passage was simply a re-expression of the
right more familiarly known as public right of way or highway. It was therefore
subject to the same rules of constitution. Any other view would cause obvious
difficulties. If a public right of passage was a new statutory concept, with new
rules of constitution, one would expect those rules to be found in the 1984 Act.
They were not. Further, if (as Lady Smith had suggested) a public right of passage
could be established by possession falling short of the prescriptive period, and
if it nonetheless conferred identical rights to those of a public right of way, it
was difficult to see what function was now performed by section 3(3) of the
Prescription Act.

Against this approach stood *Cowie v Strathclyde Council*,[4] which seemed to
support a statutory right of passage of the very kind that the Extra Division
was now rejecting; and, as a decision of the First Division, it was binding on the
court in *Hamilton*. The Extra Division disposed of *Cowie* firmly if not entirely
convincingly.[5] *Cowie* was, admittedly, a decision which 'appears to have caused

---

1 Paragraphs 38–39 and 56.
2 R Wellbeloved, *A Treatise on the Law relating to Highways* (1829) p 41. Note that access rights under
  part 1 of the Land Reform (Scotland) Act 2003 are declared, by s 5(6) of that Act, *not* to constitute
  public rights of passage for the purposes of the Roads (Scotland) Act 1984.
3 Paragraph 45.
4 8 July 1986, First Division (unreported).
5 Paragraph 56.

difficulty'. But not only was it decided without consideration of authority, but 'properly understood' it was not inconsistent with the approach now being adopted by the Extra Division.[1]

In *Hamilton* the use by the house owners fell short of the necessary 20 years. It followed, therefore, that no 'public right of passage' was in existence. As the disputed section was not therefore a 'road', it could not, the Extra Division concluded, be adopted by the Council.

If, however, the logic is compelling, the result is an unhappy one, not just for the Council (which must now pick up the bill – reputedly £300,000 – for the expenses of a long litigation) but also for the owners of the houses in the Townhead Park estate. Their reaction was reported in the *Dumfries & Galloway Standard* in this way:[2]

> Former community councillor Jim Dalziel who lives on the estate said he had spoken to about half the people there and they were 'sick as parrots'. 'Everybody is worried,' he said. 'This has lasted for five years. Our houses have been valueless. We have two young couples who wanted to sell but couldn't. They have had to build extensions instead. The time it has taken to get to this point is ridiculous. The people I have spoken to are questioning what the council and the solicitors did. The solicitors took our money. They are supposed to have checked the Land Registry but we were not told of any problems. Then this man comes along and suddenly it's not okay. They think the solicitors did not do their research of the Land Registry properly but they took our money.

Rather than pay anything to Mr Hamilton there was apparently talk of the Council obtaining an alternative access to the public road by buying and then knocking down one of the houses. But we understand that this has not happened, and that instead the Council has bought the road from Mr Hamilton.

Constitution by grant

Before leaving this topic, it seems worth saying just a little about one of the other methods of creating public rights over roads: constitution by grant. Grant may be express or implied, and a moment's reflection suggests that implied grant, at least, is of some significance. It is what happens, presumably, when a developer builds a road and asks the council to take it over, but potentially it extends to other cases where a road is made available to the public in general, whether by a private individual or by a public authority.[3] In England, implied grant was once a

---

1 The statement that the right did not have to be between public places should not, the Extra Division said, be taken as indicating some right which fell short of a public right of way. Rather, the First Division had in mind the methods of constitution other than prescription; it was only for the latter that the requirement of public places applied. This seems an optimistic reading of the passage in question. There is no mention of other methods of constitution, and no suggestion that the First Division had those in mind.

2 *Dumfries & Galloway Standard* 25 Feb 2009.

3 In *Hamilton* (para 39), Lord Reed quotes Lord Kinnear in *Magistrates of Edinburgh v North British Rly* (1904) 6 F 620 at 639: 'landowners within burghs may lay out ground for streets in such a way as to create an indefeasible right in the public'.

particularly important doctrine (on account of a very long period of prescription), and so there is in that country a substantial case law on 'dedication' of roads to the public.[1] And in Scotland there was a longstanding confusion between implied grant and prescription, leading to the idea, now abandoned,[2] that prescription was properly explained on the basis of an implied grant.

In the context so far discussed, a grant is permanent and irrevocable. But in principle such a grant might also be temporary and revocable. Suppose, for example, an owner makes clear by words or by conduct (i) that the public is welcome to use his road for the foreseeable future but (ii) that nevertheless he reserves the right to close the road to the public should he wish to do so. Since the owner is (until revocation) under an obligation to allow the public to use the road, it must follow that the public has a corresponding right to do so. No doubt that right is personal and revocable. Yet, for all that, it is arguably a 'public right of passage' within the meaning of the 2004 Act. That conclusion, however, is resisted by the Extra Division in *Hamilton*: a public right of passage cannot, the court says, be 'dependent on the licence or tolerance of the owner of the solum of the way in question'.[3] For that reason, the court found it necessary to disapprove two statements to the contrary in recent case law.[4]

This view may not take account of the difference between 'licence' and 'tolerance'. The latter, doubtless, imposes no obligations and confers no rights. It is merely a reaction to present events. But the former is an undertaking as to future conduct. It is an undertaking that, for as long as the licence remains in place, the public can make use of the road. In short it is what in Roman law was called a *precarium*.[5] It seems plausible to characterise a licence as a public right of passage. Of course, a grant which is revocable can always be revoked.[6] Indeed Mr Hamilton sought to do precisely that when, in order to forestall any argument that a grant could be inferred from his (previous) conduct in allowing the road to be used, he wrote through his solicitors to each of the owners at Townhead Park. The letter said:[7]

> We are therefore writing to confirm that with immediate effect you should consider yourselves prohibited from using that area of road which was the subject of the previous purported adoption order, without Mr Hamilton's express permission. For the avoidance of doubt our client will be happy to grant such permission when met by your written intimation of a willingness to negotiate terms.

1 See eg R Megarry and W Wade, *The Law of Real Property* (7th edn by C Harpum, S Bridge and M Dixon, 2008) paras 27–026 and 27–027. 'Dedication' may also be express. As to whether Scots law recognises the principle of 'dedication', see most recently *Hamilton v Nairn* [2009] CSOH 163 at para 22 per Lord Glennie (summarising the arguments of counsel).
2 The turning point was *Mann v Brodie* (1885) 12 R (HL) 52.
3 Paragraph 40.
4 *Viewpoint Housing Association Ltd v Lothian Regional Council* 1993 SLT 921 at 927 per Lord Cameron of Lochbroom; *MacKinnon v Argyll and Bute Council* 2001 SLT 1275 at 1293 per Lord Osborne.
5 For a discussion of the equivalent doctrine in Scotland, see K G C Reid, *The Law of Property in Scotland* (1996) para 128.
6 *MacKinnon v Argyll and Bute Council* 2001 SLT 1275 at 1293 per Lord Osborne.
7 Presumably such a letter could be sent after as well as before adoption of the road.

But unless or until there is revocation, there is much to be said for the view that a road which is subject to such a right is a 'road' within the 1984 Act, with all that that entails.

PUBLIC ACCESS RIGHTS

The commercial dimension

Part 1 of the Land Reform (Scotland) Act 2003 introduced what is commonly called the right to roam.[1] The mental picture this calls up is that of the weekend and holiday walker: Ordnance Survey map, thermos of tea, packet of sandwiches, compass, binoculars, field-guides to the British flora and British birds, anorak, 'stout footwear', woolly hat, and walking stick. All very respectable, and not someone that reasonable landowners would ever have objected to. Had all landowners been reasonable, part 1 of the 2003 Act might never have been passed, because the need for it would never have been felt. But not all landowners were reasonable, the need was felt, and the Act was passed.

What about access rights being used commercially? That sounds a startling idea. But the 2003 Act allows it to some extent. Section 1(3) says:

> (3) The right set out ... above may be exercised only –
>   (a) for recreational purposes;
>   (b) for the purposes of carrying on a relevant educational activity; or
>   (c) for the purposes of carrying on, commercially or for profit, an activity which the person exercising the right could carry on otherwise than commercially or for profit.

Paragraph (c) is not easy to understand at first sight. The *Scottish Outdoor Access Code*[2] has a useful explanation:[3]

> Access rights extend to activities carried out commercially or for profit, provided that these activities could also be carried on other than commercially or for profit (ie by the general public for recreational purposes or for educational activities or for crossing land). For example, a mountain guide who is taking a customer out hill-walking is carrying on a commercial activity but this falls within access rights because the activity involved – hill-walking – could be done by anyone else exercising access rights. The same would apply to a canoe instructor from a commercial outdoor pursuits centre with a party of canoeists. Other examples would be a commercial writer or photographer writing about or taking photographs of the natural or cultural heritage.

The example of the mountain guide is, of course, one that paragraph (c) is obviously meant to cover. But the rule means that anyone can make commercial

---

1 See *Conveyancing 2003* pp 132–35; T Guthrie, 'Access rights', in R Rennie (ed), *The Promised Land: Property Law Reform* (2008) p 125.
2 Available at http://www.snh.org.uk/pdfs/access/approvedcode050604.pdf. The Code was made under s 10 of the Land Reform (Scotland) Act 2003.
3 Paragraph 2.9.

use of another person's land, without paying for it, so long as the use can be shoehorned into paragraph (c). Two cases from 2009 are illustrative: *Creelman v Argyll and Bute Council*[1] and *Tuley v Highland Council*.[2]

Creelman

Mr and Mrs Creelman were the owners of a six-acre property at Glendaruel, Argyll. It had two houses on it, and indeed had previously been two separate plots. The Creelmans lived in one of the houses ('Stronardron') and let out the other ('Dunans Lodge') as a holiday house. When they bought the properties (in 2000 as to one part and in 2004 as to the other) the grounds had run wild and become generally impenetrable. The Creelmans were keen gardeners and gradually turned the grounds into attractive gardens. Next door was Dunans Castle, owned by Mr Dickson Spain. We quote the sheriff:[3]

> This dispute ... started as a result of the Pursuers [the Creelmans] refusing the owner of the neighbouring property at Dunans Castle permission to use their land for a commercial venture. It seemed that Mr Dickson Spain the owner thereof wanted to take visitors to his castle through the Pursuers' land as part of a tour. When the Pursuers intimated they were not agreeable to this Mr Dickson Spain had stated, 'There is always land reform'. Mr Creelman believed that Mr Dickson Spain had made a complaint to the Defenders [Argyll and Bute Council] who had then carried out certain investigations and gone ahead with the service of the notices.

When the Creelmans put up a notice saying that there was no public access along the track leading through their ground, and blocked it off with wire, the Council served a notice under section 14(2) of the 2003 Act requiring them to remove the sign and the wire. The Creelmans appealed against the notice, arguing that their entire property was free from access rights on the basis of the privacy rule found in section 6(1)(b)(iv). This says that, where there is a house, there is exempt from access rights:

> ... sufficient adjacent land to enable persons living there to have reasonable measures of privacy in that house ... and to ensure that their enjoyment of that house ... is not unreasonably disturbed.

The sheriff's task was how to apply this necessarily vague formula to the facts of the case. The case was thus essentially similar to such cases as *Gloag v Perth and Kinross Council*[4] and *Snowie v Stirling Council*.[5]

One bit of guidance given by the 2003 Act is section 7(5) which says:

> There are included among the factors which go to determine what extent of land is sufficient for the purposes mentioned in section 6(1)(b)(iv) above, the location and other characteristics of the house or other place.

---

1 2009 SLT (Sh Ct) 165.
2 [2009] CSIH 31A, 2009 SC 456, 2009 SLT 616.
3 Sheriff D Livingston, at para 5 of his note.
4 2007 SCLR 530. See *Conveyancing 2007* pp 127–35.
5 2008 SLT (Sh Ct) 61. See *Conveyancing 2008* pp 112–14.

The sheriff noted that 'the land here was small for a house the size of Stronardron in that type of locality'.[1] He also noted:[2]

> The access track runs close to Dunans Lodge. It is only about 13 metres or so away from the house at Stronardron. I cannot see how having people walking up and down that path can possibly afford reasonable privacy at these points. Persons using the path can see into the two houses at various points on the path.

So the Creelmans prevailed.[3]

Tuley

In the *Tuley* case landowners had been unsuccessful in the sheriff court.[4] The case is an astonishing one, and indeed the sort of case that gives access rights a bad name. We quote from the sheriff's fifth finding in fact:

> Since acquiring Feddonhill Wood the pursuers have developed it as an amenity and recreational area. They have created an area for use by mountain bikers within the woodland. They have actively encouraged walkers, including walkers with dogs both on and off the lead to use the woodland. The woodland is used by members of the public for recreational walking. The pursuers have incurred time and expense in making various tracks in the woodland suitable for walkers. They have kept the tracks clear and well drained. They have cultivated flora and provided seats for walkers.

So the Tuleys were the model landowners. That they should have been dragged through the courts under part 1 of the 2003 Act seems almost incredible. The reason is that the neighbouring property was a riding school. The altruistic Tuleys were happy for the riding school to use their land without paying for it. All the paths in the wood were open to walkers, and some were open to riders. The Tuleys asked riders to keep off certain paths, notably the 'Red Path', because it was unsuitable for riding. A path can easily break up under regular riding, and this path did not have a suitable surface. For it to continue to be suitable for walkers, riding was not allowed. At each end of this path there was a gate that walkers could get through but horses could not.

The local authority served a notice under section 14 of the 2003 Act requiring the Tuleys to unlock the gates so that the path would be open for riding. After a proof, the sheriff found that very light usage would not be a problem, but medium or heavy usage would be. Since very light usage would not be a problem, such usage would be 'responsible' and hence the Tuleys could not lawfully prevent it. The sheriff commented:[5]

---

1 Paragraph 63.
2 Paragraph 61.
3 For a case in which a path similarly situated, but in a suburb, was held not to be exempt from access rights, see *Forbes v Fife Council* 2009 SLT (Sh Ct) 71, discussed below.
4 *Tuley v Highland Council* 2007 SLT (Sh Ct) 97. See *Conveyancing 2007* pp 135–39.
5 Paragraph 126. The sheriff was A L Macfadyen.

The pursuers have a genuine apprehension. However, in my view, their remedy lies in co-operation with the defenders in the erection of signs warning horse riders not to enter the network of paths to the north of the red path at any time and warning against riding in weather or soil conditions when the creation of mud is an obvious risk of the presence of horses on the red path.

The Tuleys appealed, and their appeal has been successful.[1] An Extra Division of the Court of Session took a different view from the sheriff. The evidence of the expert witness led by the pursuers before the sheriff, about the vulnerability of the paths in question, had not been challenged by the Council. In the view of the court:[2]

> It makes little sense to say that the landowner must allow a mode of access which will be likely to prove productive of damage to the land and suffer that damage without being able to take preventative steps. Additionally, as counsel for the defenders appeared to recognise, the contention that no preventative steps could be taken prior to the occurrence of damage raised difficult practical issues as to the extent of the predictable damage which the landowner must endure (without compensation) before he could take measures to prevent the occurrence of yet further damage. Counsel vaguely suggested that there might be 'discussions' but was not able to offer any satisfactory answer to the problem which he recognised to lie within his own proposition.

Hence:[3]

> The pursuers were acting responsibly in preventing equestrian access (and also, incidentally, motorised access by motorcycles or 'quad bikes') to the northern sector which they intended for the enjoyment of their pedestrian visitors.

While the result seems correct, the court does not seem to tie it in particularly closely with specific provisions of the Act. Presumably if the landowner is acting responsibly in preventing a mode of access, access takers would be acting irresponsibly if they insisted on taking it. Here sections 2 and 3 are key.

Having reached this conclusion on the basis of evaluation of the expert evidence, the court had no need to consider the meaning of section 14.[4] Happily, however, it did so. Section 14 of the 2003 Act says:

(1) The owner of land in respect of which access rights are exercisable shall not, for the purpose or for the main purpose of preventing or deterring any person entitled to exercise these rights from doing so –

  (a) put up any sign or notice;

  (b) put up any fence or wall, or plant, grow or permit to grow any hedge, tree or other vegetation;

---

1 *Tuley v Highland Council* [2009] CSIH 31A, 2009 SC 456, 2009 SLT 616. The opinion of the court is given by Lord Eassie.
2 Paragraph 33.
3 Paragraph 34. As for the reference to motorcycles and quad bikes, see s 9(f) of the 2003 Act.
4 As the court itself notes at para 36.

    (c) position or leave at large any animal;

    (d) carry out any agricultural or other operation on the land; or

    (e) take, or fail to take, any other action.

(2)   Where the local authority consider that anything has been done in contravention of subsection (1) above they may, by written notice served on the owner of the land, require that such remedial action as is specified in the notice be taken by the owner of the land within such reasonable time as is so specified.

The Council had taken enforcement action under section 14(2). But a section 14(2) notice is valid only if there has been an infraction of section 14(1), and there can be a section 14(1) infraction only if the obstruction (etc) is 'for the purpose or for the main purpose of preventing or deterring' the exercise of responsible access. As the court said, the 2003 Act:[1]

> envisages many agricultural activities which may have the foreseeable result of preventing responsible access but which are done for the wider purposes of the agricultural management of the land. Thus, by way of example, the establishment of a hedge may have the foreseeable and direct result of preventing access across what was otherwise open land but yet be done for the genuine purpose of enabling the enclosure of livestock, the provision to the livestock of shelter, and the provision of habitat for birds and other wildlife.

It added:[2]

There is no suggestion that the pursuers' concern to prevent damage to the red track (and the other paths), and thereby maintain an appropriate and pleasant environment for the walking public was other than genuine.

Hence there was no breach of section 14(1) and hence the section 14(2) notice failed.

Since local authorities typically seek to enforce access rights through section 14 notices, this usefully highlights a limitation in the scope of the provision.[3] But it is worth noting in this connection that section 13, which imposes on local authorities the duty to uphold access rights, does not have the limitation to be found in section 14. No doubt local authorities tend to use the latter rather than the former because it has an easy-to-use enforcement method – the section 14 notice – whereas section 13 is silent about enforcement.[4] So: section 13 is broader, but harder to enforce, and section 14 is narrower, but easier to enforce.

It seems worth adding that the question of whether horse-riding is a permissible way of exercising access rights was not raised in this case. In our view the point is not wholly clear.[5] If it is permissible, then it is difficult to see

---

1 Paragraph 42.
2 Paragraph 43.
3 Another limitation is highlighted in *Aviemore Highland Resort Ltd v Cairngorms National Park Authority* 2009 SLT (Sh Ct) 97, discussed below.
4 It might be argued that s 13 is merely ancillary to s 14, and so not capable of separate enforcement, but that is not how we read the two sections.
5 See *Conveyancing 2007* pp 138–39.

why huntsmen, with red jackets, jodhpurs and breeches, accompanied by hounds, are not free (as they were not before the 2003 Act) to pursue foxes over farmland regardless of the owner's objections, unless the owner can come up with some good reason[1] as the Tuleys did.

As an addendum, it should be mentioned that the Scotways website[2] notes an interim interdict decision, *Williamson v Highland Activities Ltd*. The defender[3] organised rafting on the River Garry and in doing so used the pursuer's land in a way that did not constitute, the pursuer argued, responsible access. One reason was damage to paths. Here there is an obvious parallel to the *Tuley* case, and yet another case of the commercial use, without payment, of land belonging to others, and of the key question of responsible versus irresponsible access. The next case to be considered also involves the latter issue, but is not a case of commercial use.[4]

Forbes

Forbes v Fife Council[5] is a case that is like *Tuley* is some ways but not in others. There was a path in Glenrothes that was not a public right of way but which was nevertheless used by the public as a route. The owners put up gates at each end and locked them.[6] The local authority issued a section 14 notice. The evidence showed that the main reason for erecting the gates was that during the hours of darkness there was antisocial behaviour.

The owners argued (a) that access rights did not cover the path, because of their privacy rights, and (b) *esto* they did cover the path, they were still entitled to close it to prevent irresponsible use. On the first point the sheriff[7] held against them. As this path was more or less as close to the houses as was the path in *Creelman*, what one is seeing here is a distinction based on what section 7(5) of the 2003 Act calls 'locality'.[8]

---

1 And so long as the Protection of Wild Mammals (Scotland) Act 2002 is not contravened.

2 http://www.scotways.com/. The case is found in the 'June 2009' entry in the 'Court Cases' section of the website. We have no further information about this beyond what is on the website.

3 Whose website at http://www.highlandactivities.co.uk/ makes for interesting reading.

4 For valuable discussion of both *Tuley* and *Forbes*, see M Combe, 'Access to land and to land-ownership' (2010) 14 *Edinburgh Law Review* 106.

5 2009 SLT (Sh Ct) 71.

6 In fact it does not appear that all the owners were involved. At common law an action of this sort would normally require unanimity. But this issue was not raised in the case.

7 Sheriff William Holligan.

8 Since the nature of a locality may change, presumably the extent of exempt ground could wax and wane. If Glendaruel were to become an urban area, the path past the Creelmans' house might cease to be exempt. (If so, then if a local authority were to grant planning permission for new houses, that could impose access rights on land that was, before the grant of planning permission, exempt.) Conversely, if the suburb of Glenrothes in which the Forbes lived were to become more rural, for instance by the demolition of houses, the path past the Forbes' house might become exempt. Hence decisions by the courts on particular cases are not, it would seem, wholly permanent decisions because the issue could be opened up by change of circumstances. Still, in practice they would tend to stick. So if a landowner knows of a grant of planning permission that would alter the locality, it might be prudent to respond by immediately seeking declarator of exempt status, and of course doing so before the new houses start to go up.

On the second point the sheriff made an interesting and creative decision. He held, against the Council, that closure at night was legitimate, but, against the owners, that closure during the day was illegitimate. The basis for this in the legislation is that the access right is one of responsible access, so that the owners were entitled to prevent irresponsible, but not responsible, access, and that could reasonably be achieved by daytime opening and night-time closure. Of course, it would also exclude some responsible access at night. One sees here a central problem for landowners. Some people using the land will do so responsibly but some will not. Only the former are acting within their 2003 Act rights, so that the landowner is entitled to exclude the latter. But in practice how does the landowner sieve them out? The six sets of co-owners of the path could in theory have hired bouncers, 24 hours a day, seven days a week, to admit the responsible and to exclude the irresponsible. But in practice that would have been out of the question. The 2003 Act does not offer a solution. Both *Tuley* and *Forbes* on their very different facts address this basic problem.

Curiously, at the very time it issued its enforcement notice to the owners, the Council was considering closing a nearby pedestrian public right of way because of antisocial behaviour. A few weeks after serving the enforcement notice it did indeed close the public right of way. It continued with the enforcement action against the owners.

Aviemore

Lastly, *Aviemore Highland Resort Ltd v Cairngorms National Park Authority*.[1] Can a section 14 notice be used by a local authority in relation to a fence, hedge etc that already existed before the 2003 Act came into force? Sheriff Principal Sir Stephen Young held that it could not be so used. The point is a short one, but important. Nevertheless, it is limited to section 14. As mentioned above, while in practice the enforcement of access rights tends to turn on section 14, that section has limitations not to be found in other provisions of the 2003 Act. It may also be noted that knowing whether a hedge etc pre-dates or post-dates the Act may not always be easy and will become more difficult as the years pass.

BOUNDARY DISPUTES

Contradiction, prescription and separate tenements

Where one at least of the titles is held on the Sasine Register,[2] positive prescription is often the surest way of resolving a boundary dispute. Victory goes to the person who was in possession – provided, of course, that this was done on the basis of a suitable title recorded in the Register of Sasines.[3]

---

1 2009 SLT (Sh Ct) 97.
2 It is not always realised that prescriptive acquisition on a Sasine title can defeat even an indemnified title in the Land Register.
3 For Land Register titles, prescription runs only in the highly unusual case of indemnity having been excluded: see Prescription and Limitation (Scotland) Act 1973 s 1(1)(b).

What makes a title suitable for this purpose? In its comfortingly familiar language, the Prescription Act requires 'a deed which is sufficient in respect of its terms to constitute in favour of that person [ie the possessor] a real right in (i) that land or (ii) land of a description *habile* to include that land'.[1] Often the issue is analysed by reference to whether the description is 'bounding', on the basis that a bounding title will exclude anything which lies outside it. But this approach is simplistic and, often, unhelpful. It risks entanglement with the highly technical question of bounding descriptions; it seems to suggest what is not true, namely that a *non*-bounding title will necessarily be *habile* for prescription; and above all, it draws attention away from the central question for discussion, which is simply whether the description in the deed can be read as including the land which is targeted for acquisition.

A more sophisticated approach is to divide descriptions into four categories, as follows:

(a) *Uncontradicted inclusion.* The words used are such that they plainly include the targeted property and there is nothing else in the description to contradict that inclusion.

(b) *Ambiguity.* The words used are such that they might or might not include the targeted property.

(c) *Uncontradicted exclusion.* The words plainly exclude the targeted property and there is nothing else in the description to contradict that exclusion.

(d) *Contradicted exclusion/inclusion.* The words plainly exclude the targeted property but other words in the description, equally plainly, include it.

In relation to the first three categories the law is well established. A description will found prescription where it includes the targeted property or where, though unclear and ambiguous, it is *capable* of being read as including the property.[2] Conversely, a description will not found prescription where there is an uncontradicted exclusion of the property.[3] This indeed is what is normally meant by a bounding description, ie one in which the targeted property falls on the wrong side of the boundary.

On the final category (contradicted exclusion/inclusion) there has until now been an unfortunate absence of authority. *Nisbet v Hogg*,[4] a decision from the middle of the last century, may be the only clear example.[5] This concerned a dispute as to whether the description in a deed was *habile* to include a triangular area of land. On the one hand, the description made express mention of this

---

1 Prescription and Limitation (Scotland) Act 1973 s 1(1).
2 The leading case is *Auld v Hay* (1880) 7 R 663.
3 Eg *Gordon v Grant* (1850) 13 D 1.
4 1950 SLT 289.
5 *Rutco Inc v Jamieson* 2004 GWD 30-620 can possibly be read as another, although on one view the competing elements of the description could be reconciled. For a discussion, see *Conveyancing 2004* pp 111–12.

area. On the other hand, the subjects were declared to be as described in a prior disposition which, on inspection, plainly excluded the triangular area. For Lord Carmont this clear exclusion was fatal to the running of prescription. The other judges, however, decided in effect that contradiction was to be treated in the same way as ambiguity – in other words, that prescription will run provided that one at least of the contradictory elements is capable of being read as including the property in question.

The new case of *Compugraphics International Ltd v Nikolic*[1] is welcome confirmation of this approach. The facts were unusual.[2] The pursuer owned a unit in Eastfield Industrial Estate in Glenrothes. Its title was in the Register of Sasines, being a split-off feu disposition by Glenrothes Development Corporation, dating from 1983, which conveyed to the pursuer:

> ALL and WHOLE that area of ground extending to 313 decimal or one-thousandth parts of a hectare or thereby lying to the south of Newark Road North forming part of the Eastfield Industrial Estate situated in the designated area of the new town of Glenrothes, ... all as the said area of ground is delineated and shown coloured pink on the plan annexed and signed as relative hereto ... Together with the factory premises and others erected on the feu ...

According to the plan, the factory premises were built exactly on the southern boundary of the feu.

The factory was serviced by an air-conditioning system which comprised an elaborate network of ducts and pipes. The ductwork ultimately passed to the outside where it was fixed to the south wall of the building and further supported by metal posts secured to the ground. It was accepted – as indeed the plan made clear – that the ground at this point was part of the adjoining unit, which was now the property of the defender. In other words, the ductwork overhung, and was supported by, the defender's land.

The pursuer sought declarator that it was heritable proprietor of the ductwork, on the basis of positive prescription.[3] The difficulty was that the 1983 deed contained contradictory statements as to whether the ductwork was included. On the one hand it conveyed 'the factory premises' which, already in 1983, included the ductwork (assuming that the ductwork can be regarded as part of the factory).[4] On the other hand, the ductwork was plainly excluded from the subjects as shown on the plan.[5] The court accepted that the title was *habile* for the purposes of prescription. 'It seems to me', said Lord Bracadale, 'that the 1983 disposition is capable of being construed as a bounding title but it is also capable of other interpretation.'[6]

---

1 [2009] CSOH 54, 2009 GWD 19-311.
2 We take the facts from the court's opinion: there has not been a proof.
3 It also claimed, in the alternative, a servitude right. For that side of the case see p 103 above.
4 The issue of accession is discussed below.
5 Unless the plan could be regarded as describing the subjects only at the level of the surface of the ground.
6 Paragraph 19.

This led on to another difficulty. The pursuer sought declarator of ownership, not of the ground on which the ductwork was secured – for that, it was accepted by both parties, was the property of the defender – but of the ductwork itself. Ordinarily, this issue would be governed by the law of accession. But from the pursuer's point of view accession was both uncertain and inadequate. It was uncertain because the ductwork was attached *both* to the wall (the property of the pursuer) *and also* to the ground (the property of the defender). Which should prevail was, we assume, unclear. And it was inadequate because it failed to deal with the airspace which the ductwork occupied. There was no value in establishing ownership of the ductwork by accession if the airspace remained the property of the defender, because in that case the ductwork would be an encroachment which the defender could insist on having removed.[1]

The pursuer's claim was accordingly a bolder one. The effect of prescription, the pursuer argued, was to establish ownership *both* of the ductwork (assuming it was not already the pursuer's by accession) *and* of the space which it occupied. In technical language, the ductwork was said to be a (conventional) separate tenement – heritable property owned separately from the ownership of the ground, rather like minerals or a flatted property. Unfortunately, the law of separate tenements is in disarray. On the basis of the rather meagre authorities, one of us has speculated that, with the firmly established exception of a tenement flat, something which is heritable by accession cannot be separated from the land to which it has acceded.[2] If that is correct, the ductwork could not be a separate tenement. Certainly that has been the conclusion reached by the courts in respect of trees, pipes and rock anchors.[3] It is of course easy to say that supported ductwork is different from items more firmly embedded in the ground, and that was the position adopted by Lord Bracadale in finding for the pursuer.[4] But that is a merely negative argument. No positive reason was advanced for the view that airspace above the ground could be owned separately, and no consideration was given to the resulting complexity in ownership patterns or to other potential disadvantages. Here, as elsewhere in the decision, the court seems favourably disposed towards the pursuer, and disinclined to allow technical considerations to obstruct what it may have regarded as a fair and commonsense result.[5] We understand that the decision has been appealed.

Three further remarks may be made about the decision in *Compugraphics*. First, the court's decision on prescription relied on the idea that the ductwork was a pertinent of the factory.[6] It is hard to see why. There is no doctrinal advantage in such an approach, for even a pertinent cannot override a bounding description;

---

1 Issues of accession were not, however, discussed in the case.
2 K G C Reid, *The Law of Property in Scotland* (1996) para 212.
3 Respectively *Paul v Cuthbertson* (1840) 2 D 1286; *Crichton v Turnbull* 1946 SC 52; *Property Selection & Investment v United Friendly Insurance plc* 1999 SLT 975.
4 Paragraph 22. Lord Bracadale also found for the pursuer in respect of an *esto* case that the ductwork could be justified as a servitude of overhang. See p 103 above.
5 'The result of the case', Professor Gordon writes, 'seems fair': see W M Gordon, 'Servitudes abounding' (2009) 13 *Edinburgh Law Review* 519 at 523. And no doubt it does.
6 Paragraph 19.

and a thing which is attached to a building is much more readily classified as a part than as a pertinent.[1]

Secondly, the pursuer might have won even without prescription. Assuming that the pursuer's unit was sold by Glenrothes Development Corporation before the defender's, the granter was in a position to confer a good title to the ductwork without the need for prescription. In other words, a separate tenement could have been created by force of the original feu disposition. This argument seems to have been put in *Compugraphics* but not insisted on.

Finally, little account seems to have been taken of the fact that the defender, having acquired the property recently, held on the basis of a title in the Land Register. Not only was his ownership guaranteed and undeniable – as a result of the Keeper's so-called Midas touch – but it was unqualified except in respect of overriding interests or in so far as expressly burdened in his title sheet.[2] It seems safe to say that the title sheet was silent on the subject of the ductwork. Must it not then follow that the defender owned the land *a coelo usque ad centrum*, ductwork and all?[3]

Descriptions in the Land Register

The advantages of a map-based system of registration are obvious; and certainly the Land Register often clarifies much that was unclear from the vague words and rough-and-ready plans – the 'sketch or plan' beloved of the Victorian conveyancer – which are so often found in the Register of Sasines. It would, however, be naïve to suppose that registration of title will, of itself, eliminate disputes as to boundaries. For mapping on the Land Register has its own inevitable limitations. Three are thrown up by case law during 2009.

The problem of tenements

Register of Scotland's *Legal Manual* identifies three methods of mapping which can be used on first registration.[4] These are (i) site plan (steading method), (ii) precise extent method, and (iii) tinting method. Method (ii), as the name suggests, applies where the property can be precisely identified and defined within a red edge on the title plan. That is the normal method. But where ownership, though clear, is complex, method (ii) gives way to method (iii), which abandons the use of a red edge in favour of a patchwork of tinting. Our present concern, however, is with method (i) – the site plan or steading method.

---

1 K G C Reid, *The Law of Property in Scotland* para 205.
2 Land Registration (Scotland) Act 1979 s 3(1)(a).
3 Or at least the airspace occupied by the ductwork. The same point is made in W M Gordon, 'Servitudes abounding' (2009) 13 *Edinburgh Law Review* 519 at 523. As the Midas touch only operates at the point of registration, giving ownership *at that time* to the defender, it would be open to the pursuer to (re)acquire that which, on this view, has passed by registration to the defender. But as the property was only 'recently purchased by the defender' (para 4), it would be the best part of 10 years before this argument was available to the pursuer.
4 *Legal Manual* (available at http://www.ros.gov.uk/foi/legal/Frame~Home.htm) para 6.9.

The *Legal Manual* gives the following account:[1]

The site plan or steading method is used where the component parts of the subjects fall within an area which can be defined, but their location and extent within that area cannot be defined. The most common example for this method is tenemental style property. Even if the deeds contain floor plans it is only in exceptionally complicated cases that a floor plan will be used in a title sheet. Agency policy is to rely on verbal descriptions of flats wherever possible. The tenement steading will be edged red on the title plan and any pertinents will be identified verbally in the property section.

> Example:
>
> *Subjects within the land edged red on the Title Plan, being the eastmost house on the second flat of the tenement 2 Falconer's Court, Elderslie, PA42 1XE, together with the westmost cellar in the common close of said tenement.*

In newer developments, it may be possible to identify pertinents belonging to an individual flat by reference to the title plan.

> Example:
>
> *Subjects within the land edged red on the Title Plan, being the eastmost house on the second flat of the tenement 2 Falconer's Court, Elderslie, PA42 1XE, together with the cellar tinted blue and the garage tinted pink on the said plan.*

The site plan method is extremely useful where it is impossible to identify the precise location and extent of a back green serving two or more tenements. In many cases, the individual back green serving a single tenement has either never been defined or has been combined with other back greens to form a collectively used area. Provided the back green falls within the legal extent of the granter of the foundation deeds' title, plans section will include the back green, along with the solum of the particular tenement, within the red edge and normal site plan methods for describing the particular flat and editing in rights can be used.

The site plan or steading method relies on identifying some larger area – itself edged red on the title plan – *within* which the flat and its pertinents are known to lie. Often, the land edged red will accurately depict the tenement building and any accompanying ground but, as the passage just quoted indicates, the site plan method is also used in circumstances where the full extent of that ground is unclear.

Under method (ii) (the precise extent method) the person registered as proprietor owns *all* of the area edged in red. A typical description reads 'Subjects 31 Russell Road, Newton Mearns, G77 1DY, edged red on the Title Plan'.[2] But what is the position under method (i)? What, in other words, is the meaning of being 'within' land edged red?

This issue arose for decision in *North Atlantic Salmon Conservation Organisation v Au Bar Pub Ltd*.[3] This was a most unusual boundary dispute. The first defender,

1 Paragraph 6.9.1.
2 *Legal Manual* para 6.9.2.
3 2009 GWD 14-222.

the Au Bar Pub, had taken to putting out tables and chairs on the ground at the rear of its property in 101 Shandwick Place, Edinburgh. The first defender leased this property from the second defender, Iona Pub Partnership (Scotland) Ltd. The pursuer, the owner of property in adjoining Rutland Square, claimed that the ground in question was actually part of a 'piece of stable ground or Court lying at the northwest corner of Rutland Square' which was conveyed as common property to various proprietors in Rutland Square by a feu charter of 1856. If that was correct, the pursuer was a *pro indiviso* owner. The form of action was a summary cause application seeking possession of the disputed ground by having the defenders removed from it.

As the title to 101 Shandwick Place was registered in the Land Register, the starting-point was with that title; for if the second defender was registered as owner of the disputed ground, then, as a matter of law, it was indeed the owner and there was nothing left to discuss.[1] The description in the property section of the title sheet was in standard form for a tenement:

> Subjects within the land edged red on the Title Plan ... comprising ... those premises ... at 101 Shandwick Place ... and also a right in common with the proprietors of the remainder of the tenement of which the subjects form part to the *solum* thereof.

The disputed ground was within the area edged red. Did that mean that it was part of the second defender's property – or at least part of the land which effeired to the tenement – and hence was the property of one or more of the proprietors in the tenement (which might or might not include the second defender)? In that case, the ground could not belong to the pursuer. Understandably, that suggestion was rejected by the sheriff.[2]

> The word 'within' is not the same as 'comprise' in ordinary language. Both words are used in the description in the land certificate. They must therefore have different meanings. It seems to me that if a property *comprising* certain described parts is referred to as *within* a certain area it does not mean that the property extends to the whole area it is within. There would be no need to describe property in that way if it extended to the whole area it was within. I do not consider that the area edged in red is the extent of the second defender's property.

In fact the use of the word 'within' gives rise to two separate but related propositions. First, the flat in question may not extend to the whole of the land edged red. Secondly, the totality of all the flats in the tenement – all described by the same method – may also not extend to the whole of that land.[3] The land edged red, in other words, may be over-inclusive.

---

1 This is the result of the so-called Midas touch of the Keeper, provided for by s 3(1)(a) of the Land Registration (Scotland) Act 1979.
2 Sheriff N M P Morrison QC. The passage quoted appears in para 9.
3 At para 9 Sheriff Morrison said that: 'Until all the titles in the tenement are registered the Keeper cannot know what the extent of any one property is.' The truth is, however, that he may remain uncertain even at the end of this process – as in the example quoted earlier from the *Legal Manual* of the back green which has been combined with other back greens.

If the title sheet fails to define boundaries, then it is necessary to have recourse to the underlying Sasine title.[1] The dispute in *North Atlantic Salmon* thus resolved into a thoroughly old-fashioned battle of Sasine titles, with the usual combination of vague language and no plans (other than one which was referred to but, as so often, not recorded). The pursuer's eventual victory was because its position seemed the more consistent with a feuing plan of 1836 and an agreement between Edinburgh Corporation and the proprietors of Rutland Square dating from 1929.

The problem of scale

On the Land Register the title plan uses the largest OS scale available for the area in question. This will be one of 1:1250, 1:2500 and 1:10,000 depending on whether the area is, respectively, urban, rural or moorland.[2] Even on the largest of these (1:1250), however, 1 millimetre on the title plan is the equivalent of 1.25 metres on the ground.[3] In theory, it is possible to scale to 0.23 metres on such a plan, but in practice the position is often not so clear-cut, and matters are not improved by the absence of written measurements. It is a standard complaint that title plans are less informative and helpful than a good quality Sasine plan. The position is further complicated by the fact that, since 2005, the OS has updated its data under the Positional Accuracy Initiative which takes account of the fact that the earth's surface is curved rather than flat. As a result, the title plans may be 'at best a rough fit for the Ordnance Survey's current interpretation of the area' in question.[4]

　　　Given these limitations, the title plans will not provide a conclusive answer to boundary disputes where the amount of land at issue is small. There were two examples in 2009. In *Clydesdale Homes Ltd v Quay*[5] the point of disagreement was whether the length of one of the defenders' boundaries was 37.5 or 40 metres. *Stuart v Stuart*[6] was a dispute as to the precise line of the boundary. The properties were separated by 19 leylandii trees, which the defenders cut down on the basis – which the sheriff found to be incorrect – that they lay on the defenders' side of the boundary. In both cases, as no clear answer could be found from the title plans in question, the court had to choose between the conflicting and highly technical evidence of the chartered surveyors engaged by each side. In *Stuart* there was disagreement as to which fixed features could best be used for measuring distances scaled from the title plan, a task which was complicated by the fact that the houses did not appear on the plans as they appeared on the ground.

---

1 Sheriff Morrison quite correctly rejected the argument, based on *Marshall v Duffy* 2002 GWD 10-318, that it was not competent to go behind the title sheet to the prior deeds: see paras 11 and 12.
2 *Registration of Title Practice Book* para 4.22.
3 *Registration of Title Practice Book* para 4.26.
4 *Clydesdale Homes Ltd v Quay* [2009] CSOH 126, 2009 GWD 31-518 at para 18 per Lord Malcolm.
5 [2009] CSOH 126, 2009 GWD 31-518.
6 27 July 2009, Stonehaven Sheriff Court.

One argument for the defenders in *Stuart* was that a court could not fix the boundary with greater precision than the limitations of OS scaling allowed. Understandably, this was rejected by the sheriff:[1]

> [M]y understanding is that the Ordnance Survey strive to work to a standard of absolute perfection – with scientific certainty – such that they would seek to achieve 100% accuracy in the preparation of their plans; and, in so far as they strive for such perfection, then they accept that they fall short of that. But the Court works to an entirely different standard. In proceedings such as this, it seeks to resolve matters applying the balance of probabilities – a very different standard to that adopted by Ordnance Survey. The Court strives to achieve a standard falling well short of scientific certainty. So, I do not see the 'margins of error' conceded by the Ordnance Survey as necessarily presenting an obstacle to the Court's determination of this dispute.

A temptation in cases like this is to take a peek at the Sasine titles. Admittedly, the boundaries must be determined from the Land Register only – except where the details in that Register are deliberately vague (as in tenements)[2] or are being challenged by means of an application for rectification of the Register. But the sheriff in *Stuart* thought that the Sasine titles were not completely irrelevant:[3]

> I recognise that views might differ as to the extent to which, in a case such as this, one can look at prior title deeds for the purpose of determining the nature of boundaries. It is my view … that one can and should, where appropriate, examine prior titles to see how, if at all, they describe boundary lines. Such titles would be irrelevant to the issue of who currently owns any property, but relevant to the line of a disputed boundary.

A final point concerns positive prescription. In the case of the Register of Sasines, both competing titles may be capable of being read as including the disputed strip, in which case matters can often be resolved by asking who has been in possession. But for Land Register titles, prescription cannot run (unless indemnity has been excluded) and possession is therefore irrelevant.[4] In *Stuart* the party that won was the party who was *not* in possession.[5]

STANDARD SECURITIES

Procedure on enforcement

Royal Bank of Scotland plc v Wilson[6] has been dragging through the courts a long time.[7] Francis and John Wilson were brothers. Francis was married to Annette.

---

1 At p 22 of the transcript (Sheriff P P Davies).
2 *North Atlantic Salmon Conservation Organisation v Au Bar Pub Ltd* 2009 GWD 14-222 at paras 11 and 12 per Sheriff Morrison.
3 At p 20 of the transcript.
4 Except for the purposes of the proprietor-in-possession exception to an application for rectification: see Land Registration (Scotland) Act 1979 s 9(3)(a).
5 See p 22 of the transcript.
6 [2009] CSIH 36, 2009 SLT 729.
7 For the previous stage see 2004 SC 153, 2003 SLT 910 digested as *Conveyancing 2003* Case (40).

John was married to Norma. In 1991 Francis and Annette borrowed from the Royal Bank of Scotland plc to buy a house. About the same time John and Norma borrowed from RBS to build a conservatory. The loans were secured on their respective houses which were next to each other in Loanhead, Midlothian, each of which was co-owned by the respective spouses.

The brothers were in partnership together, and indeed they had two firms, F J Wilson Associates and Wilson Brothers. After the two loans just mentioned were taken out, these firms also borrowed from the same bank, RBS. Both firms eventually defaulted. The bank then called on the partners to pay, but the partners defaulted too. When the bank was unable to recover the partnership loans, it sought to enforce the two standard securities.

Both standard securities provided:

> We … and … spouses … (hereinafter referred to as 'the Obligant') hereby undertake to pay to The Royal Bank of Scotland plc (hereinafter referred to as 'the Bank', which expression includes its successors and assignees whomsoever) on demand all sums of principal, interest and charges which are now and which may at any time hereafter become due to the Bank by the Obligant whether solely or jointly with any other person, corporation, firm or other body and whether as principal or surety; declaring that … in the event of the foregoing personal obligation being granted by more than one person the expression 'the Obligant' means all such persons together and/or any one or more of them; and in all cases the obligations hereby undertaken by the Obligant shall bind all person(s) included in the expression 'the Obligant' and his, her or their executors and representatives whomsoever all jointly and severally without the necessity of discussing them in their order.

This is a thicket of words, whose appropriateness may be questioned. That it means that each granter is liable without limit for all debts, including future debts, due by the other granter is hardly obvious at first reading. But that indeed is its meaning. 'A lender', it has been said, 'who makes advances to B without the consent of A on the basis of an earlier security, entered into by A and B for another purpose entirely, is at least engaged in extremely questionable practice.'[1] Be that as it may, when the bank sought to enforce the securities, the two wives pled that they had been the victim of misrepresentations by their husbands to the effect that the securities related purely to the house purchase (in one case) or house extension (in the other), and that had it not been for this misrepresentation they would never have signed. There were also averments that the bank manager had been guilty of misrepresentation. They founded on *Smith v Bank of Scotland*.[2] Eventually this defence was repelled, and the decision was a landmark one in that it came close to killing off the *Smith* doctrine.[3]

But whilst this defence failed, the case did not end there. The defenders continued to resist, and in 2008 the sheriff dismissed the action, in which the bank

---

1 S Eden, 'Cautionary tales – the continued development of *Smith v Bank of Scotland*' (2003) 7 *Edinburgh Law Review* 107 at 114.
2 1997 SC (HL) 111.
3 2004 SC 153, 2003 SLT 910. See *Conveyancing 2003* pp 74–77.

sought decree of ejection, for three reasons.[1] (a) The certificate of indebtedness that it had served had contained no demand for payment and hence there had been no default. (b) The certificate had been sent to only one of the two owners. (c) The action was procedurally flawed because it should have been taken under the Heritable Securities (Scotland) Act 1894. The bank appealed, and the Inner House has now reversed the sheriff's decision on all three points and granted decree to the bank. As for (a) it held that the certificate was sufficient. As for (b) it held that:[2]

> the expression 'the Obligant' meant both of the debtors together 'and/or any one or more of them'. It is clear that a demand made of any one of the debtors is sufficient to entitle the bank to exercise the remedies open to it against all of them.

As for (c) it held that a crave for ejection can be included in a section 24 application, and it held that the certificate of indebtedness was sufficient.

We offer no particular comments, other than that this case highlights yet again the labyrinthine complexity of the law about the enforcement of standard securities.

Registering in the Companies Register

Part 25 of the Companies Act 2006, and before it Part XII of the Companies Act 1985, say that a standard security must be registered in the Companies Register within 21 days of its creation. The requirement is easy to overlook. If the deadline is missed, it is possible to apply to the court for permission to register late. In *Salvesen Ptr*[3] the creditor petitioned for this permission. But by this time the company debtor had already gone into administration. Not surprisingly, permission was refused. It is worth noting that in this case the securities were not standard securities over property in Scotland but mortgages over property in England. That, however, makes no difference: registration is mandatory and since the company was a Scottish company, registration should have happened in the Scottish Companies Register.

The Companies Act 2006, unlike previous legislation, enables the Secretary of State to disapply this requirement for double registration,[4] but no such order has yet been made.

Home Owner and Debtor Protection (Scotland) Bill

At the beginning of 2009 the Scottish Ministers set up a 'Debt Action Forum'. Its report[5] led to the Home Owner and Debtor Protection (Scotland) Bill.[6] This

---

1 2008 GWD 2-35.
2 Paragraph 47 per Lord Nimmo Smith, giving the Opinion of the Court.
3 [2009] CSOH 161, 2010 GWD 4-57.
4 Section 893.
5 http://www.scotland.gov.uk/Publications/2009/06/08164837/0.
6 For background see http://www.scottish.parliament.uk/business/research/briefings-09/SB09-73.pdf. See also M Higgins, 'Homing instinct' (2009) 54 *Journal of the Law Society of Scotland* Dec/16. The Bill was passed on 11 February 2010.

enhances the protection given to debtors in relation to residential property both
(a) as against a standard security holder seeking to enforce and (b) in the context
of sequestrations and trust deeds for creditors.

WARRANDICE

You buy a flat with a dedicated car-parking space at the rear. But when you come
to park your car, you find that it cannot be done if another car-parking space, at
right angles to your own, is also in use. Or if you do manage to park your car, you
cannot extricate it from the space if, in the meantime, the neighbouring space has
been taken. The result makes for great unhappiness. But do you have a remedy
and, if so, against whom? In *Holms v Ashford Estates Ltd*[1] the remedy sought was
the inventive one of a claim in warrandice for damages against the seller of the
flat. But the alleged breach of warrandice concerned, not the car-parking space
itself – the title to which was indisputably good – but the accompanying servitude
of access in order to reach that space.

The facts of *Holms v Ashford Estates Ltd* were these. The defender converted
a former office at 24 Manor Place, Edinburgh into five flats. In 1999 one of those
flats was sold to the pursuers. The disposition conveyed both the flat and also
car-parking space number 42 at the rear of the building. At the time of the
purchase, the pursuers were under the impression that there were only to be
three car-parking spaces (numbers 40, 41 and 42), all in a row. In fact there was
also a fourth, number 43, which was at right angles to number 42 and separated
from it by a small unallocated area. At the original proof, which took place in
Edinburgh Sheriff Court in 2006,[2] the evidence was that, when spaces 41 and 43
were both being used, it was impossible to park in space 42 – or at least impossible
to park anything other than a tiny vehicle such as a Smart Car. As it happened,
the pursuers owned a Mercedes estate.

In theory, the pursuers were protected by a servitude of access which was
included in their disposition. This conferred:

> a heritable and irredeemable servitude right of access for both pedestrian and
> vehicular traffic over the lane known as Bishops Lane from Manor Place and the
> common Car Parking Area more particularly described in the Deed of Conditions
> aftermentioned.

It was clear from the deed of conditions that the 'Car-Parking Area' over
which the servitude was granted included not just the unallocated parts but also
the individual car-parking spaces themselves. In other words, the disposition
granted the pursuers a servitude over, among other things, car-parking space
number 43. But in practice this servitude had proved of little avail, for the owner
of space 43 (Fenella Mason) used it to park her car, thus preventing the pursuers
from parking theirs.

---

1 [2009] CSIH 28, 2009 SLT 389, 2009 SCLR 428. The Opinion of the Court was delivered by Lord
Eassie.
2 2006 SLT (Sh Ct) 70.

Warrandice is not an altogether easy cause of action. It does not guarantee title as such. Rather, it guarantees that there will be no *eviction* on the basis of a competing title. In order to succeed, therefore, it was necessary for the pursuers in *Holms* to show that they had been evicted. 'Eviction' in this context is a technical term. Normally it requires that the competing title is successfully asserted by court action. But, as Viscount Stair recognised, there can be eviction without a court decree if the challenger's claim is based on an 'unquestionable ground' which could not sensibly be resisted.[1] That is a high standard. In *Holms* an Extra Division of the Court of Session glossed it in this way:[2]

> No doubt other equivalent expressions to 'unquestionable' may equally be deployed, but in our view one way of putting the matter is by posing the question whether, were proceedings by way of action of declarator or interdict to take place between the party to whom warrandice had been granted and the competing proprietor ... it could immediately be affirmed that the title of the competing proprietor was so plainly preferable as to render the position of the party claiming warrandice unstateable. In other words, there would be nothing that could properly be disputed or argued in such a hypothetical action on behalf of the person to whom the warrandice has been granted.

In *Holms* there had been no judicial eviction. The most that the owner of space 43 had done was to continue to park her car. But, or so the pursuers argued, there had been extra-judicial eviction. So far as we are aware, this is the first case ever to have turned on that issue.

The pursuers' argument was this. Ms Mason owned space 43. That could not be disputed. And since the whole purpose of a parking space is to park a car, it followed that Ms Mason could use her space to park her car. But if she did so, the pursuers could not park theirs. In the result they had suffered 'practical eviction'.[3] Their rights and those of Ms Mason were incompatible, and the exercise of the latter prevented the exercise of the former.

At first instance, and again on appeal to the sheriff principal, this argument prevailed.[4] The pursuers, it was held, had been evicted, and the defender was liable in damages for breach of warrandice, which the court assessed at £15,000. The defender appealed, and an Extra Division of the Court of Session has now upheld the appeal.[5] The grounds for doing so are of considerable interest.

The assumption underlying the pursuers' case was that, in a conflict between Ms Mason's ownership and their own servitude, the right of ownership would necessarily prevail. By parking, and thus blocking the pursuers' space, Ms Mason was only acting within her rights. But that, said the Extra Division, was not self-evidently true. On the contrary, if the pursuers held a good servitude of access, then Ms Mason must use her property in a way which allowed the servitude to be exercised to the full. Ownership must give way to the servitude and not the other

---

1 Stair, *Institutions* II.3.46.
2 Paragraph 46.
3 Paragraph 49.
4 2006 SLT (Sh Ct) 70, 2006 SLT (Sh Ct) 161. For a discussion, see *Conveyancing 2006* pp 141–44.
5 [2009] CSIH 28, 2009 SLT 389, 2009 SCLR 428.

way around, and if the exercise of the servitude was inconsistent with parking by Ms Mason, then Ms Mason must cease to park. It was thus Ms Mason's parking, and not that of the pursuers, which was on the line.

Naturally, this approach presupposed that the servitude granted to the pursuers was a good one. In argument, it was suggested that it might not be good, because of what is known in England as the 'ouster' principle but in Scotland is better expressed – as indeed now in statutory language[1] – as the principle that a servitude must not be repugnant with ownership. If that principle ever formed much of an impediment to servitudes in Scotland, the impediment was largely removed in *Moncrieff v Jamieson*,[2] where the House of Lords took a distinctly relaxed view of what counted as repugnancy. On the facts of *Holms*, therefore, the Extra Division was, properly, sceptical on this point. It might well be the case, the court said, that the servitude would prevent Ms Mason from using her property to park her car. But the mere fact that it was described as a 'car-parking space' in her disposition was no guarantee that it could be used for that purpose. Even if Ms Mason could not park her car, she could still use the space for other purposes. As counsel had suggested, the space 'might accommodate the parking of a motorcycle or a pedal cycle, or the setting out of potted plants and a seat whereby to enjoy the fresh air and sunshine, all compatibly with the pursuers' right of vehicular access'.[3] At the very least, therefore, the argument that the servitude was repugnant with ownership, and that Ms Mason's right must necessarily prevail over it, was not 'so obviously sound and indisputable' as to form an 'unquestionable' challenge to the pursuers' title.[4] Hence the warrandice claim must fail for lack of eviction, or at any rate was premature.

One other point may be mentioned. By the time that the servitude was granted to the pursuers, the defender had already conveyed space 43 to Ms Mason. In principle, therefore, any grant of servitude over space 43 would be void as *a non domino*. The deed of conditions, however, reserved to the defender a power to grant 'rights of access and egress and other servitudes or wayleaves over any part of the Car-Parking Area'. Although the validity of such a power was questioned by the court, the pursuers chose not to argue the point.[5] The question is indeed an interesting one. Presumably such a power is enforceable at least on a contractual basis, thus conferring what amounts to a mandate or power of attorney on the disponer. If that is correct, then for as long as Ms Mason owned space 43, the defender could grant a servitude over it. Whether such a power could be exercised once Ms Mason had disposed of her property – whether, in other words, the power is real and not merely personal – is a more difficult question. At one time there was a practice, particularly in family transactions, by which disponers reserved the power to burden the land being disponed with a subsequent heritable security,

---

1 Title Conditions (Scotland) Act 2003 s 76(2).
2 [2007] UKHL 42, 2008 SC (HL) 1. For a discussion of this point, see *Conveyancing 2007* pp 109–10.
3 Paragraph 54.
4 Paragraph 54.
5 Paragraph 48.

and in certain circumstances it appears that such a 'faculty to burden' was real. Bell wrote that:[1]

> It may appear to be anomalous, and contrary to feudal principles, that a disponer who divests himself, or a third party who never was feudally invested, should have power to grant a precept on which infeftment may proceed. But the principle is this, that the conveyance to the disponee is limited by a condition, viz. That the disponer shall still retain the power of constituting a real security over the lands, by his own act, or by that of another appointed by him, and named in the deed.

Whether – 200 years later – that principle could now be extended to the grant of other limited real rights, such as a servitude, is uncertain but must perhaps be regarded as doubtful.

SDLT AND OTHER TAX ISSUES[2]

SDLT

The increase in the zero rate threshold for residential property from £125,000 to £175,000 has come and gone. As originally announced, it was due to come to an end on 3 September 2009.[3] This was extended until 31 December 2009 by the Finance Act 2009.[4] Despite much speculation and some lobbying, the state of the country's finances made it unlikely that it would be further extended and the Pre-Budget Report on 9 December 2009 confirmed this. So it will now be necessary again to distinguish between property located in disadvantaged areas and otherwise, as the increased threshold of £150,000 for residential property located in a disadvantaged area becomes relevant again.[5] The restoration of the level of the first threshold takes effect for transactions with an effective date on or after 1 January 2010.

The administrative framework of the whole UK tax system has been subject to extensive revision over the last few Finance Acts. Finance Act 2009 extends this process to many aspects of stamp duty land tax (although some of the provisions are not yet in force). Thus new information and inspection powers are extended to SDLT, along with a number of other taxes,[6] and significant amendments are made to record-keeping requirements.[7]

An important change has been consolidation of the time limits affecting both HMRC and taxpayers in relation to such matters as making assessments and claims. The general move is from a limit of six years to one of four years.[8]

---

1 Bell, *Commentaries* I, 40–41.
2 This part is contributed by Alan Barr of the University of Edinburgh.
3 See the Stamp Duty Land Tax (Exemption of Certain Acquisitions of Residential Property) Regulations 2008, SI 2008/2339.
4 Finance Act 2009 s 10.
5 See Finance Act 2003 s 57, sch 6.
6 Finance Act 2009 s 96, sch 48, extending Finance Act 2008 sch 36.
7 Finance Act 2009 s 98, sch 50, amending Finance Act 2003 schs 10, 11 and 11A.
8 Finance Act 2009 s 99, sch 51, amending Finance Act 2003 sch 10.

Penalties are another area where a significant effort at consolidation and equalisation is taking place. This too is extended to SDLT, with new rules on penalties for failure to make returns[1] or to pay tax.[2] Many of these penalties are tax-geared; and particularly in relation to failure to make a return, the threat of a late payment penalty of 5% of the tax due (in addition to statutory interest) is a very serious one.[3] Like inheritance tax, SDLT is a one-off, 'event' tax, and administrative failures are perhaps more likely than in situations where regular compliance is required.

Other changes in Finance Act 2009 were mainly of interest south of the border, affecting collective owners of (primarily) flats, acting under leasehold enfranchisement and shared ownership rules.[4] There was a small extension of the exemption for registered social landlords;[5] and substantial rules allowing exemption (with relief from other taxes in addition) for alternative finance investment bonds.[6]

The 2009 Pre-Budget Report brought little in the way of proposed changes to SDLT. However, there is to be an extension to the rules on the disclosure of tax avoidance schemes so that they will cover residential property with a value of at least £1 million. Currently, these disclosure rules only cover non-residential property but, according to HMRC, there is growing evidence of avoidance schemes being promoted in relation to high-value residential property.[7]

Furnished holiday lettings

It was confirmed in the 2009 Pre-Budget Report that the special rules applicable to furnished holiday lettings are to be withdrawn with effect from 6 April 2010. This follows the extension of these rules from UK property to property located within the European Economic Area, which was announced in the 2009 Budget. The rules in question allow furnished holiday lettings to be treated in the same way as a trade for the purpose of a number of reliefs. These include rules on losses; certain capital allowances; a number of capital gains tax reliefs (including roll-over relief, entrepreneurs' relief and relief for gifts of business assets); and the rules for relief for pension contributions.[8] The initial extension of the geographical basis of the rules and their subsequent total withdrawal are both consequences of the need to comply with European Community rules on such reliefs.

---

1 Finance Act 2009 s 106, sch 55.
2 Finance Act 2009 s 107, sch 56.
3 See Finance Act 2009 sch 55 para 5.
4 Finance Act 2009 ss 80–82.
5 Finance Act 2009 s 81.
6 Finance Act 2009 s 123, sch 61.
7 See PBR Note 35, 9 Dec 2009. And see currently Finance Act 2004 pt 7; Stamp Duty Land Tax Avoidance Schemes (Prescribed Descriptions of Arrangements) Regulations 2005, SI 2005/1868; and Tax Avoidance Schemes (Information) Regulations 2004, SI 2004/1864.
8 See PBR Note 24, 9 Dec 2009.

❧ PART V ❧
TABLES

TABLES

CUMULATIVE TABLE OF DECISIONS ON VARIATION OR DISCHARGE OF TITLE CONDITIONS

This table lists all opposed applications under the Title Conditions (Scotland) Act 2003 for variation or discharge of title conditions. Decisions on expenses are omitted. Note that the full opinions in Lands Tribunal cases are often available at http://www.lands-tribunal-scotland.org.uk/records.html.

Restriction on building

Name of case	Burden	Applicant's project in breach of burden	Application granted or refused
Ord v Mashford 2006 SLT (Lands Tr) 15; *Lawrie v Mashford*, 21 Dec 2007	1938. No building.	Erection of single-storey house and garage.	Granted. Claim for compensation refused.
Daly v Bryce 2006 GWD 25-565	1961 feu charter. No further building.	Replace existing house with two houses.	Granted.
J & L Leisure Ltd v Shaw 2007 GWD 28-489	1958 disposition. No new buildings higher than 15 feet 6 inches.	Replace derelict building with two-storey housing.	Granted subject to compensation of £5,600.
West Coast Property Developments Ltd v Clarke 2007 GWD 29-511	1875 feu contract. Terraced houses. No further building.	Erection of second, two-storey house.	Granted. Claim for compensation refused.
Smith v Prior 2007 GWD 30-523	1934 feu charter. No building.	Erection of modest rear extension.	Granted.
Anderson v McKinnon 2007 GWD 29-513	1993 deed of conditions in modern housing estate.	Erection of rear extension.	Granted.
Smith v Elrick 2007 GWD 29-515	1996 feu disposition. No new house. The feu had been subdivided.	Conversion of barn into a house.	Granted.

Name of case	Burden	Applicant's project in breach of burden	Application granted or refused
Brown v Richardson 2007 GWD 28-490	1888 feu charter. No alterations/new buildings	Erection of rear extension.	Granted. This was an application for renewal, following service of a notice of termination.
Gallacher v Wood 2008 SLT (Lands Tr) 31	1933 feu contract. No alterations/new buildings.	Erection of rear extension, including extension at roof level which went beyond bungalow's footprint.	Granted. Claim for compensation refused.
Blackman v Best 2008 GWD 11-214	1934 disposition. No building other than a greenhouse.	Erection of a double garage.	Granted.
McClumpha v Bradie 2009 GWD 31-519	1984 disposition allowing the erection of only one house.	Erection of four further houses.	Granted but restricted to four houses.
McGregor v Collins-Taylor 14 May 2009	1988 disposition prohibiting the erection of dwellinghouses without consent.	Erection of four further houses.	Granted but restricted to four houses.
Faeley v Clark 2006 GWD 28-626	1967 disposition. No further building.	Erection of second house.	Refused.
Cattanach v Vine-Hall	1996 deed of conditions in favour of neighbouring property. No building within 7 metres of that property.	Erection of substantial house within 2 metres.	Refused, subject to the possibility of the applicants bringing a revised proposal.
Hamilton v Robertson, 10 Jan 2008	1984 deed of conditions affecting 5-house development. No further building.	Erection of 2nd house on site, but no firm plans.	Refused, although possibility of later success once plans firmed up was not excluded.
Cocozza v Rutherford 2008 SLT (Lands Tr) 6	1977 deed of conditions. No alterations.	Substantial alterations which would more than double the footprint of the house.	Refused.
Scott v Teasdale 22 Dec 2009	1962 feu disposition. No building.	New house in garden.	Refused.
Hollinshead v Gilchrist 2010 GWD 5-87	1990 disposition and 1997 feu disposition. No building or alterations.	Internal alterations.	Granted.

Other restriction on use

Name of case	Burden	Applicant's project in breach of burden	Application granted or refused
Church of Scotland General Trs v McLaren 2006 SLT (Lands Tr) 27	Use as a church.	Possible development for flats.	Granted.
Wilson v McNamee, 16 Sept 2007	Use for religious purposes.	Use for a children's nursery.	Granted
Verrico v Tomlinson 2008 SLT (Lands Tr) 2	1950 disposition. Use as a private residence for the occupation of one family.	Separation of mews cottage from ground floor flat.	Granted.
Matnic Ltd v Armstrong 2009 GWD 31-520	2004 deed of conditions. Use for the sale of alcohol.	Use of units in a largely residential estate for retail purposes.	Granted but restricted to small units and no sale of alcohol after 8 pm.
Clarke v Grantham 2009 GWD 38-645	2004 disposition. No parking on an area of courtyard.	A desire to park (though other areas were available).	Granted.
Hollinshead v Gilchrist 2010 GWD 5-87	1990 disposition and 1997 feu disposition. No caravans, commercial or other vehicles to be parked in front of the building line.	Parking of cars.	Granted and claim for compensation refused.
Perth & Kinross Council v Chapman 13 Aug 2009	1945 disposition. Plot to be used only for outdoor recreational purposes.	Sale for redevelopment.	Granted.

Flatted property

Name of case	Burden	Applicant's project in breach of burden	Application granted or refused
Regan v Mullen 2006 GWD 25-564	1989. No subdivision of flat.	Subdivision of flat.	Granted.
Melville v Crabbe 19 Jan 2009	1880 feu disposition. No additional flat.	Creation of a flat in the basement.	Refused.

Sheltered and retirement housing

Name of case	Burden	Applicant's project in breach of burden	Application granted or refused
At.Home Nationwide Ltd v Morris 2007 GWD 31-535	1993 deed of conditions. On sale, must satisfy superior that flat will continue to be used for the elderly.	No project: just removal of an inconvenient restriction.	Burden held to be void. Otherwise application would have been refused.

Miscellaneous

Name of case	Burden	Applicant's project in breach of burden	Application granted or refused
McPherson v Mackie 2006 GWD 27-606 rev [2007] CSIH 7, 2007 SCLR 351	1990. Housing estate: maintenance of house.	Demolition of house to allow the building of a road for access to proposed new development.	Discharged by agreement on 25 April 2007.

Applications for renewal of real burdens following service of a notice of termination

Name of case	Burden	Respondent's project in breach of burden	Application granted or refused
Brown v Richardson 2007 GWD 28-490	1888 feu charter. No buildings.	Substantial rear extension	Refused.
Council for Music in Hospitals v Trustees for Richard Gerald Associates 2008 SLT (Lands Tr) 17	1838 instrument of sasine. No building in garden.	None.	Refused.

Applications for preservation of community burdens following deeds of variation or discharge under s 33 or s 35

Name of case	Burden	Respondent's project in breach of burden	Application granted or refused
Fleeman v Lyon 2009 GWD 32-539	1982 deed of conditions. No building, trade, livestock etc.	Erection of a second house.	Granted.

Applications for variation of community burdens (s 91)

Name of case	Burden	Applicant's project in breach of burden	Application granted or refused
Fenwick v National Trust for Scotland 2009 GWD 32-538	1989 deed of conditions.	None. The application was for the complete discharge of the deed with the idea that a new deed would eventually be drawn up.	Refused.

Servitudes

Name of case	Servitude	Applicant's project in breach of servitude	Application granted or refused
George Wimpey East Scotland Ltd v Fleming 2006 SLT (Lands Tr) 27 and 59	1988 disposition. Right of way.	Diversion of right of way to allow major development for residential houses.	Granted (opposed). Claim for compensation for temporary disturbance refused.
Ventureline Ltd, 2 Aug 2006	1972 disposition. 'Right to use' certain ground.	Possible redevelopment.	Granted (unopposed).
Graham v Parker 2007 GWD 30-524	1990 feu disposition. Right of way from mid-terraced house over garden of end-terraced house to the street.	Small re-routing of right of way, away from the burdened owner's rear wall, so as to allow an extension to be built.	Granted (opposed).
MacNab v McDowall, 24 Oct 2007	1994 feu disposition reserved a servitude of way from the back garden to the front street in favour of two neighbouring house.	Small re-rerouting, on to the land of one of the neighbours, to allow a rear extension to be built.	Granted (opposed).
Jensen v Tyler 2008 SLT (Lands Tr) 39	1985 feu disposition granted a servitude of way.	Re-routing of part of the road in order to allow (unspecified) development of steading.	Granted (opposed).

Name of case	Servitude	Applicant's project in breach of servitude	Application granted or refused
Gibb v Kerr 2009 GWD 38-646	1981 feu disposition granted a servitude of way.	Re-routing to homologate what had already taken place as a result of the building of a conservatory.	Granted (opposed).
Colecliffe v Thompson 2009 GWD 23-375	1997 disposition granted a servitude of way.	None. But the owners of the benefited property had since acquired a more convenient access, secured by a new servitude.	Granted (opposed).
G v A 26 Nov 2009	1974 disposition granted a servitude of way.	None. But the owner of the benefited property had since acquired a more convenient access (although not to his garage).	Granted (opposed) but on the basis that the respondent should apply for compensation.
Graham v Lee 18 June 2009	2001 disposition granted (a) a servitude of way and (b) of drainage.	None.	(a) was granted provided the applicants discharged a reciprocal servitude of their own, and compensation was considered. (b) was refused.
McKenzie v Scott 19 May 2009	Dispositions from 1944 and 1957 granted a servitude of bleaching and drying clothes.	None. But the servitude had not in practice been exercised for many years.	Granted (opposed).

TABLE OF APPEALS FROM 2009

A table at the end of *Conveyancing 2008* listed all cases digested in *Conveyancing 1999* and subsequent annual volumes in respect of which an appeal was subsequently heard, and gave the result of the appeal. This table is a continuation of the earlier table, beginning with appeals heard during 2009.

Euring David Ayre of Kilmarnock, Baron of Kilmarnock Ptr
[2008] CSOH 35, 2008 Case (82) *rev* [2009] CSIH 61, 2009 SLT 759, 2009 Case (93)

Christie Owen & Davies plc v Campbell
2007 GWD 24-397, Sh Ct, 2007 Case (53) *affd* 18 Dec 2007, Glasgow Sheriff Court, 2007 Case (53) *rev* [2009] CSIH 26, 2009 SLT 518, 2009 Case (82)

Martin Stephen James Goldstraw of Whitecairns Ptr
[2008] CSOH 34, 2008 Case (81) *rev* [2009] CSIH 61, 2009 SLT 759, 2009 Case (93)

Hamilton v Dumfries and Galloway Council
[2008] CSOH 65, 2008 SLT 531, 2008 Case (37) *rev* [2009] CSIH 13, 2009 SC 277, 2009 SLT 337, 2009 SCLR 392, 2009 Case (50)

Holms v Ashford Estates Ltd
2006 SLT (Sh Ct) 70, 2006 Case (40) *affd* 2006 SLT (Sh Ct) 161, 2006 Case (40) *rev* [2009] CSIH 28, 2009 SLT 389, 2009 SCLR 428, 2009 Cases (19) and (52)

Kerr of Ardgowan, Ptr
[2008] CSOH 36, 2008 SLT 251, 2008 Case (80) *rev* [2009] CSIH 61, 2009 SLT 759, 2009 Case (93)

Royal Bank of Scotland v Wilson
2008 GWD 2-35, Sh Ct, 2008 Case (61) *rev* [2009] CSIH 36, 2009 SLT 729, 2009 Case (75)

Tuley v Highland Council
2007 SLT (Sh Ct) 97, 2007 Case (24) *rev* [2009] CSIH 31A, 2009 SC 456, 2009 SLT 616, 2009 Case (48)

Wright v Shoreline Manangement Ltd
Oct 2008, Arbroath Sheriff Court, 2008 Case (60) *rev* 2009 SLT (Sh Ct) 83, 2009 Case (74)

TABLE OF CASES DIGESTED IN EARLIER VOLUMES
BUT REPORTED IN 2009

A number of cases which were digested in *Conveyancing 2008* or earlier volumes but were at that time unreported have been reported in 2009. A number of other cases have been reported in an additional series of reports. For the convenience of those using earlier volumes all the cases in question are listed below, together with a complete list of citations.

Aisling Developments Ltd v Persimmon Homes Ltd
[2008] CSOH 140, 2008 SLT 494

Parvaiz v Thresher Wines Acquisition Ltd
[2008] CSOH 160, 2009 SC 151

Smith (Ballantyne Property Services Trs) v Lawrence
2009 GWD 6-104

Trygort (No 2) Ltd v UK Home Finance Ltd
[2008] CSIH 56, 2008 SLT 1065, 2008 Hous LR 62, 2009 SC 100, 2009 SCLR 58

Turnberry Homes Ltd v Keeper of the Registers of Scotland
2009 GWD 1-11